THE END OF AMERICAN HISTORY

The publication of this book was assisted by
a bequest from Josiah H. Chase to honor his parents,
Ellen Rankin Chase and Josiah Hook Chase,
Minnesota territorial pioneers.

THE END OF AMERICAN HISTORY

Democracy, capitalism, and
the metaphor of two worlds
in Anglo-American historical
writing, 1880-1980

DAVID W. NOBLE

University of Minnesota Press • Minneapolis

Published by the University of Minnesota Press,
2037 University Avenue Southeast, Minneapolis MN 55414
Printed in the United States of America

Library of Congress Cataloging in Publication Data

Noble, David W.
  The End of American History.
  Includes index.
  1. United States—Historiography. I. Title.
E175.N63 1986   973'.072   85-1077
ISBN 0-8166-1415-6
ISBN 0-8166-1416-4 (pbk.)

The University of Minnesota
is an equal-opportunity
educator and employer.

For Martha, Tasslyn, Alice, Andrew,
Matthew, Joshua, and Jonathan
Our grandchildren

Contents

Acknowledgments

The greatest influence on my approach to the history of ideas came from Carl Becker's *The Heavenly City of the Eighteenth-Century Philosophers*, which I read as an undergraduate in 1947. Undergraduate courses from Eric Goldman and Stow Persons also were crucial in giving me a perspective on the years between 1890 and 1940 and the place of that period within the larger context of the history of ideas in America. Both taught me to think about the 1890s and 1940s as watershed decades. In graduate school, Merle Curti shared his sense of the crisis of Progressive historiography in the 1940s and encouraged my study of the assumptions that underlay the Progressive outlook. Henry Nash Smith's *Virgin Land* added a significant dimension to the concept of crises in particular climates of opinion which I had learned from Becker and Persons. Then Thomas Kuhn's *The Structure of Scientific Revolutions* provided another language for discerning such crises. Correspondence with Gene Wise, as well as his book, *American Historical Explanations*, encouraged me to apply Kuhn's language to the work I had already done for my 1965 book, *Historians against History*, and to reconsider the importance of the 1940s as a decade of dramatic change.

Friends, colleagues, and students who have been particularly helpful in sharpening my ideas on the crises of the 1890s and 1940s, and on the issue of paradigmatic change, are Robert Schneider, Gayle Graham Yates, Harry Boyte, Joseph Amato, Peter Carroll, Bruce Stuart, Richard Chase, James Youngdale, Earl Shaw, Lary May, Susan Beck, John Plomondon, Darryl Hattenhauer, Garvin Davenport, Michael Passi, Ralph Brauer, Richard Nigro, David Howard-Pitney, Colette Wanless, David Fields, Deanne Lundell, Heather Huyck, Richard Nelson, Robert Lerfald, Ruth Townsend, Thomas Woods, David Horowitz, Terrence Ball, Steven Trauman, Sue Beckam, and Karin McGinnis. Marlene Tungseth of the University of Minnesota Press has greatly improved the style of the book. The help of my wife, Lois K. Noble, has been, as always, invaluable in editing and preparing the manuscript for publication.

THE END OF AMERICAN HISTORY

Reformation and Renaissance: Republican Virtue and the American Promised Land

1

This book explores the role played by political philosophy in providing structure and meaning to the narratives of four major American historians whose writings span the century from the 1880s to the present decade: Frederick Jackson Turner (1861–1932), Charles A. Beard (1874–1948), Richard Hofstadter (1916–70), and William Appleman Williams (1921–). I also discuss Reinhold Niebuhr (1892–1971), whose reputation is that of a political philosopher and theologian and not that of a historian. I have included Niebuhr in my analysis because I believe an examination of his political philosophy and theology illuminates the crucial position that a theory of history has in any modern political philosophy or theology. At the same time, I suggest that Niebuhr's writings provide perspective on the political philosophies that are implicit in the writings of these professional historians, especially since their philosophies changed rapidly in the 1940s.

My approach has been strongly influenced by Gene Wise's application of ideas from Thomas Kuhn's *The Structure of Scientific Revolutions* to the writings of professional historians. Wise contended in his 1973 book, *American Historical Explanations*, that the radical restructuring of fundamental assumptions, which Kuhn believed was a periodic phenomenon in scientific communities, provided a theoretical model for describing the dramatic shift of perspective taking place among historians in the 1940s. During that decade, a Progressive paradigm, most fully represented by Charles A. Beard and dominant among American historians in the 1930s, was challenged by a Counter-Progressive, or Consensus, school of younger historians. Wise used the metaphor of an earthquake to suggest the intensity with which an established set of assumptions was so shaken that a theoretical edifice, which seemed intelletually sound and aesthetically pleasing in 1940, was in such ruins a decade later that a subsequent generation of historians strenuously avoided the shambles and began to construct a new structure to give meaning to their narratives.[1]

I see my volume, therefore, as a supplement to *American Historical Explanations*, as well as a revision of my 1965 book, *Historians against History*. Since their publication, seminal scholarship by Sacvan Bercovitch and J. G. A. Pocock has appeared that makes it possible to suggest a larger historical context for the Progressive worldview that Wise presented as a relatively self-contained system during the half-century from 1890 to 1940.[2] I believe that this scholarship clarifies the internal tensions that Wise identified in Turner's writings and points toward the great differences between Turner and Beard even while it demonstrates the important areas of continuity. Above all, the work of Bercovitch and Pocock indicates that the "earthquake" of the 1940s had begun by the 1890s. If this is true, Turner and Beard, two of the more influential American historians, were desperate conservatives who from the 1890s into the 1940s tried to shore up a pattern of meaning whose collapse would leave them in the midst of intellectual chaos. The writings of Bercovitch and Pocock, therefore, add great intensity and drama to Wise's identification of the 1940s as the decade when many younger historians abandoned the terrible responsibility felt by Turner and Beard to patch up a disintegrating world view and instead seemed compelled to take up the equally terrifying responsibility of creating an alternative narrative structure for American history.[3]

In *The American Jeremiad*, Sacvan Bercovitch identifies what he believes is the crucial rhetorical ritual that has characterized the major writings of Anglo-American culture from the Puritans to the present day. Frederick Jackson Turner became famous among historians as the author of the "frontier thesis" as an explanation for the sweep of American history when he presented a paper to the American Historical Association in 1893 entitled "The Signficance of the Frontier in American History." Bercovitch has no patience for those scholars who have ignored the Puritan roots of Turner's belief in two totally separate worlds, European and American, as well as Turner's use of the metaphor of an exodus from the Old World of Europe to the New World of America to give structure and meaning to his narration of American history.

It is important to be aware of the dramatic differences between Turner's and Bercovitch's understanding of American history and to consider these differences as an expression of the crisis of American history felt by Turner and Beard between 1890 and 1940, as well as of the new stage that characterized that crisis after America entered World War II. Turner's writings, as we shall see in detail in the next chapter, accepted as reality the rebirth of Europeans when they crossed the boundary separating Europe from America. That boundary had become a frontier threshold into a new order of meaning. In this exodus from the oppressive social and political systems of Europe, they had become free within an American Promised Land.

Bercovitch, however, does not share Turner's belief that American geography offered such an alternative to European culture. On the contrary, he believes that the key division of a New from an Old World took place in the developing Protestant cultures of Europe. Specifically, by the beginning of the seventeenth century, English Puritans had defined themselves as a New Israel, trapped within the Egyptian bondage of the medieval establishment. They knew, however, that as a Chosen People they could engage in an exodus that would lead them to the Promised Land. Their conversions, their rebirth, had taken place, however, within the boundaries of the corrupt status quo.

For Bercovitch, therefore, the Puritans defined an Old and a New England on the basis of an elaborate theory of history that they brought with them across the Atlantic. They had disassociated themselves from the medieval doctrine that meaning and salvation were to be found within the boundaries of Catholic Christendom. The sacred did not exist within that circle of which Rome was the center; only the profane existed there. The sacred was to be found outside, in the future that lay across the frontier threshold.

In Bercovitch's analysis, the Puritans had denied the validity of the Augustinian doctrine that history, time as experienced in this world, was essentially mysterious and beyond human control. The medieval jeremiad warned against the acts of pride by which individuals or groups attempted to predict and control history; it warned that such acts of pride, which gave priority to earthly rather than heavenly goals, would be punished. But the Puritans knew that as a Chosen People they had the responsibility of bringing earthly and heavenly time together. Their task was to prepare for the millennium when God's Kingdom would be established on earth. They were not acting in pride but in responsibility when they predicted and attempted to control history.

The knowledge that they had been chosen to replace medieval corruption with an environment suitable for the Kingdom was the foundation for what Bercovitch has designated the American jeremiad. According to him, this rhetorical ritual began with the promise. The exodus of the Puritans as a New Israel was leading toward the millennium. The second element of the jeremiad, however, was the assertion of declension. Although the Puritans as a Chosen People had crossed the frontier threshold from the medieval past in which history had no meaning, they, as individuals and as a group, had not fully accepted their responsibility to make history a progressive path toward the future Kingdom. They were slothful. They were distracted and pursued false and evil values. And they received divine punishments for their failures to act as a Chosen People.

This Progressive jeremiad, as Bercovitch describes it, established great tension in the community of saints as the distance between the perfection of the promise and the imperfection of daily activity was examined and deplored. The preachers of the jeremiad concluded their criticism with the third and final part of the jeremiad: a prophecy that the Chosen People would accept their responsibility, reject their sinful life-styles which looked so similar to those of the corrupt medieval past, and construct the environment for the Kingdom in the immediate future.

Having identified this rhetorical ritual of promise, declension, and prophecy brought from England to New England, Bercovitch then challenged the interpretation of Puritan declension proposed in the 1940s by the influential historian Perry Miller. Miller would have agreed with Bercovitch that the Puritans brought with them a Protestant culture developed in Europe. But according to Bercovitch, Miller did not emphasize the significance of this division between an Old Catholic and a New Protestant World within Puritan theology. Instead, Miller established a drama in whch the Puritans attempted to preserve their European culture, to live within social boundaries, to sustain a circle that would protect them from the profanity of the external world. For Miller and Turner, therefore, the frontier as threshold lay between a decadent Europe and a vital America, and it was inevitable that Puritan culture would decline throughout the seventeenth century and disappear in the eighteenth century. During this period, increasing numbers of Puritans rejected their responsibility to live within the boundary of their Old World culture and crossed the frontier threshold to become free individuals, to become Americans. In 1940, Miller shared Turner's 1890 view that American nature in 1700 had been stronger than European culture.[4]

But implicit in Bercovitch's analysis is the irony that Miller, like Turner, could imagine two worlds and the possibility of a liberating exodus from the Old to the New only because these key metaphors of Puritan theology had become secularized and then widely accepted throughout the English colonies at the beginning of the eighteenth century. All Protestants, not just Congregationalists and Presbyterians, had become the Chosen People. North America, not just New England, provided the geographical space for the Promised Land. The Puritan jeremiad had become American. And the specific form of the Progressive jeremiad was political by 1776. The promise was a virtuous republic. The Revolution was the exodus from the Egyptian bondage of monarchy. And the new citizen saints found themselves living in a state of declension, the gap between the ideal republic and their imperfect political experience. But political prophets pointed out their failings, explained their sufferings as punishment for those failures, and pointed toward the fulfillment of the promise in the future.

I hope that the subsequent chapters on Turner and Beard will illuminate how Bercovitch's analysis of the American jeremiad as a product of English culture is a dramatic confrontation, not only with those historians or with Perry Miller, but with the commonsense understanding of American history that is so much a part of our current popular culture. Throughout the opening pages of this chapter, I have used the term American history. For most of us, as for Turner, Beard, and Miller, we begin to define what is American by making the negative statement that it is not European. In our everyday conversation, we often draw lines that separate America from Europe. We contrast American and European art, music, and architecture. We compare American and European cars, clothing, and food. We also separate American and European politics and history. These linguistic divisions come to our tongues so easily that they seem natural and therefore inevitable. We are startled, bewildered, even angered if it is suggested that such divisions represent a set of social conventions that developed within a specific historical context, rather than existing as an immutable, extrasocial reality.[5]

But once we raise the question of the givenness of this metaphor of two worlds, as Bercovitch has, serious logical inconsistencies immediately appear. When we say Europe, our usual meaning is that of a civilization, a set of shared values and artistic expressions, as well as shared social and economic institutions that are expressed in a wide variety of politically independent nations. When we say America, our usual meaning is not that of a comparable civilization. We do not mean a common culture that includes Canada, Mexico, and Brazil as Europe would include Sweden, France, and Greece. When we say America, therefore, we mean a single nation, the United States. Presumably, our meaning is that our nation is more than politically independent, as England or Spain or Venezuela or Argentina is politically independent. By isolating the United States from the nations of the European and American continents, we are implying that it is culturally independent, standing outside the Western civilization that gives cultural unity to those other nations.

Therefore, implicit in our common usage of the term, America, is a profound commitment to isolating our national culture. It is not enough for us that the political independence of 1776 should signify the development of a unique national culture that modified its colonial inheritance from its mother country, England. Such an emphasis would make it possible to think and talk about the United States as an independent nation, as England also is, within a common Western civilization that includes the many nations of Europe as well as those of North and South America. But American historians from the Puritans in the 1630s through the writings of Charles Beard in the 1930s have not used a concept that combines political independence with cultural interdependence to define our national identity. They have thought and written as if the United States was absolutely independent, standing apart in its uniqueness from the rest of human experience.

Although popular culture since the 1940s has continued to assume that an exodus experience has separated the United States from the rest of the world, it has been increasingly difficult for professional historians to do so. Beard, whose writings on American history embodied the metaphor of exodus from an Old to a New World and were immensely popular with the reading public of the 1920s and 1930s, defined the American entry into World War II as a reversal of the exodus that had created American cultural identity. If the United States entered World War II, Beard warned, the Chosen People would be leaving the Promised Land and returning to the Old World of Egyptian bondage.

Beard was as influential within the historical profession as he was popular with nonprofessional readers of history, and the younger professionals who wrote narratives after 1945 had to find ways of avoiding the stark confrontation that he had constructed by 1941 between a corrupt Old and an innocent New World. It is an indication, however, of the cultural persuasiveness of the metaphor of exodus that the revolutionary shift in the national political identity from "isolationism" in 1940 to "internationalism" in 1945 did not result in the kind of self-conscious analysis of the metaphor that is represented by Bercovitch's *The American Jeremiad* until a generation had passed. In the 1940s, Perry Miller explicitly criticized the exodus metaphor as part of a Puritan culture timebound in the seventeenth century and then implicitly accepted the metaphor when he discussed the eighteenth and nineteenth centuries. Henry Nash Smith in *Virgin Land: The American West as Symbol and Myth* quickly followed with an analysis of the exodus metaphor as central to Anglo-American culture from 1830 to 1890. But he argued that the metaphor died with Turner in the 1890s. He failed, therefore, to see that it was as important to Beard's narratives written in the 1930s as it had been for Turner a generation earlier. This pattern of scholarship, which demythologized the exodus metaphor held by particular generations, continued until Bercovitch's writings in the 1970s pointed to the continual presence of the metaphor from the Puritans into the twentieth century.[6]

The explicit attack on Beard that developed among younger historians between 1945 and 1955, however, did not focus on his assumption that there was an American history separate from European history and from that of the other American nations. Instead, these critics denied the validity of the distinction and conflict that Beard had found between democracy and capitalism throughout American history from the Revolution of 1776 to the New Deal of 1936. They focused their criticism on Beard's 1913 book, *An Economic Interpretation of the Constitution of the United States*, his most influential historical work.[7]

They questioned the emphasis he had given to differences between "real" property in land and "unreal" property in the form of paper securities. Beard associated democracy with property holders who were engaged in production, and an antidemocratic capitalism with economic parasites engaged in speculation rather than production.

Consensus, or Counter-Progressive, historians who challenged Beard as a spokesman for a Conflict, or Progressive, school of historians, were suggesting that he and other Progressive historians had constructed a world of illusion that obscured the essential homogeneity of American culture in which democratic and capitalist values were complementary. This theme of illusion or self-deception in imagining conflict where there was really consensus was broadened in the 1950s by young historians such as Marvin Meyers and Richard Hofstadter. Meyers's *The Jacksonian Persuasion* found that the political rhetoric of the Jacksonians at the beginning of the nineteenth century asserted that they were defending the republican virtue of the founding fathers against a capitalist conspiracy. But, for Meyers, although the Jacksonians spoke as anticapitalists, they behaved as capitalists. Richard Hofstadter had already described a similar pattern of an anticapitalist rhetoric that obscured capitalist behavior during the late nineteenth century in the analysis of populism he had presented in *The Age of Reform*.[8]

A significant parallel exists, therefore, between the development of this scholarship in the 1950s, which was critical of the rhetoric of republican virtue, and the scholarship that had criticized the metaphor of exodus from an Old to a New World. It, too, focused on limited episodes in American history without suggesting that this rhetorical convention had been a central part of Anglo-American culture from at least the time of the American Revolution through the writings of Beard in the 1930s. It is fascinating, therefore, that at almost the same time in the late 1960s and early 1970s when Bercovitch began to argue that the particular examples of the metaphor of exodus from an Old to a New World represented a fundamental presupposition of Anglo-American culture, J. G. A. Pocock pointed to the similar significance and role for the tradition of republican virtue. For Pocock, the fear of capitalism expressed by American property holders was not merely the eccentric interpretation of Beard, or the provincial outlook of nineteenth-century farmers; it represented the continued persuasiveness of the political imagination that was dominant in the English colonies on the eve of the Revolution in 1776.[9]

It has been noted that many of the younger historians who rejected the dominant Progressive school of 1940 were aware that they, unlike the Progressive historians, were using irony. The irony that they included in their criticisms of specific uses of the exodus metaphor and of the tradition of republican virtue was, however, limited to the particular generations that they analyzed. One waited for the writings of Bercovitch and Pocock in the 1970s to find an overarching ironic interpretation of American history. Pocock, like Bercovitch, was arguing that the idea of American uniqueness, its separation from Europe, was developed in Europe. The pervasiveness of that idea in the United States was an indication, to Pocock, of how deeply a Renaissance understanding of history had become part of the American political imagination. And the vision of an Old and New World with which American historians have declared the cultural independence of America was, for Bercovitch, the product of the Reformation in Europe.

Part of the irony of these two major interpretations set forth in the 1970s was that they undercut much of the irony used by the Counter-Progressive and Consensus scholars of the 1940s and 1950s to destroy the credibility of Beard and the Progressive position of 1940. The young historians of the decade 1945–55 were not aware of the possibility that in criticizing the metaphor of two worlds and the tradition of republican virtue, they were engaged in the most fundamental kind of intellectual revolution. They were not self-conscious that they had begun to demythologize and to desacralize the understanding of Anglo-American history that had been dominant for almost three centuries.

Instead, they suggested that it was Beard, rather than themselves, who stood outside the most basic American traditions. One of the major strategies employed by the Counter-Progressive, or Consensus, historians to portray themselves as conservatives, rather than revolutionaries, was to argue that the central American tradition was that of pragmatism. Mainstream Americans were so intellectually flexible that they would never assert that the world was sharply divided between good and evil, virtue and corruption, democracy and capitalism. Free from such a dualistic outlook, they would never imagine that conspiracy, the key weapon of evil against good, was a central part of historical experience.

As someone who was a Counter-Progressive, or Consensus, historian in the 1950s, I can say that we were not consciously conspiring to obscure the devastating implications that the American entry into World War II posed for the metaphor of two worlds and the tradition of republican virtue, the two elements most important in providing structure and meaning to the narratives of American historians from the Revolution of 1776 until Pearl Harbor. In retrospect, I would suggest something that I hope will become clearer in the chapters on Niebuhr, Hofstadter, and Williams; my generation was led to trivialize the tradition of republican virtue to which Beard and so many other Americans were passionately committed in 1940 because we were overwhelmed by the political implications of the nation's conversion from "innocence" and "isolation" in 1940 to "realism" and "internationalism" by 1945. As Pocock describes that tradition, it embodied a powerful, pre-Marxist criticism of capitalism dating back to seventeenth-century England. As most historians experienced a conversion from "isolationism" to "internationalism," many also converted to support of a cold war against Marxist Russia as part of their escape from "innocence" to "realism." Within this atmosphere, which came to identify patriotism with a defense of American capitalism against external Marxist criticism, it no longer seemed respectable to sustain a tradition of internal criticism of capitalism, especially a tradition associated with a discredited "isolationism."

The argument of this book is that the rhetorical ritual of the American jeremiad as described by Bercovitch provided the structure for the narratives of Turner and Beard, as it had for the most influential historians of the nineteenth century, among them George Bancroft. Turner and Beard began to write their histories on the assumption that there was a promise that separated American from European history. Most of their descriptive detail, however, was about experience that represented a declension, the failure to live by the principles of the promise. Both expected to be prophets and to complete the rhetorical ritual with a prophecy that would reveal when and how the promise would be fulfilled.

The great tension in Turner's and Beard's histories comes from the problem they faced in being able to complete the ritual; they found it difficult to prophesy the fulfillment of the promise. It is here that we must turn to Pocock's analysis of the tradition of republican virtue in order to understand the profound pessimism that Turner and Beard struggled to contain in their narratives. Bercovitch recognizes that there were major American intellectuals, among them Herman Melville, who lost faith in America as a Promised Land and who began to write what Bercovitch calls the antijeremiad. Since the American jeremiad is, for Bercovitch, a self-fulfilling prophecy which is able to isolate negative feedback within the declension category, a category insignificant to true believers in comparison to the categories of promise and prophecy, he has no way to explain why any particular figure such as a Melville or Henry Adams, after their initiation into the ritual, should come to think that it is inadequate.

But Pocock makes it possible to see that the secularized promise of a democratic America, which formed the basis for Turner's narratives, had a very specific content. Turner believed that democracy could exist only when a particular form of property was predominant in a society. Exodus from Europe in the seventeenth century brought a Chosen People into conditions that made that kind of freehold property holding possible and therefore brought political democracy into existence. Turner could prophesy that declension from the democratic promise would be overcome as long as more freehold property could be added to the nation. For Turner, however, the future that stretched beyond 1890 was one in which capitalist, rather than freehold, property would predominate. Then the democratic promise of the nation would be lost; the undemocratic social and political patterns of Europe would spread across the Atlantic, and American uniqueness would end.

Turner's language, which identified freehold property with democracy and America, and capitalist, speculative property with aristocracy and Europe, now seems so exotic or eccentric that it is difficult to believe that into the 1940s this was the commonsense language of most of the professional historians as well as much of the public and was an essential aspect of the Progressive paradigm represented by Beard. Beard, as we shall see in chapter two, argued that property that was productive and rational, in contrast to the nonproductive and irrational qualities of capitalist property, was possible in the twentieth century even though Turner's frontier of freehold property had ended.

But Turner's continued loyalty to the strong commitment in the tradition of republican virtue to a necessary economic base for political democracy was not the only source for his pessimism about the future of democracy in 1890. Pocock has argued that when Italian humanists such as Machiavelli rejected the Augustinian doctrine that an individual found greater fulfillment within the sacraments of the Church of Rome than as a citizen in politics, they did not develop a dynamic theory of history comparable to that of the Puritans which fused sacred and profane time. They did not claim to be able to predict and control time. As they turned back to the lost world of classical republicanism, which had preceded what the humanists defined as the Dark Ages that followed the collapse of the Roman republic, they defined two realms, one of history and one of natural law. Natural law was universal, rational, static. The citizens of a republic, as long as they were virtuous, lived by those principles. History, in contrast, was particular, irrational, dynamic. And the political life of the many monarchies of history was always a corrupt expression of that history.

Therefore, the republican theory of the Italian humanists, according to Pocock, was necessarily tragic. The norm of human existence was history, the dynamic flow of irrational particulars. Republics were exceptional. They emerged out of the sea of time. For brief periods, they were able to embody the timeless characteristics of natural law. But the foundation of this island of rationality was unstable because no republic could completely escape time. Its appearance had to be dated; and the question asked, when did the republic replace a monarchy? Asking that question led to the next question: At what date did the republic fall? Unable to fully separate themselves from the dynamic history out of which they had emerged, the republican structures that had embodied, so briefly, the characteristics of the timeless and rational universals were inevitably eroded by the tides of time.

For Pocock, this dramatic metaphysical combat between time and natural law had been given particular economic and political form in seventeenth-century England. There freehold property was dissociated from the changing complexities of society that had made medieval patterns of property so timebound and artificial. Ownership of freehold property brought one into harmony with the universal and rational, which stood outside history. The politics of the freeholders, therefore, was virtuous because, sharing an understanding of the universal, they were able to achieve a public interest that did not depend on the ability of some individuals to use power to force other individuals to accept their values. Such a use of arbitrary power symbolized, at a deep metaphysical level, the victory of the particular over the universal, and the political expression of that victory was corruption.

The great fear of the English republican theorists in the seventeenth and eighteenth centuries was not that the political virtue of freehold property would be lost to a resurgence of medieval property patterns, but that another post-medieval form of property, that of capitalism, would be the major force destroying the relationship of the republic to the universal. For the republicans, capitalist property was, in contrast to freehold property, clearly an artificial creation. Capitalist property existed only in the symbolic form of paper: paper money, paper securities, paper contracts. Freehold property was conservative, committed to the timeless perfection of natural law, but capitalist property was impatient with the status quo. It was future-oriented; it necessarily looked forward to future profits. Because capitalists were involved in time, they represented the particular, not the universal. No universal public interest was possible when capitalists had power. Capitalists spoke only for the particular, their self-interest. A capitalist establishment would have to impose its selfish definition of the public interest on the rest of the community. Such an artificial and artful public interest depended on power, the coercion of some individuals by others. And that was the definition, for the English republicans, of political corruption. The tragedy of all republics, the loss of their relationship with the universal and the return to the relativity of historical particulars, would come to freehold republics when capitalist property gained control.

Pocock argues that the founding fathers used this Anglo-American tradition when they gave meaning to their republican experiment. He believes this is why American historians in the 1950s and 1960s found such strident political language in the Anti-Federalists, the Jeffersonians, and the Jacksonians. They believed that the aggressive capitalism announced by men such as Alexander Hamilton must destroy the virtue of their freehold republic by pushing the United States off its foundation in natural law back into the flow of history.

Drawing on the scholarship of Henry Nash Smith and John William Ward, among others, Pocock suggests, however, that the Jacksonians could temporarily escape from the pessimism of the Anti-Federalists and Jeffersonians by focusing on the great expanse of land that lay west of the Appalachian Mountains. James Harrington, one of the major republican theoreticians in seventeenth-century England, had proposed that the freeholders could counter the dynamism of capitalism by creating a freehold empire outside the boundaries of England. According to Pocock, Jacksonians adopted this idea to stretch their empire of liberty in the land from the boundaries of the republic of 1789 onward to the Pacific. It was their "manifest destiny" to expand the freehold base of the republic of the founding fathers. But the conditions necessary for freehold property were finite, whereas capitalism represented the perpetual dynamism of history. Sooner or later, the empire of liberty would reach its limits and then the virtue of the republic would be lost to the selfishness and arbitrary power of capitalism. This seemed to be the fate of the republic as the nineteenth century came to an end.

At a grass-roots level, the Populist movement expressed this profound sense of cultural despair while Turner captured the attention of the entire historical profession by using the census of 1890 to dramatize the closing of the western frontier. For the Populists, as well as Turner, the United States had existed as an island of political and economic virtue in the surrounding sea of world corruption. Pocock, however, had found some Americans who, early in the nineteenth century, proposed that the American republic might prove immortal if it could spread its political and economic patterns to the rest of the world. All previous republics, like nineteenth-century America, were isolated exceptions vulnerable to both internal and external decay. But there was the possibility that the rational principles of natural law could overcome the irrational particulars of history and become universal. The key to Beard's ability to replace Turner's pessimism with an exuberant optimism came from his belief that what he called "the industrial revolution" offered the same kind of economic base for political virtue that freehold property had. "Industrialism," for Beard, embodied the same characteristics of productivity and rationality. Best of all, Beard had discovered that nature was not static. Nature was dynamic; it had a history. And that history was not one of particularities and irrationalities. It was rational, universal, and predictable. Industrialism was an expression of the progressive unfolding of natural law. As 1917 approached, Beard anticipated the exodus of all the peoples of the world into a universal Promised Land because industrialism could achieve on every continent the kind of egalitarian public interest that Turner had believed was limited to the freehold property of the American frontier.[10]

Beard prophesied, therefore, that World War I would provide the revolutionary opportunity for the victory of the natural and rational dynamism of industrialism over both the unnatural vestiges of the medieval past and the unnatural and irrational dynamism of capitalism. But the world as he saw it in 1919 bore no resemblance to his prophecy. As he lost faith in a historical dynamism that was rational and universal, he found himself returning to Turner's view of America as an island of political virtue in the sea of world corruption. To him, this meant that capitalism had again become the major threat to erode the foundations of that virtue. And he was certain that American entry into another world war would destroy all the protective barriers for its democracy. Participating in a European war would mean political suicide as America voluntarily joined the corruption of the rest of the world.

In 1940, Beard returned to the impasse felt by Turner in 1890 when he could no longer complete the rhetorical ritual of promise, declension, and prophecy that had provided the structure for his historical narratives. Beard could not prophesy that a democracy or republic, free from coercive power because its property system encouraged each citizen to have a rational commitment to the public interest, would exist in the American future. This was the core of the crisis for what Wise has called the Progressive school of historical writing. And in the 1940s, Reinhold Niebuhr made his reputation as a political theorist by arguing that democracy could exist without the kind of consensus on the public interest demanded by the tradition of republican virtue. Such a "realistic" democracy, for Niebuhr, would recognize that no exodus had ever delivered Americans into a Promised Land where they would be free from the kinds of problems faced by the peoples of an Old World.

As we will see, the young historians Richard Hofstadter and William Appleman Williams also felt compelled in the 1940s to radically rethink the relationship between democracy and capitalism and the place of the metaphor of two worlds in their narratives. But first, in the next two chapters, we will explore in detail how Turner and Beard identified capitalism with Europe and democracy with America, in order to illuminate the severity of the intellectual problems faced by political philosophers and historians in the 1940s. Only then can we fully appreciate the intensity of the struggle of Niebuhr, Hofstadter, and Williams to replace the exodus metaphor as the structural foundation for the narratives recounting the history of the United States.

Frederick Jackson Turner and Charles Beard: International Capitalism or International Democracy, 1880–1920

2

Frederick Jackson Turner gained instant fame and leadership within the first generation of professional historians because his essays, appearing regularly after 1890, focused on issues that were of crucial importance to these men. "The Significance of the Frontier in American History" and his subsequent essays, which continued to explore the same themes, were the single most discussed interpretation of the American past by academic historians because if Turner's thesis was correct, they could no longer write and teach that American history represented a successful exodus from the European past. And if the metaphor of an exodus from an Old to a New World ceased to provide the structure for their narratives in 1900, its disintegration also meant the end of the United States as a virtuous republic.

Subsequent generations of historians have wondered how Turner could have achieved such a commanding role within the profession since he produced so few book-length narratives. From the 1830s until the appearance of professional historians in the 1880s, the most influential historian of the American past was George Bancroft, who established his leadership by writing a multivolume history of the United States that was very popular with the public. Not until Charles Beard's *The Rise of American Civilization* appeared at the end of the 1920s did a historian get such a response from the general public.

The issues that Turner raised and that gained the attention of his fellow professionals were, of course, those that kept him from writing narratives comparable to those of Bancroft before him or Beard after him. Turner, unlike Bancroft or Beard, found it difficult to use the rhetorical ritual of promise, declension, and prophecy contained in the American jeremiad to provide structure for book-length narratives. In contrast, Bancroft's histories had begun with a very clear premise. The English coming to America were entering the Promised Land of a Protestant republic. Transformed as Americans, a Chosen People, they had the responsibility to continue their pilgrimage, constantly making progress. Periodically, their progressive history was challenged by major external foes: French Catholicism before 1750, English monarchy in 1776, and English capitalism after 1789. The stage of declension from the promise was expressed in the failure of the people to recognize the threat, to be so absorbed in everyday activity that they forgot their responsibility to fulfill the promise. Always, for Bancroft, a new Moses figure, like John Winthrop in 1630, inspired his people to shake off their decadence, which made their condition comparable to the original Egyptian bondage, and move forward once again. In the crisis of the American Revolution, George Washington and Thomas Jefferson were such figures, leading the nation toward the future when the gap between the promise and the declension of everyday life would be closed.

Although he affirmed the role of God in separating the New World of Protestantism from the Old World of Catholicism, Bancroft, an ardent supporter of President Andrew Jackson in the 1830s, sang the praises of Jefferson who was often attacked for his deism by the evangelical Protestants who were coming to dominate religious life in the United States during the first decades of the nineteenth century. Bancroft linked Jackson to Jefferson. To him, both were defenders of a producer's democracy, based on freehold property, against the conspiracy of English capitalism to infiltrate the country with a parasitic and undemocratic form of property. Although Jefferson struggled to preserve the purity of the republic as it had emerged from the Revolution, the power of capitalism and English influence seemed to increase until Andrew Jackson appeared to play the role of Moses as powerfully as Winthrop had in 1630 or Washington in 1776.

Leading his people away from the corrupt establishment in the old America along the Atlantic seaboard, he guided them across the Appalachian Mountains into the great "valley of democracy" where freehold property would not be contaminated by the capitalist forms of property that had come from England and had become part of the life of eastern cities. Marching westward, fulfilling their "manifest destiny," Americans had needed still another Moses figure, Abraham Lincoln, to awaken them from a state of declension and lead them forward to fulfill the promise in the future. American citizens had not been morally sensitive to the fact that property in slaves also contradicted freehold property and gave rise to another form of aristocratic, Old World politics. Lincoln, the great spiritual teacher of his people, as well as a mighty warrior, destroyed the threat that the slavocracy might control the West and frustrate its destiny as the empire of liberty for freeholders.

The movement of history as progress began for Bancroft with the Protestant Reformation, but the fulfillment of the exodus from the Catholic past, when the passage of time was not progressive, depended upon the existence of a New World, a Promised Land, a West. The Moses figures in his narratives, Winthrop, Washington, Jackson, and Lincoln, all faced West. Declension was overcome when prophecy could point toward a new frontier where the promise could be fulfilled. Time, as the progress of the Chosen People, flowed along a horizontal line from east to west.

Bancroft's long life, filled with the writing of many narratives, ended just as the young Frederick Jackson Turner was calling attention to the disappearance of that West to which Jackson and Lincoln had called the Chosen People to repeat the exodus of 1630 and to experience once more the ritual of purification as one crossed the frontier threshold from the corruption of the Old World to the purity of the New. And Turner inherited the belief that Bancroft had shared with so many Jacksonians: the future of a democracy, based on freehold property and threatened by European capitalism, depended upon the continued westward expansion of an empire of liberty.[1]

Turner's particular role in the historical profession then was that of a messenger bearing news of defeat. Bancroft, in his lifetime, had seen the Moses figures, Jackson and Lincoln, and he had filled his histories with the good news of their victories. But Turner shared Bancroft's belief that these victories were linked to the particular characteristics of the ground on which they fought. They won because they were fighting for the future, not the past; the West, not the East; the New World, not the Old. Turner would write as lovingly about Jefferson, Jackson, and Lincoln as Bancroft had, but he could not find the Moses figure to lead his own generation out of declension because he could not see a future, a New World in the West. For Turner in 1890, the future, the vital patterns of urban and industrial development, was coming from Europe to the East Coast and then spreading across the Appalachians; capitalist property was overrunning freehold property; and the ghost of Alexander Hamilton was conjuring up a European-style empire to replace the empire of liberty created by Jefferson, Jackson, and Lincoln, the men who had once inflicted political defeat on Hamilton's principles.

Turner faced the closing of Bancroft's West, the freehold empire of liberty, without some of Bancroft's resources for dealing with time. Bancroft believed that Jackson was the leader of a Protestant democracy whose history began with the Reformation. The "manifest destiny" of the American democracy of the 1830s and 1840s represented the unfolding of God's plan for the redemption of humanity. Perhaps, if Turner had fully shared Bancroft's Protestantism, he could have experienced the American jeremiad as the self-contained symbol system, described by Bercovitch, which was invulnerable to negative feedback. But the 1880s were a decade when the historical profession was established as part of a larger movement to professionalize American society. Crucial to this experience of professionalization was the rejection of an explicit dependence upon divine authority. The only authority for the new professionals of the 1880s and 1890s was human reason using the tool of the scientific method.[2]

When Turner self-consciously broke from the tradition of Protestant historical writing, which had been predominant in nineteenth-century Anglo-American culture, he seemed to be left with only a negative attitude toward time developed by the tradition of republican virtue during the Renaissance. Here, in contrast to the Reformation, the appeal to authority was an appeal to human reason that could apprehend the rational laws of nature outside the irrational flux of historical time. That apprehension, according to republican tradition, was always tenuous and temporary. For Turner, if the American landscape was, as a virgin land, a direct manifestation of that state of nature that was the opposite of history, its existence as the foundation for freehold property was also tenuous and temporary. Seeing Europe as a symbol of the flux of time and political corruption that constantly threatened to wash over the American island of rationality and political virtue, Turner in 1890, unlike Bancroft in 1830, could not find a way to prophesy that a secular promise of a virtuous democracy would be fulfilled in the future when the present state of declension would be overcome. It is possible, therefore, that Turner did not duplicate Bancroft's prolific production of narrative history because the rhetorical structure of Bancroft's narratives – promise, declension, and prophesy – had been reduced for Turner to only promise and declension.

Turner had drawn the quantifiable evidence for American political declension from the census of 1890, which reported there was no longer an area of unsettled land within the boundaries of the United States. "This brief official statement," Turner wrote, "marks the closing of a great historic movement. Up to our own day, American history has been in a large degree the history of the colonization of the Great West. The existence of an area of free land, its continuous recession and the advance of American settlement westward explain American development."[3] Throughout this essay and his other writings as well, he stressed the identification of what was uniquely American with the timeless space of physical nature. Turner could not have accepted Bercovitch's argument that the concept of America as a space that differed dramatically from Europe was developed by European Protestants, or Pocock's argument that Turner's definition of "an area of free land" depended upon concepts developed in England by James Harrington. Instead, Turner constantly asserted that "American democracy was born of no theorist's dream. It came stark and strong and full of life out of the American forest and it gained new strength each time it touched a new frontier."[4]

But Turner, working within the Renaissance conventions identified by Pocock, always assumed that the escape from European time to American space was temporary and that time was more powerful than space. Even when he was most poetic in evoking what Henry Nash Smith calls the myth of virgin land, one can detect Turner's almost stoic acceptance of the eroding influence of time on American exceptionalism. "Into this vast shaggy continent of ours poured the first feeble tide of European settlement. European men, institutions and ideas were lodged in the American wilderness, and this great American West took them to her bosom, taught them a new way of looking upon the destiny of the common man, trained them in adaptation to the conditions of the New World,"

Turner exuberantly declared. But then he continued, "and ever as society on her eastern border grew to resemble the Old World in its social forms and its industry, ever, as it began to lose faith in the ideal of democracy, she opened new provinces, and dowered new democracies in her most distant domains with her material treasures and with the enobling influence that the fierce love of freedom furnished to the pioneer."[5]

The significant point to notice in this passage is that Turner balances the political plenitude of the American West with the political entropy of the American East. This is the major theme in his writings. America as frontier lies just to the west of the first English settlements on the Atlantic coast. After English colonists became American democrats by crossing this frontier into the first West, however, it was inevitable that their democracy would regress into aristocratic European politics. This was a cycle that Turner traced from the seventeenth to the nineteenth centuries. When discussing the rise and fall of virtuous frontier governments, he always used the language of Jacksonian America. To a large extent, the term republic had been replaced by that of democracy, and the spatial alternative to the environment of time was known as the West. Jacksonians also insisted that American national identity was synonomous with the West. For Turner, the initial colonial settlements had not been American, and when the social conditions of a colonial frontier area became like those of Europe, that area could no longer be defined as American. In Turner's metaphysical geography, a large part of the United States along the eastern seaboard had, by 1789, ceased to be democratic and American. But that region, now dominated by the particulars of time rather than the universals of space, was unfortunately also expanding westward.

Turner, expressing the Jacksonian culture in which he was raised, gave historical substance to these abstract categories of political philosophy in precisely the same way that James Harrington had—by linking time and space to two absolutely different kinds of property, freehold and commercial. For Turner, Europeans in 1600 were committed to commercial property and therefore to the dynamism of time. But Europeans could become Americans by moving into a West characterized by freehold property, property which expressed the static perfection of universal laws. Describing the development of the first West in the seventeenth century, Turner had written that "a new society had been established," on the colonial frontiers, "differing in essentials from the colonial society of the coast. It was a democractic, self-sufficing, primitive agricultural society." And this new society was in constant conflict with "the party of privilege, chiefly the Eastern men of property allied with the English authorities."[6]

When Turner wrote about "Eastern men of property," he was not contrasting them with propertyless men of the West. Rather, he was contrasting the freehold property of the West with the eastern property of commerce, finance, and speculation. It was the property of power and dependence that corrupted political virtue; freehold property sustained virtue because of the autonomy of its owners. Turner argued that before the American Revolution there had been several cycles in which people had escaped the corruption of eastern, or European, politics and achieved a virtuous western, or American, democracy on the frontier, only to have the corrupting pattern of the Old World dependence supplant New World independence.

The American Revolution, for Turner, was the defense of the most recent of these frontier democracies against the aggressiveness of an English government that was attempting to impose its corrupt political patterns on American virtue. But as a Jacksonian, Turner did not believe the founding fathers had institutionalized that virtue in a balanced Constitution. Pocock has suggested that the Jacksonians differed from Harrington, who saw the expansion of a freehold empire supporting a Constitution that necessarily included the one, the few, and the many in a framework of checks and balances. The Jacksonians put much less stress than the founding fathers did on finding virtue in such a balanced Constitution. Instead, for Pocock, they placed their hope for virtue almost completely on the dynamism of the freehold empire. Turner, therefore, as a Jacksonian, saw the Constitution with its checks and balances as an attempt to frustrate the direct expression of the will of the already virtuous freeholding people. According to Turner, most of the founding fathers, symbolized by Hamilton, were advocates of commerce, and the Constitution was designed to impose their speculative and corrupting property on the agrarian democrats. The replacement of the Articles of Confederation by the Constitution, therefore, represented one more instance of the cyclical decline of virtue before the onslaught of corruption.

But this gathering darkness of 1789 gave way to the dawning light of 1828. Like Bancroft, Turner could prophesy that the antidemocratic declension of the early nineteenth century was about to be overcome. Turner's enthusiasm for the triumph of Jacksonian democracy over the antidemocratic forces of 1789 was, of course, related to what Henry Nash Smith identified as the concept of the fee-simple empire that stretched from the Appalachians westward to the Pacific. "The settlement from the mountains to the seaboard kept connection with the rear," Turner emphasized, "and it was only from the time the mountains rose between the pioneer and the seaboard that a new order of Americanism arose." The vast expanse of this virgin land increased the number of freeholders until they were able to defeat the descendants of the founding fathers. "An agricultural society, strongest in the areas of rural isolation rather than in the areas of greater density of population and of greater wealth," Turner continued, "had triumphed, for the time, over the conservative, industrial, commerical, and manufacturing society of the New England type. It meant that a new aggressive, expansive democracy emphasizing human rights and individualism as against the old established order which emphasized vested rights and corporate action, had come into control."[7]

Working within the republican tradition, Turner again qualified his description of the triumph of Jacksonian democracy with the phrase "for the time." Following close behind the westward expansion of freehold property came the westward expansion of an industrialism imported from Europe. Its property patterns, like those of commerce, were the corrupting ones of power and dependence. Therefore, when he announced the closing of the frontier in 1893, his commitment to the Harringtonian tradition compelled him to write, "The free lands are gone. The material forces that gave vitality to Western democracy are passing away." And so he posed the rhetorical question, "Under the forms of the American democracy is there in reality evolving such a concentration of economic and social power in the hands of a comparatively few men as may make political democracy an appearance rather than a reality?"[8]

The series of Machiavellian cycles, which Turner saw as the fundamental characteristic of American history, was now over. Exodus into a sequence of agricultural frontiers had made possible an equal number of politically virtuous communities. But always the people in those communities had developed forms of commercial property that undermined the freehold property that was the necessary economic foundation for a virtuous democracy. Until 1890, it had been possible for new generations to move westward, to renew the cycle from corruption to virtue, leaving the people in the East to suffer the culmination of the cycle as it moved from virtue to corruption. The political future of the entire American nation, for Turner, was one of complete entropy. No space remained as a refuge from time. No virtuous America as West remained independent from European corruption.

Gene Wise has written perceptively about the contradictions and tensions that characterized Turner's writings from the 1893 essay until his death in 1930. Turner, as Wise points out, insisted that an American historian should be a prophet of democracy. But, although his essays expressed hope for the future of democracy, Turner could provide no substantial evidence why that future would not be undemocratic. He never deviated from his argument that freehold property was the necessary economic base for democracy. Turner always reiterated that "not the Constitution, but free land made the democratic type of society in America for three centuries while it occupied its empire." Wise, therefore, invites us to see a direct parallel between Turner's rhetoric of hope and Perry Miller's description of Cotton Mather's rhetoric of hope two hundred years earlier. Like Mather who tried to overcome a sense of declension with an optimism about the future, Turner could not tie such optimism to any concrete experience in the present situation. Instead, like Mather, he implored, "Let us dream as our fathers dreamt and let us make our dreams come true." Wise quotes Miller's description of Cotton Mather so that we may feel the emptiness and futility of Turner's rhetorical asurance that democracy would be fulfilled in the future. "We avert our gaze," Miller wrote, "while he fled up the ladder of the jeremiad and soothed himself with fresh dreams of the New Jerusalem."[9]

Although Turner never wavered from his belief that an economy of freehold property was a necessary precondition for virtuous politics, his writings do reveal a significant change in the Harringtonian understanding of time. When Turner's generation of professional historians rejected the divine authority of Protestantism, they also self-consciously accepted evolution as a scientific truth. Turner, like so many other late Victorians, believed that evolution could replace Protestantism as the authority for progress in history. According to this secular faith, evolutionary progress, when applied to humans, revealed that society had developed through a series of stages from primitive savagery to the pinnacle of modern civilization.[10]

Henry Nash Smith has pointed out the contradiction in Turner's identifying political democracy with the simple economic pattern of freehold property while associating modern civilization with complexity. Turner, in Smith's analysis, had a love-hate relationship with the West because he defined it as a primitive stage of social development that must give way to more sophisticated and complex patterns. It is important to remember that Turner, before his conversion to a belief in evolutionary progress, held that seventeenth-century perspective that associated time with history and corruption and the timeless with nature and virtue. It appears that he never gave up that perspective when he thought about politics, but he embraced time as orderly and meaningful within the framework of social evolution. Turner and many of his contemporaries shared the belief that the impersonal forces of physical evolution influenced society most directly through the economic environment. Humans built social and political patterns to adjust to that environment. But because the underlying economic reality continued to develop through time, it constantly moved away from existing social and political patterns. For Turner's generation of social scientists, the primary, active role of economic forces and the secondary, reflective role of social and political patterns always caused cultural lag. As soon as a culture adjusted to its economic environment, that environment was moving again. The culture, then, had lost touch with reality and had to be reconstructed to catch up with economic progress.[11]

This internally divided Turner looked at American political democracy in 1890 as the victim of the triumph of time, symbolized by the Old World of Europe, over the universal principles of space as they had been temporarily embodied in the American landscape. But he also celebrated the spread of sophisticated civilization across the Atlantic to the East Coast of the United States and then westward across the Appalachians. Cultural progress, relecting the dynamic qualities of natural law, was overcoming the cultural lag of the provincial societies of the West. When he thought about democracy, it was the East that was unnatural and the West that was natural. But socially the East was natural and the West unnatural.

There is an amazing symmetry about the way in which Turner used these two contradictory understandings of the natural in his writings. When he wrote about the period from 1600 to 1828, he contrasted the unreality of European time against the reality of American space. His ability to use the rhetorical ritual of the American jeremiad to structure his historical narratives was based on that contrast. The promise of the colonial democracies, which were threatened by the undemocratic men who had written the Constitution, would be fulfilled by the democracy of the trans-Appalachian West. "Jefferson," Turner wrote, "was the first prophet of American democracy, he was the John the Baptist of democracy, not its Moses." It was Andrew Jackson who led the exodus that finally separated American democracy from the European past. Americans in 1828 "were rallying around the man who personified their passion for democracy and nationalism – the fiery Jackson."[12]

Turner had plans for many books, but the only one he was able to complete described this triumph of Jackson and the West over the framers of the Constitution and the East. He structured his narrative to anticipate Jackson as the greatest American Moses. Each colonial frontier pointed toward the ultimate frontier of the trans-Appalachian West. After the exodus of 1828, however, time, aristocracy, the East, and Europe were no longer the past; and space, democracy, the West, and America, no longer the future. The symbolism was reversed as the American spatial future faded into the past and its plenitude was transformed into entropy. It was Europe that had ceased to be entropic and commanded the future as it expressed the energy of the evolutionary process.

When Turner declared that the problem of the Populists in the 1890s "is not to create democracy, but to conserve democratic institutions and ideals," we might expect that he was prepared to describe his own generation in tragic terms. All Americans shared with the Populists the problem of defending an inexorably shrinking space; the West, democracy, and America were in decline. All Americans were now defenders of a lost cause. But, although there is much that is somber in Turner's discussion of the decline of the West and democracy, he did not describe his own period as he had that of the Revolution. He had explicitly related the democracy of 1776 to freehold property and the undemocratic Federalists to commercial property. Because commercial property, unlike freehold property, did not represent the reality of universal laws, it fought its battles through subterfuge and conspiracy. And after 1800, the victorious Federalist conspiracy was overthrown by the power of the trans-Appalachian West with its vast expansion of freehold property, a power expressed by the honest and direct politics of Jackson and the Democratic party.

In the 1890s, however, Turner saw the Populists being defeated by the rational and universal forces of evolution. It is significant that he did not relate the waning of democracy to a conspiracy. The natural was not being overcome by the unnatural. The plenitude of American space that prevailed in Turner's writings when he described the years before the Civil War was replaced by the plenitude of evolution when he discussed the period after 1865. From this perspective, the yeoman politics of late nineteenth-century America could be seen as the life-style of a primitive people who were destined to move from this early and simple stage of society to higher and more complex stages of civilization. From this perspective, the decline of the American West was not a tragedy but a sign of progress. Turner quoted the Italian economist Achille Loria who had argued that all societies go through a series of fixed stages as they move from childhood to an adult state. According to this theory, American space had allowed Americans to abandon an advanced level of European sophistication and regress to a primitive, childlike society. "Loria," Turner wrote, "has urged the study of colonial life as an aid to understanding the stages of European development. There is much truth in this. The United States lies like a huge page in the history of society. Line by line as we read this continental page from West to East, we find the record of social evolution."[13]

By accepting this idea of social evolution, Turner could partially escape from the Jacksonian and Populist commitment to the Harringtonian tradition that defined the economic forces defeating freehold property as symbolic of the meaningless flux of time. If one assumed that the patterns of industrial capitalism that had spread from Europe to the United States represented the rational progress of evolutionary nature, it was the Populists whose economic theories expressed fantasy and unreality and not their opponents. Thus, Turner wrote about the Populists that "a primitive society can hardly be expected to show the intelligent appreciation of the complexity of business interests in a developed society."[14]

But Turner, throughout his academic career, struggled with this contradictory understanding of American democracy. When he looked at the period from 1600 to 1828, he found democracy the most fulfilling and virtuous political life available to humankind. He accepted fully the Machiavellian tradition as modified first by Harrington and then by the Jacksonians. And his understanding of nature was that of timeless universals. But when he looked at the period after 1865, after the conventions of republican thought told him that virtuous politics would begin to decay under the dynamism of historical change, he redefined Western democracy as a primitive stage of human civilization. His understanding of nature was that of an evolutionary development from lower to higher forms. Although Turner could predict an exodus of Americans from a childlike to a more mature society, he could not link that exodus to the promise of a democratic, exceptional America. Ironically, that exodus would not fulfill the promise; it would end it. There would be a new promise of a progressive, but undemocratic, civilization that from its center in Europe would control the American future. It is not surprising, then, that Turner, unlike Bancroft before him or Beard after him, did not write an epochal narrative of the sweep of American history.

There is little evidence that Turner brought his dilemma to self-consciousness, but rather continued, as Gene Wise has pointed out, to agonize over the contradictions without achieving a resolution. Charles Beard, like Turner from the Midwest but almost a generation younger, was, however, able to create an argument that linked the agricultural democracy of colonial America with social evolution. Beard, in contrast to Turner, was able to bring the good news that democracy need not be equated with primitivism. In so doing, he revitalized the American jeremiad as the narrative structure for American historical writing. Beard, therefore, could be as prolific as Bancroft because, unlike Turner, he was able to complete the rhetorical ritual of the jeremiad. He presented evidence that convinced his readers that the declension of 1900, although it seemed to contradict the democratic promise of 1600, would be overcome. Beard's prophecy of a fulfilled democracy in the future was convincing to his contemporaries because he announced that the highest stage of economic evolution, industrialism, provided a material foundation that supported political democracy as fully as freehold property had in the past.[15]

It is clear, then, that Beard in 1890 was less committed than Turner to the identification of political virtue with the experience of a timeless space, symbolized by the American geographic landscape, and that he was much more comfortable with the concept of social evolution. Beard, however, did not completely abandon the Puritan heritage that had identified the Promised Land with American space; nor did he completely abandon Harrington's identification of virtuous politics with freehold property and corruption with capitalist property.

His synthesis of the history of a unique American democracy, standing apart from the aristocracies of Europe because of the virgin characteristics of American geography, with the history of a progressive civilization spreading from Europe to the backward areas of the world was, unlike Turner's, fully optimistic. He was able to suggest that colonial democracy was a preview of the future toward which social evolution was proceeding rather than merely a return to uncivilized primitivism.

It is of great symbolic significance that Beard's first book, *The Industrial Revolution* (1901), was about nineteenth-century Europe. While Turner was lamenting the decline of American democracy because the complexity of European civilization was spreading across the United States, Beard was celebrating the upsurge of democracy in England. Immediately after his graduation from DePauw College in Indiana, Beard went to England where he participated in the creation of a college for working men. Ruskin Hall, for young midwestern Americans, symbolized the liberation of the common people from their centuries-old subservience to an aristocracy. Surely Turner was wrong that the 1890s were the decade when hope for democracy died.[16]

In examining English history, Beard identified capitalism as the evolutionary stage that succeeded medievalism. He described the capitalist period in England from the seventeenth to the nineteenth centuries as a chaotic time when individuals seemed to pursue their own self-interests in a war against their neighbors. But Beard argued that the economic poverty and social misery of the capitalist era was giving way to a higher stage of evolution. The undemocratic unity of the medieval past was being replaced by the democratic unity of modern industrialism.

Crucial to Beard's analysis, and to Turner's, was the association of political democracy and economic resources. There was no possibility of democracy during the medieval and capitalist periods, Beard stated, because limited wealth caused classes or individuals to act selfishly and oppress other classes or individuals. But in the eighteenth century, the Industrial Revolution began, opening up a magnificent future of plenitude. "Man, who through the long centuries had toiled with his hands, aided by crude implements, to wrest a pitiful substance from nature, suddenly discovered that the blind forces against which he had been struggling could be chained to do his work," Beard exulted. "Suddenly, almost like a thunderbolt from a clear sky, were ushered in the storm and stress of the Industrial Revolution, the mechanical inventions of the centuries were eclipsed in less than one hundred years."[17] Turner, like the English republican thinkers of the seventeenth century, saw America as the only source of economic plenitude, land, on which to base virtuous politics. But the American frontier was a finite resource that inevitably would be used up. Beard visualized a much more powerful frontier of economic plenitude, one whose vitality was infinite because it was in harmony with the dynamism of evolutionary physical nature. Time was not the enemy of such a nature, as it had been of the American landscape. Time, as endless progress, was a characteristic of evolution where nature was perpetually young.

An ecstatic Beard, therefore, did not define this Industrial Revolution in Harringtonian terms as an island of meaning within the sea of historical chaos. There was, he affirmed, a law of progress running throughout history. The first part of this law, immediately apparent at the beginning of the Industrial Revolution, was "the substitution of intelligence for precedent." The second part of the law, which was gradually becoming clear during the nineteenth century, was the substitution of "organization for chaos and anarchy."

At the very moment when Turner was describing the diminishing abundance of the American agricultural frontier, Beard was describing the expanding plenitude of an industrial frontier in England. Turner had linked the entropy of the American West with the entropy of American democracy. Democracy, for Turner, could not exist without a dynamic supply of freehold property. But

Beard insisted that industrialism did provide the economic foundation for political democracy. Looking at England, the first country to experience what he called the Industrial Revolution, Beard declared that "just as the political history of the past one hundred years has centered in political democracy, so the industrial history has centered in Industrial Democracy." There seems, he concluded, "to be but little doubt that the trusts are merely pointing the way to higher forms of industrial methods in which the people, instead of a few capitalists, will reap the benefits."[18]

Beard had overcome Turner's pessimism about the future of democracy through this dramatic challenge to the tradition of the separation of a vigorous New American World from an Old and decadent Europe. Anticipating the modernization theory that has influenced so many American historians in the 1960s and 1970s, Beard, in 1900, was primarily concerned with the transition from medieval to modern Europe. Beard described that change as an exodus that was emancipating the common people of Europe from the Egyptian bondage they had suffered when their lives were controlled by the medieval aristocracy. After the Renaissance and Reformation, the people had wandered in the wilderness, experiencing great suffering at the hands of capitalists who took advantage of the breakdown of shared moral principles and exploited the people even more viciously than had the feudal aristocrats. But they were reaching the Promised Land of industrial democracy. The march of humanity into the twentieth century symbolized the transition from the wilderness to the Promised Land.

Upon his return to the United States, Beard completed a dissertation, "The Office of the Justice of the Peace in England," in the political science department at Columbia University, where he began his teaching career. He was delighted to find a member of the history department, James Harvey Robinson, who shared his understanding of modern European history as a progressive movement toward democracy. In 1907, Beard and Robinson published a textbook, *The Development of Modern Europe*. Its narrative structure expressed a rhetorical ritual very similar to that identified by Bercovitch as the American jeremiad. Theirs, however, was a modern jeremiad.

In the preface, the authors called attention to what they believed was the uniqueness of their book. It represented a "new history." "New history" differed from "old history" by beginning with a discussion of the current situation. Then the "new historian" wrote about the past in such a way that the patterns of development that linked the past and the present could be clarified. Beard and Robinson asked their readers to consider the eighteenth century as the critical moment in the past when the foundations of the present and the future were established. In that century of the Enlightenment, a group of prophets appeared who gave people the vision that history was more than chaos or the repetition of cycles. History, for the Enlightenment *philosophes*, was progress. This was the first parallel to the American jeremiad. The promise of the modern world was established, and it was inevitable that the promise would be fulfilled. But Beard and Robinson, as militant secularists, did not identify the promise with the theology of the Reformation. The promise came from people like themselves who looked to reason and science, not faith and religion, for the proof that humanity was being liberated from the peasantry, the aristocracy, the monarchy, and, above all, from the Roman Catholic church of the Middle Ages. It was the scientists of the Age of Enlightenment who proved "that man was by nature good; that he should freely use his own God-given reason; that he was capable of becoming increasingly wise by a study of nature's laws; and that he could indefinitely better his own condition and that of his fellows if he would free himself from the shackles of error and superstition."[19]

The promise of the Enlightenment had seemed to be fulfilled in the exodus experience of the French Revolution when the medieval past was left behind. But, for Beard and Robinson, political fanatics had unfortunately gained control of the Revolution and replaced democracy with tyranny. Gradually, however, France began to move again toward fulfillment of the promise. By 1850, there was evidence that all of Europe was moving toward democracy. Because the suffering that inevitably accompanied such a major social transformation was intensified by the selfishness of capitalists, Beard and Robinson were not surprised that the Enlightenment promise that democratic means could achieve a liberated society was challenged during the nineteenth century by Karl Marx. For Marx, the fulfillment of the Enlightenment promise demanded the use of political tyranny and revolutionary violence to overthrow capitalism and achieve a producers' democracy. But Beard and Robinson did not believe that capitalism was a fully organized stage in human evolution comparable to that of the medieval past or the democratic future. Capitalism represented the kind of anarchy and selfishness of an era of transition that would give way to democratic political means. Since capitalism represented, in their analysis, chaos and irrationality, one of the factors working for its replacement was the Enlightenment commitment to rationality and the scientific method. Beard and Robinson therefore rejected Marx's theory of the necessity of class warfare and the dictatorship of the proletariat. "It is clear," they wrote, "that the evils of our present organization are being more and more generally understood and there is hope that many shocking inequalities may gradually be done away with."[20] They, not Marx, were the true prophets of how the promise of the Enlightenment and the Industrial Revolution would overcome the current undemocratic experience and be fulfilled in the future.

Like the Anglo-Americans of the eighteenth century, Beard identified rationality with political virtue and irrationality with political corruption. But unlike those republicans and also unlike Turner, Beard was certain that industrialism was the highest economic stage of evolution and that its triumph over earlier stages of economic activity also marked the triumph of the rationality of a mature humanity over the irrationality of the childhood of the human race. Anglo-American republicans had defined all of history as chaotic and irrational, but Beard knew that human history as part of natural history was becoming more organized and rational. In 1909, he published an article entitled "Politics" that summarized his views on the relationship of politics and evolution. In it, Beard engaged in an implicit debate with the republican tradition. He began by suggesting that his discipline of political science was undergoing a revolution as it became open to influences from history, economics, and sociology. For Beard, this meant that finally "solid foundations are being laid in reality in place of the shifting sands of speculation. We are getting away from metaphysics, from artificialities." The most important liberation, in his view, was from the belief in static laws of nature, from the belief in a state of nature from whose rational principles humankind had fallen into the irrationality of history. Implicitly addressing Turner's sense of the declension of American democracy, Beard declared that political scientists had learned that history was not decline but an upward movement out of "a dim and dateless past into an illimitable future which many of us believe will not be hideous and mean, but beautiful and magnificent."[21]

If history represented the inevitability of evolutionary progress, Beard argued, the nineteenth-century English and American political scientists who believed that the political and legal patterns of that society represented the immutable laws of a timeless state of nature were mistaken. And Beard pointed most forcefully to the conservative defense of freedom and contract and private property on the grounds that they represented immutable natural law. Confronting capitalism with democracy as he had done in *The Industrial Revolution and the Development of Modern Europe*, Beard urged that democracy represented the higher stage of evolution and that capitalist property had no claim to legitimacy. We must remember, he declared, that the focus of political life is sovereignty. In the history of Western civilization, there had occurred the progressive shift of sovereignty from the monarchy to the people. We in the United States, he continued, have assumed that we achieved democracy before the rest of the world. But, he declared, if democracy means the sovereignty of the people, we Americans do not now have a democracy. Our Constitution with its checks and balances makes such popular sovereignty impossible. Compare this undemocratic Constitution, he urged, with an ideal democratic one "where the rule of the majority is frankly recognized (a condition of affairs gravely feared by the framers of our Constitution), government tends toward a type, unified in internal structure, emancipated from formal limitations, and charged with direct responsibility to the source of power."[22]

Looking at the United States from the perspective of a Europe becoming more democratic because of the growing influence of the scientific method and industrialism, Beard could not share Turner's view that an exceptional American democracy was being lost in the 1890s because Europe had begun to influence American history. Reversing the situation, Beard insisted that it was because of European influences that Americans would achieve a democracy. The prophetic fulfillment of a democratic future in the United States depended upon the promise that had emerged during the Enlightenment in eighteenth-century Europe. Turner was right that American provincialism was giving way to European sophistication, but it was an undemocratic capitalist provincialism that was surrendering to the forces of social evolution spreading from Europe to the rest of the world.

Such major contemporary political scientists as Woodrow Wilson, Henry Jones Ford, and Frank Goodnow, Beard reported, "have conclusively shown the unreality of the doctrine of divided powers, and the positive fashion in which our democratic political society seeks through extra-legal party organization to overcome the friction of a disjointed machine." Americans, by 1900, were creating a democratic political society despite the undemocratic aspects of the Constitution because the country was being industrialized. Americans were sharing in the worldwide exodus from an undemocratic status quo. Industrialism, unlike the freehold frontier of the American West, could sustain virtuous rational democratic politics in every corner of the world. Beard therefore ended his essay with a dramatic affirmation that American industrial democracy was a part of a worldwide pattern. "A new division of political research may be denominated world politics," he wrote. "The shuttle of trade and intercourse flies ever faster and it may be weaving the web for a world state. It may be that steam and electricity are to achieve that unity of mankind which rests on the expansion of a common consciousness of rights and wrongs through the extension of identical modes of economic activity."[23]

In 1909, it appeared that the only significant similarity between Beard's and Turner's understanding of American history was their agreement on the existence of a freehold democracy at the time of the American Revolution. Although Beard agreed with Turner that the unprecedented number of yeoman farmers in the English colonies caused them to be more democratic than any European societies in the eighteenth century, he did not separate a sacred American space from profane European history as Turner had when he wrote about the years before 1865. Beard's primary focus was on his concept of social evolution from the evils of the medieval past, through the sufferings of the era of capitalism toward a humanity redeemed by industrial democracy.

In his first major scholarly work that dealt with the United States, the text-book *American Government and Politics*, which appeared in 1910, Beard stressed the domination of colonial politics by capitalist elites similar to those who were in control of English political institutions. For Beard, the ironic cause for the beginning of the Revolution was to be found in the competition between the American and the English elites because of "discontent with economic restrictions, not with their fundamental political institutions." Certainly, he continued, they were "not motivated by the levelling doctrines with which the French middle class undermined the bulwarks of feudalism."[24] Once the Revolution began, however, and shattered existing patterns of authority between the English and the colonial elites, democratic ideas could gain a reception throughout the newly independent states.

As a prophet of a democratic future on a worldwide scale that would fulfill the international promise of the Enlightenment and industrialism, Beard found nothing sacred about the American Revolution. The competition between English and American capitalists momentarily so shook the patterns of established authority in the new independent American states that spokespeople for the freehold democracies that had existed at the local level within the colonies were able to influence the shape of the Articles of Confederation. But when the Revolution ended, the American capitalist elites were able to once more consolidate their authority and power and replace the decentralized and democratic Articles of Confederation with the centralized and undemocratic Constitution. They attacked the Articles of Confederation, Beard wrote, because they had no quarrel with the system of class rule and the strong centralization of government that existed in England. American capitalists "were not seeking to realize any fine notions about democracy and equality. They were anxious above everything else to safeguard the rights of property against any levelling tendencies."[25]

In 1910, Beard was certain that he understood the pattern of social evolution. He was, after all, a political scientist and, for him, "political science is to be the greatest of all the sciences. Physics and politics are to be united." Political scientists, Beard continued, utilized "the economic interpretation of history" that "rests upon the concept that social progress in general is the result of contending interests in society."[26] As a political scientist who was a prophet of industrial democracy, Beard took a dispassionate pose in describing the defeat of freehold democracy in the 1780s. The democracy of colonial America was an anomaly outside the major pattern of social evolution that had to move from the medieval past through capitalism until it reached industrial democracy. And it was the accident of the civil war between English and colonial capitalists that had allowed freehold democracy to momentarily capture political leadership from the capitalists. But it was inevitable that capitalists would regain control in the United States. As in England, capitalism had to prepare the historical context for the industrialism that would replace it.

Turner saw the trans-Appalachian West as a spatial force that could temporarily overcome the undemocratic capitalism of the founding fathers. The freehold democracy of Andrew Jackson was powerful enough to seize the national identity and to protect it in 1861, under the leadership of Abraham Lincoln, against the reactionary aggressiveness of the neomedieval slaveholders of the South. But when Beard wrote about the Civil War, he described it as another victory of capitalism over a vestige of the medieval past. Between 1900 and 1919, whenever Beard wrote about the nineteenth century, he described the continuing control of the capitalist elite that had been able to defeat the anomalous freehold democracy of the 1780s.

Since Beard believed that the United States, like England and all of western Europe, was participating in the inevitable transition from capitalism to industrial democracy, he defined his responsibility as a political scientist and historian as that of clarifying the extent to which capitalism had become an example of cultural lag, out of touch with the new economic reality of industrialism. There was, however, a special irony in this situation of cultural lag in the United States. In the first place, for Beard, most Americans shared Turner's belief that their country was already a democracy. They were not aware of the entrenched social and economic power of the capitalist aristocracy. This ignorance was making it possible for capitalism in America to effectively delay the inevitable transition to industrial democracy. In the second place, Beard asserted, American capitalists had a constitutional weapon at their disposal that was more powerful than any available to English capitalists. Ironically, it was because capitalism had been prematurely challenged by the chance existence of freehold democracy in the English colonies that American capitalists had forged the powerful weapon of judicial review, written into the Constitution in 1787, to guard against any democratic uprising in the future. In his 1912 book, *The Supreme Court and the Constitution*, Beard presented this thesis, arguing that the founding fathers "regarded it as their chief duty, in drafting the new Constitution, to find a way of preventing the renewal of what they deemed 'legislative tyranny'." "Under the Articles of Confederation," he continued, "populism had a free hand, for majorities in the state legislatures were omnipotent. Anyone who reads the economic history of the time will see why the solid conservative interests of the country were weary of talk about the 'rights of the people' and bent upon establishing firm guarantees for the rights of property." To overcome the unexpected upsurge of democracy in the newly independent states, the capitalist aristocracy invented judicial review, the power of the courts to block the will of the people expressed through the legislatures. "Judicial control," Beard concluded, "was really a new and radical departure which did not spring from Anglo-Saxon 'ideas' but from the practical necessity of creating a foil for the rights of property against belligerent democracy."[27]

Whereas Turner is best known for his essay of 1893, Beard's next book, *An Economic Interpretation of the Constitution of the United States*, which appeared in 1913, is the one for which he is best remembered. It brought to a climax themes he had been developing in *American Government and Politics* and *The Supreme Court and the Constitution*.[28] All of his scholarly energies between 1909 and 1915 were directed toward the clarification of the unique relationship of the United States to the universal pattern of social evolution that was moving humanity from medieval darkness, through the necessary sufferings of capitalism, to the Promised Land of industrial democracy. The exodus in America, one of the most industrialized nations in the world, was being delayed because Americans erroneously believed they already had democracy. Americans vastly exaggerated the experience of freehold democracy during the Revolution and the era of Andrew Jackson. They blindly associated the Constitution with what they assumed was the nation's fundamental identity as a democracy. They ignored the ability of the capitalist aristocracy to directly control the major economic developments and indirectly control politics throughout the nineteenth century. As industrialism began to encourage a true upsurge of political democracy at the beginning of the twentieth century, the will of the people expressed in state and national legislation was being effectively blocked by the power of judicial review.

Beard's modern, industrial jeremiad was full of confidence in 1913, and one can feel the prophetic tension with which he infused *An Economic Interpretation of the Constitution*. In 1789, the promise of a democratic future existed in the Enlightenment and the Industrial Revolution that had begun in England. Ironically, therefore, there had to be a declension from the freehold democracy of the Articles of Confederation if undemocratic capitalists were to create the foundations for the industrialism that was the necessary base for modern democracy. The further irony was that most Americans believed, with Turner, that freehold democracy had been restored with much greater vigor by Andrew Jackson. They were not aware, therefore, that capitalists had controlled the country since 1789. Instead of lamenting, as Turner was, that freehold democracy was being lost in 1890, they needed to understand the desperate way in which capitalists were using the political and judicial weapons they had developed in the 1780s to fight a rear-guard action against the industrial democracy whose victory was inevitable. The purpose of *An Economic Interpretation of the Constitution*, therefore, was twofold. Beard had to complete his education of the public to convince them that the new nation that emerged in 1789 was the antithesis of democracy. He also had to demonstrate that the capitalist victory over the freehold democracy of the Articles of Confederation was inevitable and therefore progressive.

In attempting to desacralize the Constitution and reveal the existence of a capitalist aristocracy that had given definition to the new nation, Beard assumed that he was conversing with readers who, like Turner, understood democracy within the Harringtonian tradition of republican virtue. J. F. A. Pocock has argued that for this tradition, a virtuous republic "must be a perfect partnership of all citizens and all values since, if it was less, a part would be ruling in the name of the whole, subjecting goods to its own particular goods and moving toward despotism and the corruption of its own values." Beard was clarifying, therefore, how some of the capitalists came to rule in the name of the whole, subjecting the freehold property of the people to their own selfish interests. The freehold democracy expressed in the Articles of Confederation was overthrown, Beard argued, because "large and important groups of economic interests were adversely affected by the system of government under the Articles of Confederation, namely, those of public securities, shipping and manufacturing, money at interest; in short, capital as opposed to land."[29]

Through brief biographies of all the members of the Constitutional convention, Beard demonstrated to his own satisfaction that all the signers were related to the dynamic property interests of capitalism. His use of the term capitalism conformed perfectly to the conventions of eighteenth-century republican theory. In contrast to the contemplative and virtuous aspects of freehold property, capitalist property was aggressive and self-interested. "The representatives of these important interests attempted to secure amendments to the Articles of Confederation which would safeguard their rights in the future," he continued, but "having failed to realize their great purposes through the regular means, the leaders in the movement set to work to secure by a circuitous route the assembling of a convention to 'revise' the Articles of Confederation with the hope of obtaining, outside of the existing legal framework, the adoption of a revolutionary programme." To facilitate this change, a coherent philosophy of self-interest was expressed in the Federalist Papers. This was class, not national, unity. "It is to the owners of personality anxious to find a foil against the attacks of levelling democracy," he concluded, "that the authors of the Federalist address their most cogent arguments in favor of ratification."[30]

As war began in Europe in 1914 – a war that Beard came to see as providing a revolutionary opportunity for a swift collapse of the mixtures of medievalism and capitalism that still obscured the evolutionary forces that were developing industrial democracy as the future for the entire world – he was almost frantically using his scholarship to destroy what Bercovitch has called the American jeremiad. Beard insisted that there was no promise in the American past that was to be fulfilled in the future. The colonial democracy that had asserted itself in the Articles of Confederation was committed to decentralization; and Beard knew that social evolution was moving humanity from decentralization toward centralization. The industrial democracy of the future was not local but universal. The founding fathers, as he had demonstrated in *American Government and Politics, The Supreme Court and the Constitution*, and *An Economic Interpretation of the Constitution*, were antidemocratic capitalists. But the president of the United States, Woodrow Wilson, elected in 1912 as the candidate of the Democratic party, insisted that the future of American democracy would be a fulfillment of the democratic promise that Turner had found in Thomas Jefferson and Andrew Jackson, those democrats who, for Turner, had overthrown the antidemocratic politics of the founding fathers at the beginning of the nineteenth century.

Beard believed, however, he had found his Moses figure in Theodore Roosevelt, who would lead the American people in an exodus from the declension of capitalism into the Promised Land of industrial democracy. Supporting Roosevelt's New Nationalism against Wilson's New Freedom in the election of 1912, Beard vehemently attacked Jefferson as the source of Wilson's erroneous political philosophy. Wilson asks us to fulfill Jeffersonian democracy, Beard wrote, but "agrarian democracy" is as fallacious "as the equally unreal and unattainable democracy of small business" that "is Wilson's goal." With great bitterness, Beard asked, "Today nearly half of us belong to the 'mobs of the great cities' — sores on the body politic. What message has the sage of Monticello for us?"[31] To prove the inadequacy of the Jeffersonian and Jacksonian democracy whose decline Turner lamented, Beard published *The Economic Origins of Jeffersonian Democracy* in 1914.[32] In it, as in *An Economic Interpretation of the Constitution*, Beard assumed that his readers defined virtue in terms of the republican tradition. Turner had found virtue in Jefferson and Jackson because he believed they represented freehold property that offered an alternative to the class bias of capitalist self-interest. But Jefferson and Jackson, Beard insisted, represented not freehold property but "an aristocracy of slave-holding planters." They fought Hamiltonian policies, not to restore freehold democracy, but to fulfill their own selfish, materialistic, and aristocratic interests. This book pointed toward Beard's well-known interpretation of the Civil War as a clash between the self-interest of northern capitalists and southern slave-holding aristocrats.

Beard provided a clear outline of his own political philosophy in another of his textbooks, *Contemporary American History, 1877–1913*, published in 1914. Because his democratic promise was to be found in eighteenth-century Europe and not in either the colonial period or the early nineteenth century, he did not write lovingly about those periods as Turner had done. But Beard, unlike Turner, could write enthusiastically about the immediate past, the present, and the future.

Our generation, he wrote, is characterized by economic revolution. We have become an industrial nation during these thirty years. And this material transformation must be accompanied by comparable changes in political and social thought, in legal and economic theory. But overcoming this cultural lag has been made difficult by the failure of the average American to see that revolution is in progress and that the country is suffering from the capitalist theory of laissez-faire. This fallacious economic philosophy was harmful enough in England but it has taken on disastrous proportions in America because of the power of the Supreme Court to enforce it as the law of the land. As the democratic upsurge during the Revolution had led American capitalists to develop judicial review, so these capitalists had used their victory in the Civil War to add the Fourteenth Amendment to their defensive armory. Capitalists then had greater protection of their property against any attempts by the national and state legislatures to regulate it in the public interest.

Mistakenly interpreting the Civil War as a defense of freehold democracy against an aggressive feudal aristocracy in the South, as they mistakenly interpreted the Revolution as a defense of democracy against an aggressive English aristocracy, Americans were not prepared to understand the relationship of their national history to the international history of capitalism and to the international force of industrialism that was succeeding capitalism as the fundamental economic reality in the world.

From the Civil War until 1896, therefore, the American people had largely ignored the massive processes of industrialization and urbanization that were accompanied by vast riches for the robber barons who controlled the giant new corporations and by grinding poverty for the new wage-earning classes in the cities. Turner's awareness of these developments caused him to become pessimistic about the future of democracy in the United States. But if Americans would only look at England, Beard urged, they would see that the logic of industrialism was overcoming these class divisions and leading to a new kind of democracy. Unlike freehold democracy, industrial democracy would be characterized by social and economic planning. This planning could achieve the goal of republican virtue, the "perfect partnership of all citizens and all values." No longer would capitalists be "ruling in the name of the whole" and "moving toward despotism and the corruption of its own values." But if Americans were to engage in such social and economic planning, they must free their legislatures from judicial control. The sovereign will of the people must become free to express itself directly and completely through its legislative bodies.

The election of 1896, according to Beard's account, marked the decisive turning point when Americans liberated themselves from the belief that they were defenders of an old, declining democracy and came to see themselves as the pioneers of a new, vigorous democracy. From 1896 to 1912, Beard wrote, the people were on the march, leaving behind the old political forms that the robber barons manipulated to their selfish advantage. The people were establishing direct methods of expressing their will. There was new emphasis on direct elections, the initiative, the referendum, the recall, the popular election of United States senators. This virtuous democracy, when it came, would, of course, be classless. The popular movement for a constitutional amendment to make an income tax possible was designed to undermine the capitalist aristocracy. Other progressive social and economic legislation was intended to lift the lower class out of their dependent situation. These progressive reforms, Beard argued, could not be understood as a fulfillment of a past agricultural democracy. These reforms were inspired by industrialism and were similar to those of other industrial nations. "It was apparent," Beard rejoiced, "from an examination of the legislation of the first decade of the twentieth century that they [the United States] were well in the paths of nations like Germany, England, and Australia."[33]

For Beard, the people had finally found in Theodore Roosevelt the leader for their exodus into this new democracy. Roosevelt understood that industrialism had created a centralized economy that required control by the national government. Roosevelt also understood that this new democracy, with its roots in the Enlightenment, offered an alternative to both capitalism and socialism. With deepest admiration, Beard pointed to Roosevelt's New Nationalism as the embodiment of this new democracy. "The New Nationalism puts the national need before sectional or personal advantages. It is impatient of the utter confusion that results from local legislatures attempting to treat national issues as local issues. It is still more impatient of the impotence which springs from overdivision of government powers, the impotence which makes it possible for local selfishness or for legal cunning, hired by wealthy special interests, to bring national activities to a deadlock. The New Nationalism regards the executive power as the steward of the public welfare. It demands of the judiciary that it shall be interested primarily in human welfare rather than in property, just as it demands that the representative body shall represent all the people."[34]

In *Contemporary American History*, Beard was clarifying how all of his scholarly writings revolved around the issue of political virtue. In the eighteenth century, defenders of republican virtue, the "country" party, had argued that freehold property encouraged rationality and harmony with natural law. It was that relationship with the universal that made virtuous politics possible when there was "a perfect partnership of all citizens and all values." For the "country" party, the triumph of their enemies, the "court" party, inevitably would bring corruption because of the characteristics of capitalist, in contrast to freehold, property. "Credit, to the observers of the new economics," Pocock has written about the eighteenth-century "country" party, "symbolized and made actual the opinion, passion, and fantasy in human affairs, where the perception of land might still appear the perception of real property and human relations as they really and naturally were." Underlying all of Beard's writing, beginning with his first book, *The Industrial Revolution*, was the assumption, which he shared with the eighteenth-century "country" party, that the essence of capitalism was the manipulation of credit for selfish interest, and that capitalism constituted a culture of transient particulars, mere "opinion, passion, and fantasy." But Beard also assumed the paradox that capitalism as a period of transition in the history of social evolution was preparing its own demise by helping to establish industrial production. For Beard, industrial production was the way of life in which all future generations throughout the world would participate. Beard believed industrial production to be, by definition, a cooperative enterprise. It was also, by definition, rational. Therefore, people who participated in industrial production were experiencing an economic community that embodied the political virtue cherished by eighteenth-century republicans. A factory, in Beard's estimation, was "a perfect parnership of all citizens and all values."

Beard, like Turner, assumed it was inevitable that capitalist property would defeat freehold property. But unlike Turner who defined capitalism as universal and freehold democracy as provincial, Beard defined capitalism as provincial and industrialism as universal. Turner, like the "country" party of the eighteenth century, pessimistically surmised that because each republic was local, its rationality and virtue must in the future be overwhelmed by the surrounding irrationality and corruption of history. However, if industrialism with its logic of rational productivity became universal, irrational and parasitic capitalism would disappear from human experience.

When the United States entered World War I in 1917, Beard was optimistic about the future of American democracy because he was completely confident about the future of industrialism as the economic base for virtuous politics. Like many of his fellow academic Progressives, such as Thorstein Veblen and John Dewey, Beard was aware that Germany had become the most industrialized of European nations. For American Progressives, the economic base for democratic politics, therefore, had been established in Germany. In 1917, that country was suffering from a particularly severe form of cultural lag because of the reactionary political power of the Kaiser and the neofeudal aristocracy. Beard shared the hope that American participation in World War I, by inflicting military defeat on these leaders, would also drive them from power. A political revolution would occur in Germany that would make it possible for politics in that country to express the virtuous democracy implicit in the rationality of industrial production. Beard also believed that the necessity of wartime planning and cooperation in England and the United States would speed up the process of overcoming the cultural lag in those countries. The undemocratic selfishness of capitalism still had political power in 1917, especially in the United States with its constitutional checks on majority rule.

To understand Beard's disillusionment with the results of World War I, one must feel the strength of his expectations in 1917 that the promise of the Enlightenment was about to be fulfilled as all the contradictions to that promise were swept away by the war. "For more than two hundred years a great ideal has been taking form and spreading throughout the earth," he declared, that "governments must derive their powers from the consent of the governed. This democratic principle has been compelled to battle every step of the long way from despotism to liberty against the ancient doctrine that government belongs by divine right to kings whom it is the duty of the people to obey in all things." But now Beard rejoiced, "those who have the faith will believe that a real change had come in the long course of history and that the years, 1917–1918, as surely as the age of the American and French Revolutions, will mark the opening of a new epoch in the rise of government by the people and in the growth of a concert among the nations."[35] In 1917, Beard, as a prophet-historian, had changed his mind about Woodrow Wilson. During his lifetime, George Bancroft had admired two Moses figures, Andrew Jackson and Abraham Lincoln, who led their people toward a future of freehold democracy. And Beard, fortunate enough to live in a progressive era, had seen Theodore Roosevelt and Woodrow Wilson inspiring not only Americans, but people everywhere, to march into the Promised Land of an international, industrial democracy.

Charles Beard: American Democracy or International Capitalism, 1920–48

3

As Charles Beard entered the 1920s, he experienced the intense pain and confusion of a failed prophet. The rational and democratic promise of the eighteenth century, the Enlightenment and the Industrial Revolution, had not been fulfilled. How then could he continue to write hopeful jeremiads that asked his readers to look beneath the surface of those current events that had seemed, for Turner, to indicate a state of permanent declension, and to recognize the underlying evidence that the promise was about to be fulfilled? How could he, as a political scientist and historian, continue to be a prophet of a democratic future for the United States and the world?

The answers to these questions are to be found in a drastic turnabout in Beard's understanding of the relationship of American history to that of the rest of the world. In 1900, he had deliberately replaced the American jeremiad with an international one to escape from Turner's pessimism about the future of American democracy. Now, after the failure of World War I to provide a threshold experience in which all the peoples of the world crossed over from the Old World of political tyranny to the New World of democracy, he began to discard his international jeremiad and return to an American one. For him, it was the only way to escape from his newfound pessimism, which sprang from his interpretation of the peace settlement.

For the remaining three decades of his long life, Beard was to insist that "if there is promise of any kind for the future of America, that promise inheres in the past and present in American history."[1] These words indicate how profoundly he had rejected, after the disheartening failure of his prophecies in 1917, the concept of a universal pattern of social evolution. Never again would Beard prophesy that humanity was responding to economic forces that were leading the peoples of the world through the wilderness of capitalism into the Promised Land of industrial democracy.

As Beard returned to what Sacvan Bercovitch has identified as the American jeremiad, as he returned to the belief that America was the New World and Europe the Old, he felt the need to systematically repudiate the philosophy of historical determinism that Turner had used to argue that capitalism, coming

41

from Europe, represented the New World of the future while the freehold democracy of the American frontier represented an outdated past. That philosophy of economic determinism, whether used pessimistically by Turner in 1890 or optimistically by Beard in 1900, had placed the United States within a modern, international history of capitalism and industrialism. Therefore, if Beard was to once again isolate American from modern European history, his task was to develop the argument that human experience in the United States was exceptional and could not be compared to the experience of people in other parts of the world. To accomplish this, he proposed during the 1920s and 1930s that the patterns of change in human history cannot be forced within the framework of universal stages of social evolution.

Scholars, especially David Marcell, have noticed the dramatic change in Beard's understanding of the physical sciences after 1920. When Beard had linked political science and physics in his essay of 1909, "Politics," he had surmised that the physical sciences had developed methods to comprehend the laws of nature and that they were now capable of predicting the patterns of natural history. He supposed that the changes in human history reflected those in nature and that economics was the part of society in which the forces of physical evolution first expressed themselves. He further assumed that the social sciences had developed methodologies comparable to those in the physical sciences and, therefore, were in a position to predict the changes in the political patterns of society caused by the changes in the underlying economy. This had been the metaphysical foundation for his theory of cultural lag.[2]

However, by the end of the 1920s, Beard was denying that either the physical or social world developed along such predictable patterns. Marcell has pointed out how Beard became increasingly enthusiastic about the realm of ideas after World War I and how this appreciation for the role of ideas was linked to his mounting criticism of philosophies of determinism. In 1927, when he visualized the possibility of a more democratic future, for example, Beard did not prophesy that economic change would necessarily bring that democracy. Instead, he stressed the necessary role of "agitation, political action, economic pressure, and the spread of ideas. A word, an article, a pamphlet, a speech or a book may set in motion forces of incalculable moment." And in an essay of 1929 discussing political science, he wrote, "If we could get enough knowledge to make a science of politics, we should imprison ourselves in an iron web of our own making."[3]

Perhaps Beard had some realization of how deeply autobiographical his current analysis was when he wrote about society's loss of faith in the ability of science to provide absolute answers. "When the Victorian age discarded theology and took up science, a certitude of empirical knowledge seemed to promise an infallible guide to life, action, practice," but, he continued, "now even the hardiest empiricists are divided forty ways on the issues of economics, politics, and culture." And, he concluded, "deprived of the certainty which it was once believed science would ultimately deliver, and of the very hope that it can in the nature of things disclose certainty, human beings must now concede their own fallibility and accept the world as a place of trial and error."[4]

By the late 1920s, Beard had become deeply involved in the writings of a number of European philosophers of history, Benedetto Croce, Karl Huessi, Karl Mannheim, and Hans Vaihinger, all of whom insisted on the pluralistic nature of historical experience and on the creative role of historians in artfully developing their narratives. At the beginning of the 1930s, aware that contemporary physicists were discussing the indeterminacy of physical nature, and being conversant with the current European scholarship of the relativity of human history, Beard was prepared to challenge what he believed was the commitment of most American historians to the myth of scientific objectivity.[5]

He presented this challenge most dramatically in his presidential address to the American Historical Association in December 1933, "Written History as an Act of Faith." He began with the firm assertion that the only valid definition of history is that it is what historians think about the past. Beard, however, tried to explain to his skeptical audience that he was not advocating the writing of history as an irresponsible act of pure imagination. It is clear, he asserted, that historians must build their narratives on empirical knowledge about the past, "authenticated by criticism and ordered by the help of the scientific method." But they must remember, he continued, that the major themes of their narratives did not emerge passively from the authenticated facts, from criticism, or from the scientific method. Rather, he insisted, the structure of their writings reflects their philosophy of history because ultimately each historian selects a particular set of facts that he or she believes are representative of the most important patterns in the past. But although we are creative philosophers of history rather than passive social scientists, he continued, we are not caught in meaningless relativity.[6]

In struggling to develop a new philosophy of history in the 1920s, Beard had read, among others, Niccolo Machiavelli. He had understood Machiavelli as an advocate of virtue in opposition to either "fortuna" or "necessita." As Beard interpreted him, the acceptance of a life of virtue was to believe that individuals can shape their destiny, whereas the acceptance of fortuna was to define the environment as so chaotic that no action could be meaningful. And the acceptance of necessita, that there was order but that it was predetermined, also robbed individuals of any role of responsible action. Building on this framework, Beard appealed to his audience to realize that they could not write history as fortuna, as chaos, and that they would not want to write history as necessita, as predetermined cycles. The logic of telling a story that unfolded through time, the logic of being a historian, he concluded, must assume progress where human action, "virtu," steered a middle course between the absurdity of chaos on one side and the absurdity of determinism on the other. Although, in Beard's estimation, no one could write history who did not accept the reality of progress, he still concluded his address with the appeal that his fellow historians make a self-conscious commitment to progress, that they become aware of their faith in progress and that they cultivate that faith. As for myself, Beard declared, my faith in progress leads me to prophesy the emergence of a "collectivist democracy" in America.[7]

In 1933, as in 1917, Beard therefore was still a prophet of a democratic future. But he had developed a philosophy of historical relativism by 1933 which seemed to be the antithesis of the philosophy of economic determinism he had used to give authority to his prophecy between 1900 and 1917. He did not assume, however, that his new prophecy demanded a leap of faith that transcended experience. Indeed, his rhetorical ritual of the original promise, declension as the current failure to fulfill the promise, and prophecy that the promise would be fulfilled in the future had come, since 1920, to emphasize that the promise of a democratic America was to be found in the historical experience of the American people. This experience, though, had no relationship to universal patterns of evolution. It was the experience of national tradition.

The narrative structure of Beard's popular multivolume history, *The Rise of American Civilization*, written with the help of his wife, Mary, was constructed around the thesis that a democratic American identity had developed in the English colonies. He now accepted Turner's thesis about the relationship of democracy to the physical nature of the New World. His discussion of colonial America, written in the late 1920s, evoked Turner's passionate statement that "American democracy was born of no theorist's dream. It came stark and strong and full of life out of the American forest and it gained new strength each time it touched a new frontier."

In the 1920s, Beard thought that he could reembrace Turner because he did not share Turner's republican commitment to the confrontation of political virtue and time. In 1900, when he had believed in industrialism as a universal force inevitably leading all humankind toward a democratic future, Beard had placed time within the predictable framework of evolutionary change and had celebrated it as the friend of democracy. From that perspective, time was running out for capitalism; it was now time for industrial democracy to replace capitalism, which had become irrelevant to the future. But his writings on relativism in physics and history after 1920 separated time from that kind of universal and predictable framework. Such a separation, however, did not mean that Beard had returned to the republican view that a virtuous politics representing static universals would always be undermined by the dynamic particulars of historical time.

Instead, Beard postulated a pluralistic world of many nations, each of which had developed particular traditions out of the interaction of the national community with its special physical environment. Time, he argued, was dynamic:

it was pluralistic but not chaotic. Time flowed within the framework of the various national traditions. Beard now identified "virtu," which he had borrowed from Machiavelli, with such tradition. Timeful tradition was not the meaningless chaos of fortuna, nor was it the rigid determinism of necessita. People had the freedom to make variations on their national traditions. But Beard also argued that they did not have the freedom to step outside their national traditions without falling out of a meaningful order into chaos, into the realm of fortuna.

There was a partial and dramatic exception to that rule. Europeans coming to America had stepped out of an Old into a New World. By accident, they had come to a new environment that forced them to create a new culture. This American environment was one of unusually rich resources; its miraculous plenitude demanded that Europeans abandon their undemocratic societies built on the experience of scarce resources and begin a democratic society that expressed the unlimited bounty of the New World. In crossing this frontier threshold, they escaped necessita without falling into fortuna.

Turner had said as much in 1890 about the American past but had reached the pessimistic conclusion that time would erode the uniqueness of American space and the abundance of nature would give way to entropy. Then he had tried to escape from this vision of an entropic future by abandoning a dying American democracy for the vitality of an undemocratic capitalism that embodied all the strength of the universal patterns of evolution. In 1930, however, Beard believed he had escaped from Turner's tragic choices by fusing American space and time as tradition. When a democratic culture had formed in response to the miracle of New World geography, it had formed a tradition that flowed from this colonial past toward modern America. All national cultures were dynamic, according to Beard in 1930, and embodied time represented in a past, a present, and a future. Because American democratic culture was in the constant process of change and development, it did not represent a static space that could be overwhelmed by time, as Turner had feared. And because it was a unique national culture, it could not be overwhelmed by international capitalism, as Turner also had feared. By 1930, Beard had designed an American jeremiad which apparently was the invulnerable symbol system discussed by Bercovitch.

If American democracy was a living tradition and was the only tradition that gave individual Americans their identity, it would be difficult to find any disjunction between the original democratic promise, the current state of democracy, and the prophecy of the fulfillment of the democratic promise. Beard's view of the inevitable and unbreakable flow of American democratic culture from the past, through the present, into the future made it almost impossible for him to find any significant declension from the original democratic promise in any particular period of American history. Beard in 1930 had the confidence of Bancroft in 1830. Like Bancroft, he defined declension only in terms of the ignorance of the people who failed to comprehend a serious, external threat to their national heritage. And he seemed to share with Bancroft, in contrast to Turner, the faith that the continuity of the national tradition would never be shattered by an alien culture.

In the first volume of *The Rise of American Civilization, The Agricultural Era*, Beard no longer portrayed colonial democracy as accidental, as he had in 1900, and based on a primitive form of agriculture that necessarily gave way to the higher stage of economic evolution, capitalism, as both he and Turner had proposed in 1900. In Beard's new universe of many nations, each developing according to its own traditions, nationalism was the fundamental reality of human history; nationalism was natural. Capitalism, within his new theoretical framework, was unnatural because it contradicted nationalism. Capitalism was an enemy of tradition. Its logic was that of abstract universals. Its concerns were completely materialistic. It denied the spirituality that was at the core of national identity.

Beard's *The Rise of American Civilization*, therefore, represented a fascinating reversal of the metaphysics embodied in the tradition of republican virtue. The republicans of the eighteenth century had asociated virtue with the republic's ability to embody rational universals. But, since all republics were particular and not universal, they were unstable islands of rationality in the surrounding sea of irrational history. Because they were particular and not universal, the waves of history, the waves of particulars, inevitably eroded the republic's tenuous hold on universals and forced the republic out of its exceptional virtue back into the large world of corrupt nations. For Beard in 1930, however, every nation was virtuous in its own way. The particular did not represent corruption. The flow of time within national traditions did not represent chaos, as the republicans had believed. Instead, chaos existed in the unnatural world outside those national bodies. Corrupt people were those who wanted to blur national boundaries and destroy national traditions. Beard saw capitalists as the most dangerous of these internationalists, although he also feared the internationalism of Marxism, Catholicism, and Judaism.

In *The Rise of American Civilization* and until the end of his life, Beard agreed with eighteenth-century republicans that capitalism was a corrupting force. But, for him, capitalism corrupted not because it expressed the dynamic flow of the particulars of history but because it tried to seduce people from their national traditions and lead them into the unnatural and artificial world of internationalism. Capitalism offered the false promise of the timeless rationality of the marketplace. Since the philosophy of the marketplace pretended to embody historical universals, it encouraged people to try to transcend the spirituality and virtue embodied in the history of their nations.

Turner, using James Harrington's concepts, had countered the dynamism of capitalism with the dynamism of spatial expansion into the West. When the West was gone in 1890, however, Turner had to admit that the virtue of American democracy would be overcome by the capitalism that, crossing the Atlantic, now placed the United States within the undemocratic, hierarchical, political traditions of Europe. Beard, in 1930, on the other hand, countered the undemocratic dynamism of international capitalism with the democratic dynamism of American national tradition. He argued that this democratic tradition was open-ended; since it embodied time, it would not collapse when the space of the western frontier vanished. He also believed that the dynamism of American democratic nationalism could defeat the dynamism of international and undemocratic capitalism because nations, as natural, had more intrinsic strength than internationalism, which was unnatural.

These metaphors of American exceptionalism were expressed in deliberately poetic prose in the first two volumes of *The Rise of American Civilization* as well as in volumes three and four, *America in Midpassage* and *The American Spirit*, which appeared a decade later. Writing at the end of the 1920s, Beard's self-image was no longer that of the precise political scientist who expressed his analysis of social evolution in the language of scientific objectivity. Such rhetorical restraint was suitable for *An Economic Interpretation of the Constitution* when he had believed in rational universals and cultural lag. Now, however, he was celebrating the spiritual heritage of the nation and he was explicitly and self-consciously a theologian for the humanistic religion of American democratic tradition.

Writing before World War I, Beard had found colonial democracy to be weak and provincial in contrast to the strength and cosmopolitanism of the capitalist aristocracy. Then, of course, he had been describing the inevitable victory of capitalism as a higher stage of social evolution over the cultural backwardness of the primitive agriculture practiced by most white farmers. But in *The Agricultural Era*, he was describing the sturdy yeoman who had founded the American democratic tradition which would live as long as the American nation sustained its cultural independence. Evoking the spirit of Turner, Beard's description of the colonial farmers was that "they were not peasants, in the European sense of the word, surrounded by agricultural resources already exploited and encircled by ruling orders of landlords and clergy armed with engines of state and church for subduing laborers to social discipline. On the contrary, these marching pioneers were confronted by land teeming with original fertility, by forests and streams alive with game and fish and they were, under the sun and the stars, their own masters. In these circumstances, a new psychology was evoked."[8]

In Beard's narrative, this new psychology, this American democratic identity, grew continually stronger from 1600 to the American Revolution to which he gave an ironic interpretation. English culture, by nature antidemocratic, had been brought, of course, to the English colonies where it survived among the elites, who did not have the redemptive and democratic experience with the American landscape enjoyed by the yeoman farmers. Controlling colonial governments, they dominated and exploited the people in the fashion of all European aristocracies. Concerned with defending their selfish, material interests, the colonial aristocrats opposed the new imperial policies instituted by the privileged classes in England. This civil war between the English and the Anglo-American vested interests, according to Beard, made it possible for the American people to impress their democratic identity on the Revolution. On the eve of the Revolution, he stated, "it seems that a very small percent of the colonists were politically active." But with the Declaration of Independence, the people became dominant in "this mass movement in which preachers, pamphleteers, committees, lawyers, and state governments advanced the revolutionary cause." It was the yeoman farmers, he continued, who were "pulling down the elaborate superstructure and making the local legislatures, in which the farmers had the majorities, supreme over all things. The radical leaders realized their ideal in a loose association of sovereign states; in the Articles of Confederation, their grand ideals were fairly mirrored."[9]

As in his pre-1920 writings, Beard had to report that the victory of the people was short-lived. In *An Economic Interpretation of the Constitution*, he had stressed that the founding fathers were capitalists; now he stressed that they were rooted in English culture. In replacing the Articles of Confederation with the Constitution, they "re-established in effect the old British system of politics, economics and judicial control."[10] For the Beard of *The Rise of American Civilization*, the battle between the people and the elites was one between American and European principles, between an organic national identity and a foreign identity which, as long as it could keep a foothold in the New World, would be a parasite attempting to exploit the people.

Continuing to develop a narrative that was similar to Turner's views of the years from 1600 to the Civil War rather than the analytical framework he himself had used between 1900 and 1917, Beard de-emphasized the antidemocratic victory of the founding fathers. It was only an external political victory by un-American people who lived by the alien principles of English national culture. What was important in 1800 was that the American democratic identity, as Bancroft and then Turner had declared, was about to be immensely strengthened by the surge of the yeoman farmers across the Appalachians into the great valley of democracy.

In *The Economic Origins of Jeffersonian Democracy*, Beard had savagely desacralized Bancroft's and Turner's heroes, Thomas Jefferson and Andrew Jackson. But Beard was no longer debunking agrarian democracy. He established a conflict in the 1790s between Alexander Hamilton, whose values were undemocratic and English, and Jefferson, whose values were democratic and American. Jefferson, Beard declared, was America's first national hero. It was Jefferson who taught us to turn our backs on Europe and on the Atlantic coast, so influenced by centuries of contact with the Old World and the home of the colonial elites. He taught us, Beard wrote, echoing Bancroft and Turner, to look forward to the settlement of the West, where the yeomen could take their democratic culture, developed during the colonial years, and have a completely American society uncompromised by the vestiges of the English heritage.

Like Turner, Beard asked his readers to stand at the crests of the mountains and look backward at the colonial past and forward to the national future:

> It was a marvelous empire of virgin country that awaited the next great wave of migration at the close of the eighteenth century. The valley of the Mississippi now summoned the peoples of the earth to make a new experiment in social economy in the full light of modern times.
>
> The rolling tide of migration that swept across the mountains and down the valleys, spreading out through the forests and over the prairies, advanced in successive waves. In the vanguard was the man with the rifle—grim, silent, and fearless. He loved the pathless forest, dense and solitary, carpeted by the fallen leaves of a thousand years and fretted by the sunlight that poured through the Gothic arches of the trees, and where the campfire at night flared into the darkness of knitted boughs as flaring candles of the altar of a cathedral cast their rays high into the traceries of the vaulted roof.
>
> In this immense domain sprang up a social order without marked class or caste, a society of people substantially equal in worldly goods, deriving their livelihood from one prime source—labor with their own hands on the soil.
>
> In its folkways and mores there was a rugged freedom—the freedom of hardy men and women, taut of muscle and bronzed by sun and rain and wind, working with their hands in abundant materials, shaping oak from their own forests and flax from their own fields to the plain uses of a plain life, content with little, and rejoicing in it, rearing in unaffected naturalness many children to face also a career of hard labor offering no goal in great riches or happiness in a multitude of things, all satisfied by the unadorned epic of Christianity inherited from their fathers.[11]

When Beard discussed the Civil War in his narrative, he had reached the place where Turner's story of the spatial expansion of American democracy into the West had turned from optimism to pessimism. It was at this point in the chronology of American history that Turner had shifted his controlling metaphor from the confrontation of American space and European time to the confrontation of the sophisticated economy of international capitalism and the provincial, primitive agriculture of the American frontier. American history after the Civil War, for Turner, was no longer the movement from European time and corruption to American space and virtue; it was now the unfolding of the successively higher stages of social evolution, climaxing in the era of international capitalism.

In the second volume of *The Rise of American Civilization, The Industrial Era*, Beard agreed with Turner that the great crisis of American democracy came after 1865, and that it was the growing strength of capitalism that caused that crisis. Before 1917, Beard had emphasized the power of capitalism in the writing of the Constitution and had refused to take seriously Turner's admiration for Jefferson and Jackson or Turner's belief that a Western democracy had existed throughout the nineteenth century. According to Beard's pre-World War I analysis, capitalism controlled America from 1789 to the 1890s, but then at the beginning of the twentieth century, industrial democracy, the higher stage of the international economy which Turner had failed to recognize, was replacing capitalism. In 1917, Beard did not perceive any great threat to a vital democratic tradition rooted in the American past. The democracy that was important was the industrial future rather than the agrarian past.

In the late 1920s, however, Beard returned to Turner's celebration of a colonial and nineteenth-century democracy that had an agricultural foundation. But, unlike Turner, in *The Rise of American Civilization*, he reached the late nineteenth-century crisis between democracy and capitalism full of optimism. The strength of colonial democracy was not limited to a constantly diminishing space, as Turner believed. That democracy had come to embody time. It had become the national tradition destined to flow inexorably out of the past, through the present, and into the future. And capitalism did not have the authority of social evolution behind it; Turner (and the early Beard) was mistaken that human development followed universal patterns of evolution. The natural experience of time, for humans, was within the boundaries of their national traditions. Capitalism, committed to the universal marketplace, was necessarily the unnatural enemy of nationalism and flourished best in times of deep and unpredictable disruptions such as wars.

Before 1920, Beard did not share Bancroft and Turner's description of the Civil War as the victory of freehold democracy over a semimedieval South; *The Rise of American Civilization* reflected this. But he did take seriously the freehold democracy of Abraham Lincoln, and he found a tragic similarity between Lincoln's experience with a war that was supposed to expand democracy and Wilson's experience in 1917. In both cases, the unexpected consequences of the revolutionary turmoil caused by war gave capitalism a chance to frustrate the American democratic tradition.

Beard could write with relative equanimity, however, about the irony that the Civil War, whose purpose had been to achieve democracy, had resulted in the triumph of antidemocratic capitalists. He and his readers understood that it was only a matter of time before the national democratic tradition shook off the external parasites who tried in vain to alter the innermost American identity. In 1927, Beard did not directly identify political virtue with a freehold economy, as Turner had, or with an industrial economy, as he himself had done before 1917. He now placed political virtue in the heart of the national tradition, where it gained rather than lost strength from time. In Beard's new metaphysics, democratic virtue was apparently invulnerable.[12]

In his chapters dealing with the years from 1865 to 1896, his prose was as vivid and dramatic in evoking the capitalists' vain attempt to corrupt the nation as it had been in describing the power and beauty of the pioneers' exodus to the Promised Land of Western democracy. The capitalist hell of the Gilded Age was garish and vulgar, comparable to the decadence of the crumbling Roman Empire. In the cycle of history, it would not be American democracy that fell but rather this empire that was in America but not of it.

"Roads from four continents now ran to the new Appian Way – Wall Street," Beard wrote, "and the pro-consuls of distant provinces paid homage to a new sovereign. The land of Washington, Franklin, Jefferson, and John Adams had become a land of millionaires and the supreme direction of its economy had passed from the owners of farms and isolated plants and banks to a few men and institutions near the center of its life."[13]

The organic metaphor Beard was constructing in *The Rise of American Civilization* implicitly defined the American people as Anglo-Saxon Protestants, the descendants of the English colonists. A few men from this stock had become traitors to their people in opting for the corrupting power of international capitalism. Beard described in bitter detail the effort of these traitors to create a new American population, one that was outside the democratic traditions of the Anglo-American Protestants. Immigrants from southern and eastern Europe, Catholics and Jews linked by their religions to international values, had been brought by the capitalists to become a dependent working class in the capitalist factories and mines. "Not since the patricians and capitalists of Rome scoured the known world for slaves," he scornfully wrote, "had the world witnessed such a deliberate overturn of a social order by masters of ceremonies." This was the system of domination and dependence that the tradition of republican virtue always associated with corruption. Master and slave were debauched by such a relationship. And Beard painted the life-style of the immigrants in the vivid colors of such decadence. "Vaudeville shows, prize fights, circuses, dime museums, and cheap theaters, like the spectacles of ancient Rome, kept countless millions happy in penury," he declared, and he added that "the Catholic Church, with its gorgeous ceremonials and its sublime consolations for suffering and wretchedness, followed the poor everywhere."[14]

Capitalists and proletarians, however, were not native to America, and they could not permanently alter the American identity. By the 1890s, the American democratic tradition was asserting its indigenous strength. "Between the urban masses with their circuses and prize fights and the plutocracy with its palatial mansions," Beard was able to report, "stretched a wide and active middle class engaged in professional, mercantile, and clerical pursuits. It was within this group that the early Puritan characteristics of thrift, sobriety, and self-denial appeared to survive and unfold in the most natural fashion."[15]

These virtuous people, in Beard's view, were not rejecting the exploitation of capitalism because they were influenced by Karl Marx's philosophy of international socialism, which was based on the same kind of materialist outlook as international capitalism. Drawing on their own democratic tradition as a productive people, Americans were able to proceed without heroic leadership to free themselves from capitalist exploitation between 1896 and 1916. "By a gradual and peaceful operation," Beard wrote, "was effected a transfer of economic goods greater in value than the rights shifted from the French nobility to the peasants by the national assembly. Historians now recorded that the theory of the public interest was being substituted for the older doctrine of laissez faire. Presidents came and went, governors and legislatures came and went but the movement of social forces that produced this legislation was continuous. It was confined to no over-powering leadership. Such were the processes and products of American democracy."[16]

Beard's narrative had reached World War I when his earlier prophecy of the triumph of a worldwide industrial democracy had been shattered. Reacting to that terrible frustration of his expectations, he had abandoned the jeremiad he had employed from 1900 to 1917 which had found its promise in Europe during the eighteenth century when the vision of the Enlightenment had been created and when the system of industrial production had been established. And he could no longer identify the Progressive Era of the early twentieth century with the Moses figures of Theodore Roosevelt and Woodrow Wilson. They had helped lead the nation into World War I, and they had advocated a permanent role for the United States outside its boundaries. Beard, after 1919, had come to believe that World War I was caused by capitalist elites who dominated most modern nations. Since capitalism, for him, symbolized the chaos that existed between the many centers of national meaning in the world, it gained strength as it was able to intensify the chaos in a wartime situation. Beard's description of the Civil War came out of this analytical framework he had developed during the 1920s. And he now applied this analysis to his discussion of World War I in *The Rise of American Civilization*.[17]

Although the plutocracy in the United States had been overwhelmed by the people after 1896, he wrote, it had managed to retain control over the foreign policy of the Republican party and had instituted an imperialistic program for world conquest. Woodrow Wilson and the Democratic party had resisted this policy, but according to Beard, Wilson, in 1917, was seduced into thinking that he could make the United States a redeemer nation, helping to spread democracy throughout the world.

When the war was over, however, the people had reasserted their Jeffersonian tradition of isolation and kept the United States from surrendering its national integrity to a world government. But they had not been able to keep the capitalists from using the Republican party to continue their pattern of covert, economic imperialism abroad. Capitalism gained material strength from the profits it made through such exploitation. It also gained spiritual strength as it weakened national traditions and increased the size of its unnatural and artificial international network.

His more recent variation of the American jeremiad, however, gave Beard the hope to prophesy that America's democratic promise would overcome this apparent pattern of declension after World War I, as it had overcome the declension after the Civil War. Democracy would triumph over capitalism in the future. After all, the great American middle class was still virtuous. According to Beard, it had developed a strong religious commitment to a public interest opposed to capitalist selfishness in the Social Gospel movement of the Progressive Era before World War I. And he reported that this faith remained strong in the 1920s, bringing a "spirit of charity, generosity, and benevolence," especially in the new field of social work. The tools of the social and physical sciences were available to those who had this religious commitment to a democratic future. Freed from the philosophy of materialism and determinism, Beard stressed, social and physical scientists were now working within the experimental philosophy of John Dewey. He credited Dewey with understanding the cooperative nature of industrial production. Dewey also realized that a cooperative, democratic politics must replace the selfish, capitalist politics of the Republican administrations of the 1920s so that the unlimited bounty of industrial production could be utilized to eliminate poverty from America.[18]

Beard still held his belief of 1900 that industrial democracy would defeat capitalism. But after his disillusionment with World War I, he thought that this could happen only in America. Industrialism, for him, was no longer a universal stage of social evolution. As a new form of economic activity, it fit into the political traditions of the nations where it developed. Since no other nation had a democratic tradition, it was only in America that industrialism could become part of a democratic future. As his narrative approached the beginning of the Great Depression in 1929, Beard's American jeremiad seemed more confident than ever. He had woven a synthesis of an agricultural past and an industrial future around the idea of a national democratic tradition whose nature was that of dynamic progress. Space and time were not incompatible, as they had been in Turner's philosophy of history. And the destiny of American democracy was not linked to the rest of the world, as Beard had believed in 1917. The revelation, stemming from the catastrophic political consequences of World War I, of how profoundly undemocratic the traditions of the other nations were was not a cause for pessimism within the United States. And the postwar Beard had also joined religion and science within the American democratic tradition. He appealed to both to establish authority for the prophecy of the triumph of democracy with which he closed the first two volumes of *The Rise of American Civilization*. America, he declared, "meant an invulnerable faith in democracy, in the ability of the undistinguished masses, as contrasted with heroes and classes."[19]

It also meant, he concluded, "a faith in the efficacy of that new and mysterious instrument of the modern mind, 'the invention of invention,' moving from one technological triumph to another, effecting an ever wider distribution of the blessings of civilization, conjuring from the vasty deeps of the nameless and unknown creative imagination of the noblest order, subduing physical things to the empire of the spirit that has summoned into being all patterns of the past and present, living and dead, to fulfill its endless destiny."[20]

Beard, therefore, greeted the coming of the Great Depression with much enthusiasm. By the end of the 1920s, he had become as optimistic about the future as he had been in 1917. Once again, he believed the American people were poised at a threshold that they would cross and escape from the Egyptian bondage of capitalism to the Promised Land of industrial democracy. Having discarded Theodore Roosevelt and Woodrow Wilson as Moses figures, Beard, in 1933, was willing to believe that Franklin D. Roosevelt was the Moses who would succeed where the Progressive presidents had failed as the leader of this exodus. During the years from 1929 to 1933, Beard was certain that he was witnessing the collapse of capitalism in the United States. Once again, as between 1910 and 1917, he wrote with controlled passion and incredible speed, as innumerable articles and books flowed from his pen, all designed to educate Americans about the existence of a capitalist establishment that had to be overthrown. He was certain that the jeremiad of promise, declension, and prophecy again gave a progressive structure to the narrative of American history.

Beard wrote that the destructive and antisocial principles of capitalism had come from England after the Civil War. An upper class of businessmen, ministers, and professors had begun an education campaign to convince the American people that competitive capitalism, not a selfless and virtuous democracy, was the authentic American tradition. Now, because of the power of this alien ideology, the Hoover administration had no intellectual or spiritual resources to establish a constructive program to deal with the collapse of the economy. Hoover, a prisoner of the English ideology of laissez faire, could not imagine that the authority for government planning was to be found in the American democratic tradition. But in *The American Leviathan*, published in 1930, Beard described the theoretical efforts being made "to unite politics, government, and technology as reflected in the federal system of the United States, with emphasis on the newer functions created under the pressures of the machine age. Natural science and machinery have set a new and complex stage for the operations of government, imposed additional functions upon it, and lifted it to a new role in the process of civilization."[21] The essence of democracy, he wrote, is a society governed by the people. Our society, he continued, is one of mass production and the people are the producers. It is natural, he concluded, that they should use government to facilitate their life as producers.

Capitalism, however, had always been the enemy of production. Capitalism was irrational and parasitical. After 1929, it had managed to disrupt the whole productive process, and only government planning could restore economic growth. In 1932, Beard advocated a "Five Year Plan for America." He felt the need to explicitly disassociate his plan from those of the Soviet Union. Once again, he argued that American Progressives were engaged in industrial planning long before the Russian Revolution of 1917. And he declared that this American tradition of democratic planning would soon "lop off the dead wood of our futile plutocracy, so sinister in its influences on politics, culture, and rational living."[22]

This essay was published in 1932 in a book entitled *America Faces the Future,* which was edited by Beard. By the end of 1933, he announced in his next book, *The Future Comes,* that Franklin D. Roosevelt had proved in his first revolutionary months that he was indeed the Moses who would lead Americans into a New World of industrial democracy, a new America that was fulfilling the promise of colonial democracy. "The Recovery Program," Beard declared, "accepts the inexorable development of combination in industry, abandons all faith in the healing power of dissolution and prosecution; and makes use of combination in planning." And he continued, "The Recovery Program calls upon millions of individuals in industry and agriculture, who have hitherto been pursuing their own interests at pleasure, to cooperate in adjusting production, setting prices, and maintaining standards. The New Deal symbolizes the coming of a future collectivist in character."[23] For Beard, the corrupting self-interest of capitalism was now overcome by the virtuous public interest of democracy as the artificial world of internationalism, represented by the Republican party, gave way to the reality of nationalism, symbolized by the Democratic party.

It is not surprising, therefore, that when Beard updated the narrative of *The Rise of American Civilization* in a third volume, *America in Midpassage,* Roosevelt was given the role of a secular saint. The president, in Beard's estimation, had liberated the people not only from the alien economy of capitalism but, equally important, from an alien culture. Notice, he wrote, the vitality of the Federal Theater project. Notice the renaissance of American painting under government sponsorship. These changes were momentous because the aristocratic art that had come from Europe had corrupted Americans by teaching them to ignore the public interest. The new democratic art, however, was reminding them that they really were members of an organic community. "Primitive art had expressed communal organization and purpose," he wrote, "now, through the patronage of the arts by the government of the United States, art was again to be a public affair." Calling attention to Roosevelt's second inaugural address in 1937, Beard declared that the president had taken "cognizance of the fundamental antithesis between the ideal and the real—and expressed the conviction that it was the function of statesmanship to bring the real into closer conformity with the ideal." The president, Beard concluded, "discussed the basic human and economic problems of American society with a courage and range displayed by no predecessor in his office. And in doing this he carried on the tradition of humanistic democracy which from colonial times had been a powerful dynamic in the whole movement of American civilization and culture—economic, political, literary, scientific and artistic."[24]

But the devastating irony of Beard's outlook in *America in Midpassage* was that when the book was published in 1939, he no longer saw the president as a salvation figure. Indeed, the image had been completely reversed. And Beard's rage was boundless as he responded to the leader who had betrayed the American people. Fear, however, was the dominating emotion with which Beard viewed this devilish president as he prepared to break tradition and run for an unprecedented third term in 1940. Beard knew the power and persuasiveness of Roosevelt's leadership. He had felt the charm and charisma. Between 1935 and 1939, however, Beard reluctantly had come to believe that all of the president's persuasive power was being used to create an anti-exodus into another world war. Just as the United States was recovering from the declension caused by its participation in World War I, the national democratic tradition would be exposed to the unpredictable and chaotic cosequences of war.

Slowly at first, Beard in 1935 and 1936 had begun to fear that Roosevelt was not sincere about his administration's foreign policy of political isolation. In 1937, however, even as his fears were intensifying, Beard had been able to write with glowing admiration about the president in the manuscript that became *America in Midpassage*. But it almost seems that in 1937 he was trying to convince himself that Roosevelt was attempting to revitalize democracy on the foundation of America's national uniqueness. In 1939, however, wishful thinking was no longer possible. Beard was certain that the president was engaged in a conspiracy to lead the country ito foreign entanglements and into the war that had begun in Europe.

The unbearable agony of this situation, for Beard, was that at the very moment in 1933 when Roosevelt had the power to lead his people out of the last vestiges of the antidemocratic corruption of international capitalism and away from the remaining fragments of European artistic influence to fulfill the democratic promise of the seventeenth century, the president had chosen to turn back from this threshold into the Promised Land. Instead, he was using his great gift of persuasion to get Congress to repeal the neutrality legislation it had passed during his first administration, legislation designed to avoid the experiences of 1914–16 that had made Americans vulnerable to the propaganda and economic pressure of the pro-English elites. If Roosevelt was successful in this course of leadership, he would plunge the nation into the chaos of the artificial world of international affairs and immeasurably strengthen the un-American aristocracy that was the implacable foe of the American democratic national tradition.

When Beard described American domestic history to 1937, his narrative was structured on that immensely optimistic rhetorical ritual that Bercovitch has called the American jeremiad. In that rhetoric, the original promise and the prophecy of future fulfillment are defined as invulnerable to the superficial signs of declension in the immediate present. Bercovitch criticized Perry Miller for stressing the characteristic of declension in Puritan rhetoric and minimizing the promise and the prophecy. But Turner's narrative, when he discussed the events in American history that occurred after 1865, dealt more with declension from the original promise than with the fulfillment of the promise of the future because expansion into the West had ceased. By 1890, international capitalism, for Turner, had become a stronger expression of the natural law embodied in the evolutionary process than the vanishing frontier of freehold property which had been the basis for American national uniqueness.

After 1919, the way for Beard to escape from Turner's pessimism was to deny that the international was natural. He denied that there was an evolutionary process that provided a common experience to all nations. He also blended time with space so that the flow of American history could incorporate those democratic traditions born in the agricultural world of the seventeenth and eighteenth centuries within the structure of an urban-industrial America. His narratives, written in the 1920s and 1930s, reported no real declension of the American community. American heroes did not call the people out of their sloth and their selfishness; instead, they fought against un-American people and worked to end their unnatural presence in America. The only major weakness Beard found in the American people was ignorance. It was difficult for them to distinguish between Americans who upheld national tradition and those who were born in America but were not truly Americans because they were committed to the destruction of that tradition. It was in the area of foreign policy, therefore, not domestic policy, that the people masquerading as Americans might subvert the national tradition. When Beard wrote about foreign policy after 1919, his rhetoric no longer minimized declension and celebrated promise and prophecy. Here was a large and important part of American history in which the original promise was endangered by a profound declension, one so deep that it called the future fulfillment of the promise into doubt.

Beard published two major books on foreign policy in 1934. The first, *The*

Idea of National Interest, read like a tragedy. Although Beard's writings from 1900 to 1917 show that he had despised Jefferson, he was now the American whom Beard admired most because he "was a nationalist in a narrow and racial sense, and looked to the development on this continent, of a homogenous people primarily engaged in agricurture—a society of people speaking a common language, knit together by ties of blood and language, capable of self-government, and so placed in a strategic geographical position as to be easily defended without large military and naval establishments—those historic menaces to liberty,"[25]

What Beard's opponents in the 1930s would call isolationism, he called continentalism. And he insisted that the promise of the American national tradition depended upon the rootedness of the people within the borders of this continent. But Jefferson's vision of an authentic American history developing according to its own inner logic, as other nations developed their own patterns of uniqueness, did not become the basis for American foreign policy.

Jefferson's true definition of national interest as an inward-looking continentalism was immediately replaced by Alexander Hamilton's false definition of national interest. This un-American outlook became the foreign policy of the Federalist, Whig, and Republican parties. It assumed that American prosperity depended upon the expansion of foreign markets for the nation's industrial and agricultural surplus. The proponents of this policy had no concern for the preservation of the virtue of the American republican experiment. Instead, they were willing to corrupt American innocence through the creation of an empire and by "bringing in immigrants still less adapted to the national heritage than many races later excluded by law, thus adding to the confusion of peoples, the babel of tongues already existing in the country." No one has ever been able to demonstrate, Beard concluded, that this Hamiltonian policy was based on economic truth. Indeed, he argued, all evidence pointed to the conclusion that if American production were distributed throughout the community by intelligent economic planning, there would be national prosperity without foreign markets.[26]

Tragically, the Democrats throughout the nineteenth century also had followed a foreign policy that ran counter to the true national interest. They too had assumed that American prosperity depended upon marketing the suplus crops of the farmers abroad. In contrast to the Hamiltonian-Whig-Republican tradition which believed that the United States must search for economic prosperity in an external world of constant war, and that America must become a warfare state to survive that kind of military competition, the Democrats believed that the peaceful influence of American overseas trade could persuade the other nations to imitate American democracy. This tradition had culminated in the leadership of Woodrow Wilson, who hoped to democratize the world and institute a new era of perpetual world peace.

But from their bitter experience in World War I, Americans had learned that it was not possible for them to redeem the world. They had also learned the costs of the Hamiltonian acceptance of an aggressive military policy as they witnessed the catastrophic escalation of war as a system of competition. The most important lesson they were learning in the 1930s, however, was that "by domestic planning and control the American machine may be kept running at a high tempo supplying the intranational market, without relying primarily upon foreign outlets for 'surpluses of goods and capital'." Beard's second book of 1934, *The Open Door at Home*, was a more detailed description of how this policy of true national interest, the intranational market, could operate. It was also a stirring tribute to Jefferson as the great prophet of American continentalism. Americans, Beard wrote, must rekindle Jefferson's vision that they were a chosen people; they must accept their responsibility to preserve and extend the virtue of their uniquely democratic tradition by isolating themselves from the corrupting influence of the Old World.[27]

By 1936, as Roosevelt was winning reelection, Beard had come to understand American history as two absolutely incompatible traditions. National history was democratic and virtuous, but the tradition of foreign policy was antidemocratic and corrupt. Republicans had carried on this un-American foreign policy because they were the descendants of Alexander Hamilton who had nothing but contempt for democracy. Democrats, however, had been internationalists because they were not aware that other nations could not be separated from their undemocratic traditions and because they did not see that planning could solve the problem of domestic surpluses. President Roosevelt was now in a position to finally restore the Democratic party to the continental principles of Jefferson since he, like Beard, had lived through the failure of Wilson's crusade and understood the possibilities of planning. America, after 1936, would have only one history, the natural history of the nation rather than that of an unnatural overseas frontier.

But in 1936, Beard had the terrifying vision that Roosevelt was really a Hamiltonian masquerading as a Jeffersonian. Was that why he was continuing the Republican policy of hostility to Japan? Was that why he asked Congress for money to enlarge the navy? Did the president plan to lead the country into war with Japan to avoid the democratic reforms that would finally eliminate the insidious influence of capitalism? Did Roosevelt hope to revitalize the plutocracy with a foreign adventure that would lead Americans away from their democratic heritage?

Between 1936 and 1938, Beard came to believe that these fears were real. Roosevelt was engaged in a conspiracy. He was trying to undermine the natural, national history and make internationalism, the unnatural, dominant. The president was going to take the United States into a war that might accomplish what the Civil War and World War I had failed to do—break the organic democratic tradition that stretched from the seventeenth to the twentieth centuries.

By 1938, Beard had shifted from an optimistic to a pessimistic jeremiad. In two books that appeared in 1939, *Giddy Minds and Foreign Quarrels* and *A Foreign Policy for Americans*, he tried to convert his readers to his analysis of Roosevelt's intentions to lead the United States into the European world of war and chaos.[28] His rhetorical strategy was to convince readers that their desire to avoid participation in a war was shared by their neighbors. Beard's writing was shrill as he demanded to know why this overwhelming majority of Americans was allowing the president and the plutocratic minority to maneuver the country out of its neutrality. His next book, *The Old Deal and the New*, published in 1940, was even angrier. But it was also characterized by a sullen stoicism, as if Beard recognized that Roosevelt, in winning an unprecedented third term, was also succeeding in his effort to take the country into World War II. Bitterly, he denounced Americans for permitting the triumph of the un-American people. "Never in all the history of the country," he preached, "not even during the long Civil War, had the people moved in such an intellectual and emotional daze as they did while these events transpired. In their easy, almost abject, acceptance of all that was handed out to them by the Administration was revealed a profound change in national temper – a deeper subservience to government policy and instruction."[29] However great the differences were between Beard's views during the years 1900 and 1920 and those he had developed between 1920 and 1937, he had always criticized the checks and balances in the Constitution and affirmed the affinity of democracy and centralized planning. But by 1937, as his fear of Roosevelt's presidential leadership in the area of foreign policy became his overwhelming concern, he dramatically broke that lifelong pattern and became a defender of the division of powers. In *The Old Deal and the New*, he denounced Roosevelt for instituting a dictatorship in 1933. "The private interests and the state and local political interests which had once exercised powerful checks on the power and momentum of the Federal Government, lost a large part of their independence," he declared, "and, as Congress escaped its responsibilities by transferring to the Executive a huge discretionary authority in relation to banking, currency, and spending, centralization proceeded rapidly. In this way the old system of checks and balances, political and economic, was profoundly altered." It was because Roosevelt had such dictatorial power, Beard insisted, that he was able to disregard the will of the majority that did not want to intervene in Europe.[30]

This revolutionary change in Beard's attitude toward the Constitution, however, facilitated his effort to finally integrate the founding fathers into his theory of organic nationalism. As the United States entered World War II, Beard, therefore, declared that "nowhere is the predominating ideal of a progressive society set forth more cogently or with greater authority than in the Constitution."[31] Making his peace with the founding fathers helped Beard escape the shrillness of *Giddy Minds and Foreign Quarrels* and *A Foreign Policy for Ameri-*

cans and the frustration and anger of *The Old Deal and the New*. In *The American Spirit*, which appeared in 1942 and provided the fourth and concluding volume to his epic history of the United States that had begun in the 1920s with the first two volumes of *The Rise of American Civilization*, Beard was able to summon the willpower to write once again within the optimistic framework of the American jeremiad. Although Roosevelt's conspiracy was successful and the un-American plutocrats who thrived on the chaos of international relations were sucking the lifeblood of the American people, although signs of declension were everywhere, he reminded himself and his readers that the American national tradition might be temporarily captured by aliens but it could never be destroyed or replaced. The particular marriage of space and time that had taken place in the seventeenth century could not be broken.

The American Spirit, therefore, expressed the same philosophy of history that Beard had developed to overcome the failure of his prophecy that World War I would provide a threshold from the Old World of capitalism to the New World of industrial democracy. Again he had prophesied such a threshold – the inauguration of Franklin Roosevelt as president in 1933. And again the prophecy had failed. However, Beard now refused to prophesy that the entry of the United States into World War II was an antithreshold marking a permanent exodus out of its democratic national tradition into the undemocratic international world of capitalism. It was merely one more episode in the long war between democratic virtue and capitalist corruption. Capitalists had won battles against the American people during the Civil War and World War I. Now the capitalists were winning another battle. But Beard reiterated in *The American Spirit* what he had written in the 1920s: nationalism, because it was natural, could never be destroyed by internationalism, which was unnatural. And the political virtue of democracy embodied in the America national tradition could never permanently be replaced by corruption.

"Calamities may come upon America or be brought upon the country by demagogic leadership. Civil storms may shake the United States. Temporary dictatorships may be set up," Beard seemed to calmly declare, but "enough of our Republic will be kept intact to restore, rebuild, and go ahead."[32] Approaching the end of his long life, disappointed that he had not seen the fulfillment of the promise of America and had experienced so much declension, he was giving *The American Spirit* to his people. In this gift, this prophecy, he hoped to achieve a level of clarification of the promise not reached by any previous American historian. In the midst of the superficial declension of World War II imposed by the devilish demagogue Roosevelt, Beard would pass a rich knowledge of the promise to a younger generation. Keeping faith in the promise, these youthful Americans, led by their historians, would create a vision of how the declension would be overcome and how the promise would be fulfilled.

Preparing this gift, Beard associated the American promise and its fulfillment in the future with the idea of progress. It was of crucial importance to him that his readers recognize the difference between the European approach to the idea of progress, which was materialistic, and the American approach, which was spiritual. It was Jefferson, the nation's greatest humanistic theologian of progress and democracy, he declared, who developed the idea of civilization as spiritual progress. Formed by revolution in 1776, the United States seemed to express the principles of the European Enlightenment. The European intellectuals were committed to the emancipation of humankind from the tyranny of the Middle Ages, and they developed an idea of progress to provide the map for the journey toward a better future. But their idea of progress was built on a belief in inevitable and mechanical states of social evolution. Jefferson, in contrast, assumed that because humans were social animals, the progressive community of emancipated human beings must be democratic and cooperative; that progress was not automatic but depended upon human will; that this will must be inspired by an ethical faith. Progress for Jefferson was a moral constraint, not a form of materialistic determinism as the Europeans believed. Jefferson, therefore, believed that the idea of civilization could serve as a national faith only in America because of the uniqueness of American social harmony. Built on the new foundations of the frontier, America's origins, "unlike those of European societies, were not lost in prehistoric darkness, in mythological time, in the dim twilight of barbarism, pagan gods, superstitions, ignorance and fears."[33] By the 1830s this idea of democratic civilization, Beard continued, was producing a great renaissance of American culture. Emerson, Whitman, Margaret Fuller, and George Bancroft all give artistic expression in diverse ways to the unique American destiny. All found their inspiration in the idea of a distinct American civilization. Even in economics, a man like Henry C. Carey expressed the uniqueness of American civilization, criticizing English classical economics for forgetting the Jeffersonian principles that human beings are ethical animals and that history is a product of human effort.

These English economists had abstracted humans from society, made them prisoners of economic law, and argued that they were motivated only by selfishness. Now Beard began to trace the tragic decline of the Jeffersonian ideal as this English ideology infiltrated Jefferson's America. The American economy began to be dominated by bankers. The bankers accepted the views of the English economists; then the bankers converted the Americans in business, whom they controlled, to this alien ideology; the people in business in turn demanded that the college professors and the clergy, whom they controlled, teach this doctrine of acquisitive individualism. And by 1865, the official doctrine of America was English classical economics.

Beard provided a dramatic footnote to the power of this new "establishment" by showing its control over two historians usually associated with Jeffersonianism, Woodrow Wilson and Frederick Jackson Turner. Both men, Beard related, thought they were Jeffersonians because they believed in the uniqueness of American civilization defined as individualism. Ironically, neither know that they were defining America in terms of an English ideology.[34]

But Beard asked his readers not to despair because almost immediately after the Civil War, Americans began to fight their way back to the real Jeffersonianism. Leaders in this movement were men like the anthropologist Lewis Henry Morgan, the sociologist Lester Frank Ward, the economists Simon Patten and Richard Ely, and the ministers of the social gospel Walter Rauschenbusch and George Herron. All defined humans not only as naturally social and cooperative but also as progressive. All believed that history moved forward constantly, giving human beings the perpetual opportunity to improve their society. The young American generation after 1900, however, would be deprived of these enduring truths by the diversion created by foreign critics of Amerian civilization. These critics asked Americans to abandon the reality of the American experience and to lose sight of American uniqueness. Catholics asked the young people to look back to the ideal absolute of medieval theology; Marxists asked them to look forward to the ideal absolute of the communist utopia.[35]

Beard blamed the great influence of these doctrines for the failure of American historians to teach the reality of America. The Catholics and the Marxists were able to win young people by criticizing the selfish materialism of the United States. But, Beard asserted, acquisitiveness, the cash nexus, is not American; it is the result of English ideology. America, the real America, is the Jeffersonian concern for human cooperation, for the selfless ethic of true civilization. Working also to alienate the young people from the Jeffersonian covenant was the doctrine of internationalism propounded by men like "Louis Finkelstein under the title of 'American Ideals and the Survival of Western Civilization' in the *Contemporary Jewish Record* of June 1941." It is no wonder, Beard wrote, that in the 1920s so many young intellectuals became cynical and pessimistic about their nation when it was defined for them in terms of alien ideologies.[36]

Beard had painted a scene of true moral drama. The good American intellectuals of the Progressive Era were locked in mortal combat with the evil representatives of European ideologies. Both sides were attempting to win the minds of young America. By 1920, the factor of American participation in the European war seemed to give the advantage to the forces of darkness. Many promising young Americans were becoming expatriates. But even in this darkest hour of the Republic, the people, the sleeping giant, awoke to strike out in blind fury against their foreign corrupters. Beard discovered the beginning of the final victory of the forces of light in the national legislation restricting immigration: "Expressing in many respects this revulsion and this determination to protect American civilization against European and Oriental invasions, immigration legislation, especially the Acts of 1921 and 1924, stood out in public discussions and in law as positive testimony to renewed concentration of the reinforcement of civilization in the United States." Now, said Beard, America was at last returning to the principles of the founding fathers. And once Americans began the rediscovery of their heritage, purged of foreign influence, their insights flourished in every area of cultural life.[37]

Even the social scientists, Beard announced, were now escaping from the bondage of English thought. In 1931, the Commission of the Social Studies had issued "A Charter for the Social Sciences," which declared that "America has never imported a large part of the Old World heritage. Having rounded out the Continent, the American people have turned in upon themselves. The great body of thinkers still agree with Emerson that we must stand fast where we are and build a civilization with characteristics sincerely our own."[38]

Beard then found this Jeffersonian continentalism to be the dominant philosophy among American thinkers in the 1930s, controlling political, economic, philosophical, and artistic thought, and he had hope. The American spirit, indeed, could not die; it was American history. Any contradictions to it were foreign intrusions, parasitical growths, which could not permanently establish themselves. "As to ultimates," Beard proclaimed, "while rejecting a total determinism, the idea of civilization predicates a partial determinism, such as an irreversible and irrevocable historical heritage, and a partially open and dynamic world in which creative intelligence can and does work; in which character can and does realize ethical values; in which virtue can and does make effective choices."[39]

This indeed was a message of hope. Jeffersonianism could never be lost; it could only be improved. True American history could never be changed but only progress because the foundation of American life was the rock of physical nature, not the ephemeral qualities of European institutions and traditions. And progress must be the restoration of the social simplicity of Jefferson's America.

Beard had denounced Europeans for holding to a materialistic view of history, for believing that human society was determined by material factors. Beard had affirmed that Americans were unique in their belief in the freedom to shape their own environment. Now he concluded his lifework by announcing that Americans were not free to destroy their Jeffersonian heritage because it had the eternal attributes of physical nature. Beard was expressing a theological tradition as old as George Bancroft—that in America, God's spiritual purpose had found final and complete expression in the virgin land of the frontier. If younger historians accepted his gift, his vision of the indestructible promise of the American democratic tradition, they could withstand even the more awful signs of declension he pointed to in his final book, *President Roosevelt and the Coming of the War* (1948). Then, in the future, they could complete the rhetorical ritual of promise, declension, and prophecy. They, like Beard and Bancroft, would find signs that the American national democracy was triumphing over international capitalism.[40]

Reinhold Niebuhr: International Marxist Democracy or American Capitalist Democracy, 1915–55

4

One reason for the great popularity of Charles Beard's writings with the public as well as with professional historians during the 1920s and 1930s was that so many Americans shared Beard's deep disappointment with the results of the United States' participation in World War I. The powerful consensus among intellectuals and average voters alike was that American entry into the war had been a tragic mistake. In the early 1930s, when Beard preached the necessity of a policy of continentalism, many Americans responded positively and enthusiastically to his symbolic separation of the American democratic experiment from an external world of undemocratic chaos. The lesson the majority of Americans felt they had learned from 1919 was that the United States must not participate in another European war. They shared Beard's belief that participation would bring a repetition of the national tragedy that had occurred when Woodrow Wilson mobilized his fellow citizens for a war that was supposed to redeem the world.[1]

The Japanese attack on Pearl Harbor in December 1941, therefore, shattered a complex and fully articulated philosophy of history for which Beard was a major spokesman. Even more abruptly than in 1919, when Beard had turned his back so dramatically on the international jeremiad that he had begun to preach in his 1901 book, *The Industrial Revolution*, many American intellectuals now felt the need to retreat from his national jeremiad. Once the United States was actually at war, they refused to interpret the war effort as a tragic declension from the necessary isolation of an organic American nationalism. It seemed to mock all the heroic sacrifices being made by young citizen-soldiers to ask them to accept Beard's gift. How could one say to them that they should fight stoically, sustained by the reassurance that once the senseless battles were over, they could return home to help rebuild an American continentalism? How could one say to them that their suffering represented only a temporary fall from the American promise, which was how Beard characterized the years from 1941 to 1945?

Many in the intellectual community, therefore, could no longer share Beard's thesis that the national war effort was without meaning, or worse, that President

Franklin Roosevelt, as a leader of the nation's defense, was actually undermining the national value system. The most powerful and persuasive voice in 1941 calling for the repudiation of Beard's continental or isolationist philosophy of American history and offering an alternative philosophy of history that did find positive meaning in America's participation in another European war was that of a Protestant theologian, Reinhold Niebuhr. Many historians younger than Beard looked to this theologian for guidance in developing a political philosophy that did not define an absolute disjunction and constant conflict between democracy and capitalism. And Niebuhr's influence was an important indication that the radical restructuring of the narrative of American history under way in the 1940s would not be based on a reversion to Beard's position in 1917. Historians such as Richard Hofstadter who were breaking away from Beard's rejection of capitalism did not return to a theory of universal stages of historical evolution which were to be revealed by a social science methodology that had achieved the certainty of the physical sciences.[2]

During the 1890s, as Turner haltingly and then Beard enthusiastically had participated in the blending of the dimension of time with the universal laws of nature, they were gaining a philosophy of inevitable progress which claimed to express Darwin's theory of evolution. Armed with this concept, Anglo-American culture no longer needed Protestant theology to provide a synthesis between the dynamism of time and what the tradition of republican virtue had understood as the static aspect of the laws of physical nature. Beard, however, after his bitter disillusionment in 1919 with the placement of American history within such a framework of universal laws, had begun in his popular writings to emphasize the crucial role of the Protestant social gospel in revitalizing and sustaining a democratic tradition in twentieth-century America. In his more theoretical writings after World War I, he also had denied that human experience could be explained as the unfolding of immutable and universal patterns of social evolution. As Beard increasingly came to describe the writing of history as an act of faith, he had moved toward the position of being a self-conscious theologian of a national religion of democracy. He explicitly included the Protestant heritage of colonial America within that democratic faith. But he was not as overtly Protestant as Bancroft had been before the members of the new historical profession in the 1880s accepted evolutionary theory. Beard continued to find the origins of the American democratic promise within a secular framework. At one time, he had observed it in the Industrial Revolution and the Enlightenment. Now, between the wars, he discovered the promise in the agricultural landscape of the English colonies and not, as did Bancroft, in the biblical prophecies of the Puritans.

These trends in Beard's writings had culminated in the gift he had tried to give to younger historians in his 1942 book, *The American Spirit*. That gift was to be a renewed faith in the American jeremiad. No matter what the signs of declension, Beard's litany of reassurance in the 1940s, like Turner's in the 1890s, insisted that the promise would not be erased and that new prophets would appear who could ensure its fulfillment in the future. If we remember, therefore, how fully Beard had defined the entry of the United States into World War II as a terrible threat to an American democratic tradition that had all the implicit characteristics of a national religion, we can begin to understand why the most important challenge to Beard's interpretation of the events of 1941 was by a Protestant theologian who for the previous decade had been denouncing American Protestants for allowing themselves to be prisoners of a secular religion of progress.

In *The Structure of Scientific Revolutions*, Thomas Kuhn has suggested that the person who provides leadership for the radical restructuring of the set of hypotheses on which a scientific community has been operating is often an outsider to that particular field. Such a person has not been fully initiated into the paradigmatic status quo and therefore has an alternative psychological space available in which to create a new set of hypotheses to replace the existing ones that the community no longer finds fruitful. In this respect, it is important to notice that Niebuhr, unlike so many professional historians, had not shared Beard's philosophy of an organic national tradition during the 1930s. And by 1930, Niebuhr had severe doubts about the possibility of achieving the kind of harmonious public interest that was central to the tradition of republican virtue and that remained a fundamental tenet of Beard's definition of industrial democracy. Indeed, it might be suggested that Niebuhr was marginal to the whole tradition of Anglo-American historical writing that stretched back to the Puritans' use of the metaphor of exodus from an Old World to a New World and to which the tradition of republican virtue was added during the Revolutionary period.

It was a long way from Niebuhr's birth in 1892 into a close-knit immigrant community in rural Missouri to his leadership role in the cosmopolitan intellectual society of New York City in the 1940s. His father, Gustave, had come from Germany and was the minister to a group of fellow immigrants who were loyal to their Old World tradition of evangelical piety. He taught his son to see the migration of the congregation as an exodus from a country that demanded that its citizens give their first loyalty to the nation and not to their Christianity. These German-Americans had escaped from Egyptian bondage, but Niebuhr was warned by his father not to substitute one national religion for another. Christian principles must take priority over those of the nation in the United States, as in Germany.

Inspired by his father's example, Niebuhr always knew that he would follow him into the ministry and that he too would serve the German-American people who shared his father's evangelical theology. But after he graduated from the denomination's small seminary in Missouri, Niebuhr experienced the cultural shock of moving from that localized German-American world into the national Anglo-American culture that informed the Divinity School at Yale University. There the religious vision of his father, which transcended national boundaries, was transformed by his teachers, who taught him a new universalism. Those who influenced him most were spokesmen for the social gospel. They looked to the theory of evolution more than to biblical prophecy for reassurance that the United States and other nations were achieving democracies that fulfilled the promise of the Kingdom of God on earth. The limitless plenty of industrial production was making it possible for the peoples of the earth to finally turn their backs on class exploitation and continual war between nations. The Peaceable Kingdom was at hand, and World War I was Armageddon, the final defeat of all the forces of darkness and evil.[3]

When the young Niebuhr left Yale to accept a call from a German-speaking congregation of his denomination, Bethel Evangelical in Detroit, he described himself as a "Christian internationalist." As a youthful enthusiast of the social gospel movement, he was committed to a Progressive jeremiad almost identical to that espoused by Beard in 1915. Niebuhr described his position in that year as standing at "a sort of watershed in time, the mark of an era like the birth of Christ."[4] The pattern of expectation he had learned at Yale was that the promise of the kingdom as an egalitarian democracy was revealed in the Old Testament teachings on social justice and in the witness to that principle which was the life of Jesus. Judged against that promise, world history was the record of a terrible state of declension. Even in the United States, the present era was one of capitalist exploitation. But the social gospel theologians had seen beneath these surface events of turmoil and suffering; they saw that evolution had brought a new economic system, industrialism, into existence, which had turned the long centuries of declension into a relatively harmless example of cultural lag. And they prophesied that humanity was stepping out of this lifeless past into a democratic future, whose social and political patterns would express the vitality of the new economic reality that was already in place. Now in the first decades of the twentieth century, the promise of the ancient Jewish prophets and Jesus was to become the everyday experience for all people. This Kingdom, of course, like the promise of the virtuous republic, would be free of power and corruption. Public interest would triumph over private interest. This reign of public interest would be based, as the social scientists of the Progressive movement such as Beard had proposed, on the cooperative nature of industrial production.

Preaching this Progressive jeremiad, Niebuhr and other ministers had the responsibility to point out the gap between the promise and society's present state of declension. They must call their fellow citizens and fellow Christians out of their ignorance and their irresponsibility. They must inspire as well as chastise, providing a clear outline in their prophecies of how the patterns of social evolution were bringing the fulfillment of the biblical promise. Americans in 1915, like the Puritans of 1630, must work furiously to help God's preordained plan become an actuality. In 1917, Niebuhr reluctantly accepted war as part of that responsibility. Although the coming Kingdom would be a place of perpetual peace, he preached to American soldiers that bloodshed was necessary to purge the last vestiges of the ungodly status quo, the last signs of the long nightmare of declension. His sadness in having to compromise his deep desire to be a pacifist was overcome by his absolute self-confidence that American entry in the war symbolized an exodus across a frontier threshold between the Old World of declension, "the pre-war, industrial, competitive civilization," and the New World of the fulfilled promise, "the post-war, industrial, cooperative era." The failure of the war to fulfill this prophecy, the failure of the exodus experience, he declared, "created my whole world view. It made me a child of the age of disillusionment."[5]

Like Beard, he too had to rethink his whole philosophy of history as he entered the 1920s. Unlike Beard, however, he was not ready to replace his Progressive international jeremiad with an American one that separated the United States from world history. Still influenced by his father's warnings about German nationalism, Niebuhr was distressed by the inward turning represented by Beard's celebration of American nationalism. "America," he warned, "is in the throes of a violent nationalism which compares with the jingoism so prevalent in Europe."[6]

Indeed, Niebuhr's writings during the early 1920s provide little evidence that the foundations of his prewar philosophy of history had been so badly shaken that he had to begin the difficult task of constructing a new one. He still defined capitalism as a sinful but dying stage of historical evolution. He still assumed that democracy would be the next stage of the evolutionary process. He continued to find room within this virtuous democracy for private property. Like Beard, he made the distinction between the private property of democracy, which was productive and rational, and the private property of capitalism, which was parasitical and irrational. In 1920, as in 1915, he believed that a middle class of virtuous and productive property holders was existing in a state of undemocratic declension because they were ignorant, for the most part, of how different the two kinds of private property were. Therefore, in the early 1920s it seemed that his disillusionment was minor. He and many of his contemporaries were wrong in their prophecies about the timing of the exodus from the chaotic capitalist stage of social evolution to the harmony of the higher, democratic stage. But the international jeremiad of the Progressive Era still made sense to him. What he and like-minded Protestant ministers had to accomplish in the 1920s was the refinement of their analysis of the chronology of social evolution. Then they could more accurately date the moment of inevitable transition.[7]

Excitement and energy flowed from Niebuhr, therefore, as he entered the

1920s. In 1915, he had known that he stood at a frontier threshold and that his preaching could help inspire the people to begin their march out of Egyptian bondage into the Promised Land. He still knew this in 1920. He dedicated the energy of an ordinary minister to his congregation in Detroit. But his extraordinary energy flowed into an outpouring of articles to a national audience of Protestants who, like him, remained loyal to the social gospel. Gustave Niebuhr had found fulfillment in leading his congregation out of Germany and helping to establish a virtuous local community in rural Missouri. His son aspired to be a leader for the exodus of all humanity into a worldwide community of peace and justice.

He was a prolific writer whose articles appeared in the journals *Biblical World, World Tomorrow*, and the *Christian Century*, which made him a contributing editor in 1924. Clearly, Niebuhr's voice was that of a spokesman for the social gospel as his Protestantism transcended denominational boundaries. And he was quickly becoming a leader among the social gospel Protestants of the 1920s by trying to determine when the lower stage of social evolution, capitalism, was to be replaced by the higher stage of democracy. What date should replace 1917 as the frontier threshold for that salvation experience? It was the recognition of this vitality and leadership that brought the invitation in 1928 to accept a professorship at Union Theological Seminary, perhaps the most prestigious center of liberal, interdenominational Protestantism in the country.

Ironically, since Niebuhr by 1928 had physically as well as psychologically separated himself from his German-American roots, a major reason why he and his brother, H. Richard, gained a special hearing in the liberal Protestant community was their ability to use their fluency in German and their knowledge of that country to bring current developments in both German theology and German social theory into their discussions of the modern condition of declension. It was also in these discussions that Niebuhr revealed that 1919 indeed had caused him to have serious doubts about the Progressive international jeremiad, doubts that he had hidden, perhaps even from himself, behind his facade of optimism. In the 1920s, while Beard was using his discovery of German social theorists and historians to strengthen his concept of an organic national tradition which defied international influences, Niebuhr was using his new German contacts to gain a deeper appreciation of what it meant for the United States to share a bourgeois culture with the nations of western Europe. By 1925, Niebuhr was clearly losing his assurance of 1915 that democracy and Protestantism were twin enemies of capitalism. He was finding it difficult to believe that one could successfully appeal to the conscience of a middle class that avowed loyalty to the ideals of democracy and Protestantism and motivate these property holders to provide leadership for a movement to overcome the selfishness, the absence of public interest, in the dominant capitalist economy. He had been shocked when he had read the German social philosopher Max Weber, who claimed that it had been the Protestant Reformation that had provided the necessary cultural context for the emergence of capitalism.[8]

Studying Weber, Niebuhr for the first time had an explanation why the jeremiad preached by the social gospelers in 1917 had failed to pull the American middle class out of its sloth and inspire them to fulfill their destiny as progressives who would fulfill the promise of a democratic and Protestant society. The social gospel preachers had expected that the middle-class owners of productive property would understand that the parasitical private property of capitalism could not support the kind of public interest necessary for a democracy. But, as Niebuhr understood it, if Weber was right and the deep loyalty of middle-class Protestants was to capitalism rather than democracy, one could never preach a successful Progressive jeremiad to the bourgeoisie which dominated not only American political and economic life, but also the Protestant denominations.

To reach this grim conclusion, it had taken Niebuhr most of the decade after the failure of his prophecy that World War I would provide the opportunity for a great exodus. He had started the 1920s less shaken than Beard. But now his decision set him, as of 1930, far apart from the hopeful American jeremiad that informed Beard's *The Rise of American Civilization*. In the early 1920s, he had called Karl Marx a cynic for insisting that the middle class could never transcend its self-interest and that it would always defend the status quo. Entering the 1930s, however, Niebuhr described Marx as a realist, not a cynic. Indeed, Marx had become a heroic figure, whose message was necessary if Niebuhr was to continue to believe in a Progressive jeremiad.

When Niebuhr wrote about Marx at the beginning of the 1930s, he asked his liberal Protestant readers to understand Marx as an Old Testament prophet who had suddenly returned to modern society. Niebuhr declared that Marx, like those prophets, had pointed to the corruption of his society and warned about the terrible judgment that awaited bourgeois civilization because it rejected the goal of social justice that was the implicit norm of historical evolution. When the stock market crashed in 1929 and a depression overwhelmed the American economy, Niebuhr did not turn, as Beard did, to another hero of the virtuous middle class who would save American democracy from international capitalism. Niebuhr agreed with Beard that the profound economic chaos provided another moment when the exodus out of the capitalist declension into the democratic future could take place. But, for Niebuhr, Beard was part of the capitalist problem, as was the American middle class that Beard lauded. Marx, Niebuhr had concluded, was correct when he insisted that only the propertyless workers, the proletariat, would respond to the prophets who urged them to destroy the corrupt, undemocratic status quo and achieve the democracy that lay at the end of the historical process. Only Marx's version of the Progressive jeremiad was true.[9]

Niebuhr did not explicitly describe Marx as a prophet for a democratic promise that had a divine origin, but he did so describe the German theologians Karl Barth and Paul Tillich, whose works were crucial in bringing Niebuhr to the point in 1927 when he declared, "Our churches are the perfect instrument of the middle classes which dominate America." When Niebuhr had supported the Progressive party of Robert La Follette, Sr., in 1924, he was still insisting that the middle class "may be enlisted through its ideals, once they are awakened, to support a program of thoroughgoing political and economic reconstruction." And he continued to share the optimism of the Progressive social scientists in their appeal to reason as a major tool for the Progressive jeremiad. "Modern sociology's demand that the social motives of primary social groups shall become the motives of secondary groups is identical with the demands of the Sermon on the Mount," and, therefore, he concluded, "reason and experience will contribute to the attainment of human brotherhood."[10] But in 1924, Niebuhr was reading Karl Barth. If he believed Barth, there was no hope in a political movement like that of La Follette because there was no hope that reason could contribute to the attainment of human brotherhood; reason could never persuade the middle class to abandon its privileges. From Barth, Niebuhr learned that his social gospel theology represented an American heresy. True Christianity, Barth declared, acknowledged that there was no redemption within history. Humanity would remain sinful until the end of time. Humans would continue to receive divine judgment and punishment in the future, as they had in the past. Nothing, Barth wrote, was more sinful than the intention of social gospel theology to place God within the limits of history. God, Barth insisted, is transcendent, existing beyond history. Modern humans, in Barth's analysis, faced with the catastrophic refutation of their belief in inevitable progress toward the Kingdom by the events of World War I, were realizing the absurdity of trying to imprison the Divine as an immanent force within history. The prideful assertion of bourgeois society that it was making moral and spiritual as well as economic and political progress toward a perfect human condition was now subject to divine judgment and punishment. The agency for this punishment would be the proletariat. The downtrodden who exposed the hypocrisy and self-centeredness of the middle class would rise up and destroy the world of ease and comfort built on the exploitation of the poor. Niebuhr, however, in 1930, did not accept Barth's conclusion that there was no democratic promise that gave meaning to the unfolding of social evolution. He did not agree with Barth that the proletariat was only an agency of divine wrath directed against bourgeois pride. Rather, he believed that the primary historical role of the proletariat was to serve as a Chosen People who would escape the bondage of capitalism and bring the democratic promise of history to its fulfillment.[11]

Armed with Barth's "crisis" theology and Marx's international jeremiad, Niebuhr was scornful of the belief of people like Beard that the election of Franklin

D. Roosevelt in 1932 meant a quick and easy victory of democracy over capitalism. The vision of American exceptionalism, that America was immune to the crisis of European history, which informed Beard's *The Rise of American Civilization*, was built on an ephemeral foundation. According to Niebuhr, America was exceptional only in the sense that the richness of its resources had postponed the impoverishment of the proletariat. But this frontier legacy of accidental bounty had intensified the refusal of the American middle class to confront the problem of social justice. Even more than the middle classes of the European nations, the American bourgeoisie suffered under a burden of "innocence" that ignored the existence of economic suffering in the United States.

Niebuhr's prolific writings, which were now appearing regularly in the *New Republic* and the *Nation* as well as in the Protestant journals where he had begun publishing, were attempting to persuade his readers to see their future in the current events taking place in Europe. Above all, he wanted to introduce the theologian Paul Tillich to his American audience because, according to Niebuhr, he was "the intellectual leader of the little group of religious Socialists in Germany who are trying to understand our modern civilization and proletarian protest against it in religious terms." Their analysis, he continued, "could not possibly have been written in America. America is still too thoroughly immersed in the illusions and superstitions of liberal middle-class culture."[12] Even as Beard was doing everything in his power to convince Americans that they could learn nothing about their past or future by looking abroad, Niebuhr was asserting that they could learn everything important about their current situation by such a cosmopolitan perspective.

When Niebuhr published *Moral Man and Immoral Society* in 1932, his first book to reach a wide secular audience, he held potentially contradictory attitudes toward history. He was persuaded by Barth's crisis theology that there was no redemption within history. But the consequence of accepting Barth's argument that God was beyond history, if carried to a logical conclusion, was to abandon the rhetorical ritual of the Progressive jeremiad, either in its American or in its international form. People could not be called out of the current declension to fulfill a promise made in the past if history was as mysterious and unpredictable as Barth insisted. Niebuhr still wanted to believe, however, that the crisis of the twentieth century symbolized more than the judgment and punishment of bourgeois civilization. He wanted to believe that the democratic society characterized by perfect social justice, which he had expected industrialism to bring so quickly in 1917, was going to be reached in the 1930s. Once he had assumed that such a society would emerge from the goodwill of the middle class; now, however, he declared that violent revolution by the proletariat was necessary to achieve the virtuous democracy. In *Moral Man and Immoral Society*, and in *Reflections on the End of an Era*, published in 1935, his narrative of modern history continued to depend on the metaphor of an exodus from a profane Old

World, the middle-class establishment in the United States and all other capitalist nations, to a sacred New World, a working-class democracy. And he wanted his readers, liberal Protestants as well as secular liberals, to be willing to join the proletariat in using force to reach the Promised Land. In *Moral Man and Immoral Society*, he insisted that the pacifist ethic of Jesus was relevant only to the Divine Kingdom that exists beyond history. Since humanity could not achieve perfection within history, it was sinful to appeal to the perfectionist ethic of Jesus as the standard for action in this world. Justice and virtue within history must always be relative. Confronting the way many of his readers recoiled at the use of violence because of the recent and bitter memory of World War I, Niebuhr defended Marx's thesis that the overthrow of the bourgeoisie must be bloody. "If a season of violence can establish a just social system," he declared, "and can create the possibilities of its preservation, there is no purely ethical ground upon which violence and revolution can be ruled out."[13]

Moral Man and Immoral Society as well as *Reflections on the End of an Era* reveal a Niebuhr struggling with a set of paradoxes within his philosophy of history. He continued to believe in 1935, as he had in 1915, that historical change was predictable because it represented the universal laws of evolution. The chaos of capitalism did not signify that the experience with time trapped humans within the realm of the particular and the irrational. Capitalism was a necessary stage in the course of progress toward industrial democracy. And the collapse of capitalism that had begun in 1929 indicated that the transition of the stages was about to take place. But Niebuhr's philosophy of history in 1935 was fundamentally different from that of 1915. He had, of course, lost confidence in middle-class owners of productive property as citizens of the coming industrial democracy. This change placed Niebuhr in a major debate with Beard who continued to see a middle-class democracy in the United States that was the enemy of capitalism. And for Niebuhr, since the large middle class would fight, if necessary, to defend the capitalist establishment, the transition to the highest stage of social evolution, industrial democracy, would not come peacefully, as he had so firmly believed in 1915, but only through a terrible class war. The proletariat would win the war after great suffering because they had the strength of history behind them; they alone were in direct harmony with the cooperative energy of industrial production.

The greatest difference, however, separating Niebuhr in 1935 from his position of 1915 came from his conception of the relationship of God to human history. In 1915, he had assumed that God was present in the process of historical evolution. It was God who provided the promise that history as progress would culminate in His Kingdom on earth, a Kingdom that Niebuhr described as a perfect industrial democracy. But the failure of his 1919 prophecy that the Kingdom was at hand seemed to have opened Niebuhr to Karl Barth's theology, which declared that God had begun human history and would end it, but that

God was transcendent to and not immanent in the history that was taking place between the beginning and the end. God's Kingdom, according to Barth, would not be reached as the culmination of historical progress, but only after God had ended history.

It is clear that Niebuhr was struggling between 1925 and 1935 with the implications of Barth's insistence that God could only be defined as transcendent. And in 1935, he was still able to find a compromise between his Progressive jeremiad and Barth's crisis theology. In *Reflections on the End of an Era*, his vision of history remained one of inevitable progress, proceeding from lower to higher stages. In it he preached that the final stage of industrial democracy would be much superior to the present capitalist era. But while Niebuhr urged Protestant ministers and secular intellectuals to join in the violent victory of the proletariat, he also asked them to recognize that the coming workers' democracy, in contradiction to Marx's prophecy, would not be a New World that escaped all the evils of the Old World. There is a great irony in Niebuhr's use of the title *Reflections on the End of an Era*. His self-conscious intention was to draw attention to the end of capitalism. And he did preach a Progressive jeremiad throughout the book, exhorting his readers to renounce their passive acceptance of the sinful capitalist establishment and assume their responsibility to fulfill the promise of a democratic future. But he also preached an anti-Progressive jeremiad. Protestants must recognize that the Kingdom would not be reached when a proletarian order was established. Secular intellectuals also must recognize that the proletarian democracy would not be one of perfect virtue. They must join the proletarian revolution because a better society than the crumbling capitalist establishment was possible, and they, as people of conscience, must always choose good over evil. But as people of conscience, they must be prepared to criticize the pretensions of the coming proletarian establishment to perfection, as Barth had criticized the pretensions of the bourgeoisie who claimed that they had brought history to its highest possible point. The proletariat, he warned, like the bourgeoisie, would identify their particular, selfish, and relative interests with the universal and the timeless, and would try to suppress all who disagreed with them. Niebuhr, therefore, was asking his readers to be in the revolution but not of it. Accepting Marx's vision of a communist democracy as the highest human achievement, they must recognize that it would not be a perfect society, free from selfishness and the oppressiveness of power. He appealed to them to be prepared to play the role of a dissenting, critical minority in the new order that they had helped to bring into existence. But they must be ready to kill other men and sacrifice their own lives for the imperfect revolution that inevitably was coming.

It is also ironic that Niebuhr's paradoxical relationship between faith and historical evolution had significant parallels to that proposed by Beard in 1935. Until the mid-1930s, both continued to expect that the development of industrialism was making capitalism an outmoded stage of historical evolution and was replacing it with democracy. Beard, after 1919, anticipated the triumph of democracy only in the United States, whereas Niebuhr believed the transition would take place in all capitalist nations. Both had reacted, however, to the failure of historical evolution to meet their prophecies about World War I. And both, after 1920, argued that a collective act of faith was necessary to force that transition. They no longer had complete confidence that there was an inevitable logic to history as progress. At the same time when Beard was insisting that the future of democracy in the United States depended upon a religious faith in the national democratic tradition, Niebuhr was declaring that the international revolution of the proletariat against capitalism could not succeed without a Marxist theology. Identifying himself as a Barthian Christian, Niebuhr stated that he could not believe in Marx's prophecy that a secular millennium was coming. But he declared that he and other Protestant ministers must encourage the workers to believe in the Marxist mythology of the Promised Land. Only such a spiritual and emotional commitment to the inevitability of the victory of democracy over capitalism could provide the psychic energy that was a necessary supplement to the inherent energy of social evolution which seemed to have faltered halfway between capitalism and democracy. "Once the religious quality of the proletarian creed is abandoned and the eschatological emphasis in Marxism is destroyed," he insisted, "evolutionary socialism may easily lose the furious energy which alone is capable of moving against the stubborn inertia of society."[14]

In 1935, then, both Beard and Niebuhr seemed confident that they could prophesy the immediate future because they understood that capitalism existed only because of cultural lag. Frustrated, however, by the unexpected delay in the inevitable victory of democracy over capitalism, they had moved together toward a greater appreciation of the role of the nonrational, the mythic in history. And both assumed that the persuasive power of the mythic would be used only by the progressive forces of history. But between 1935 and 1941, Beard's expectations about the course of American history were shattered by the charismatic power of President Roosevelt. For Beard, Roosevelt demonstrated a frightening capacity for manipulating the emotions of the public. Beard's reaction to what he saw as the terrifying demagogic and despotic influence of Roosevelt was to jettison his lifelong commitment to a strong presidency as well as his critique of the checks and balances of the Constitution. During the last ten years of his life, he reversed the tenets of the previous thirty-five and urged an appreciation of the system of divided powers constructed by the founding fathers. Roosevelt's ability to mobilize psychic energy to overcome the inertia of society was, in Beard's opinion, catastrophic because he was overthrowing a democratic tradition in an attempt to impose an antidemocratic capitalist society on America.

Niebuhr saw the American establishment in 1935 as capitalist and not democratic. But, like Beard, his confidence in his understanding of the evolutionary patterns of history was shattered by a charismatic figure who used his power to manipulate myths to destroy and not enhance democracy. And, like Beard, Niebuhr was so shocked by the power of a demagogue to shape history in an antidemocratic direction, that his priority after 1936 was no longer the achievement of a better democracy but the defense of whatever imperfect democracy existed.

In Niebuhr's case, the political figure of unpredictable power and energy who broke his confidence in an inevitably progressive history was Adolph Hitler, who assumed authority in Germany in 1933 at the same time Roosevelt became the president of the United States. In contrast to Beard, Niebuhr had assumed that Roosevelt, like Hoover, was a spokesman for the capitalist establishment. He also assumed that American workers were so inculcated with the myth of American exceptionalism that they were not able to take advantage of the collapse of the economy to construct a strong Marxist political party. He believed, however, that Hitler's fascism represented that final and desperate stage all capitalist goverments were destined to reach as bourgeois civilization fell apart. He was certain that, unlike American workers, those in Germany were educated into a Marxist understanding of class exploitation and class conflict. For Niebuhr, therefore, the first victory of the proletariat would take place in Germany sometime between 1933 and 1936 as Hitler and fascism were overthrown in a bloody revolution.

In 1936, Beard feared that Roosevelt had more political energy than those who, like himself, were loyal to the American democratic tradition. And by 1936, Niebuhr was horrified to discover that Hitler had more political energy than his socialist opponents. Although Niebuhr continued to write articles until 1944 suggesting that since industrialism had developed in England earlier than in the United States, the development of a socially responsible democracy in England would necessarily move to America, it is clear that his understanding of history as progressive social evolution was rapidly disintegrating. Beard's crisis of faith in the inevitable expansion of democracy within the United States caused him to be stridently conservative about what he saw as the existing foreign policy of continentalism, or "isolation." Niebuhr's crisis of faith was in the inevitable expansion of democracy within Western civilization. He became vehemently protective of the incomplete social democracy that had been achieved in all the capitalist nations. Hitler proved that democracy could be destroyed. What he had done in Germany could be done elsewhere. And so the logic of Niebuhr's conservative international concerns caused him to challenge Beard's attempt to keep the United States out of world history.[15]

No longer able to promise the inevitable victory of democracy, Niebuhr was developing a rhetoric that prophesied an unthinkable future if the demagogue

Hitler was not stopped. The structure of his historical narrative, the Progressive jeremiad of democratic promise, capitalist declension, and democratic future, collapsed when Hitler's fascism proved more powerful than socialism. Niebuhr, by 1937, could no longer define fascism as the final stage of a disintegrating capitalism. Fascism was an unpredicted novelty erupting in history. And it seemed to have the strength to destroy both democracy and capitalism. Demonic and destructive, fascism threatened the pattern of Western history that had seen capitalism begin the liberation of humanity from medieval darkness. And capitalism, Niebuhr believed, unlike fascism, tolerated the expansion of political democracy. That democracy, in turn, had forced capitalism to accept significant patterns of social justice. So Niebuhr came to associate capitalism and democracy, once incompatible elements in his philosophy of history, as interrelated parts of a Western civilization that must be preserved against the horrible anti-civilization that Hitler was trying to create.

Niebuhr, however, was in a quandary between 1936 and 1940 about how best to keep Hitler from expanding his initiative in defining the shape of the future. Hitler's successful use of violence to destroy German socialism had left Niebuhr bewildered. Until 1935, he had imagined capitalists using violence to sustain the status quo and socialists using violence to construct the future industrial democracy. The Nazi use of violence to bring an unpredicted future, one that violated all the conventional wisdom about the stages of social evolution, left him stunned.

As he quickly changed from an advocate of a violent revolution that was to bring modern history to its logical conclusion, to a dedicated conservative, he expressed fear that any use of violence would add to the chaos brought by Hitler's rise to power. War to contain Hitler might only feed the destructive fury of fascism in its larger war against human progress. Niebuhr's many articles in the late 1930s reveal a deep confusion and equally deep anguish. For a moment, he almost sounded like Beard as he advocated that the United States should remain isolated when war broke out in Europe in 1939. The United States, he suggested, might provide an island of order where the progressive principles of Western civilization could be preserved as the rest of the world collapsed into chaos. One could then hope that someday those principles would help the rest of humanity to again attempt the long climb out of darkness.[16]

But Niebuhr's fleeting advocacy of isolation from the European war was based on a very different philosophy of history from that of Beard. Beard, in 1940, found capitalism to be an alien enemy of the American organic national tradition. His great task, therefore, was to stop those capitalists who had gained a foothold in the United States from forcing the nation into the realm of international chaos where capitalists flourished best. Niebuhr, however, assumed that the establishment in the United States was only a national variation of an international bourgeoisie. For him, to advocate isolation in 1939 was to sacrifice his immediate hopes that a socialist democracy would soon replace the bourgeois status quo in America. "It may be that such neutrality will serve to fasten the capitalistic system upon the United States for additional decades," he declared, "but even that result would be preferable to the general destruction of all the physical and moral bases of our present civilization, which, whatever its defects, is surely preferable to the complete chaos which would result from a world war."[17]

All his adult life, however, Niebuhr had placed the United States within an international framework; progress, Protestantism, capitalism, and socialism were all international. Early in the 1920s, he had expressed his antipathy for the kind of organic nationalism that he saw advocated in the United States as well as in Germany. When he suggested isolation in 1939, it was an act of expediency rather than an abandonment of his philosophy of history built on the shared experiences of Western civilization. It is not surprising, then, that a year later he decided that the United States must become a military ally of England. Niebuhr, in 1940, still saw himself as a socialist, and he was deeply disappointed that socialists in England, France, and now the United States had not provided the leadership to mobilize their fellow citizens against Hitler's aggressions. Instead, it was conservatives, even men such as Winston Churchill whom Niebuhr considered a reactionary, who had sounded the alarm. He was especially angry that many of his radical American friends, secular and Protestant, were isolationists. But the conservative capitalist Roosevelt understood the danger that Hitler represented and was trying to inform the public that it was in the national interest to seek the collective security of a military alliance with England.

After 1936, when Niebuhr had so suddenly developed his conservative commitment to the preservation of the heritage of Western civilization against the nihilistic fury of Nazism, he had begun to blur the dichotomy between capitalism and democracy that had been central to his philosophy of history for the previous twenty years. It is probable that in 1940 he still believed that democracy was going to replace capitalism sometime in the future. But democracy and capitalism were no longer the major symbols of the forces of good and evil which were locked in mortal combat, a war from which democracy would emerge victorious after the unconditional surrender of capitalism. In Niebuhr's imagination, the war had become that of a good Western civilization, containing both capitalism and democracy, against the absolute evil of Hitler's Germany. This sense of capitalism and democracy as natural allies made it possible for Niebuhr to support President Roosevelt in his tradition-shattering campaign for a third term in 1940.

As a socialist, Niebuhr was still critical of the New Deal economic philosophy which patched up a faltering capitalism rather than engaging in the rigorous planning of a socialist democracy. In 1939, he had written that "the Rooseveltian doctors are quacks in the sense that they hold out the prospect of an ultimate recovery which lies completely beyond the potency of their medicine." When he celebrated the president's reelection in 1940, however, he identified Roosevelt with democracy and not capitalism. "Despite the ambiguities of Rooseveltian liberalism," Niebuhr declared, "the reelection of the president was a heartening revelation of the ability of democracy to arrive at a right decision in a crisis. . . . No election in our history had validated the principles of universal suffrage more than this one." He concluded that "the 'good' people and the 'wise' people, the 'leaders' voted generally for Willkie."[18] Such rhetoric sounds surprisingly like that of Beard in 1932. Then Beard had assumed that democracy was the fundamental cultural and political reality in the United States, while Niebuhr had seen capitalism as that reality. In 1940, Beard believed that American democracy was critically endangered by international capitalism and that it must be protected from the chaos of the outside world. But, in 1940, Niebuhr was in the process of fusing capitalism and democracy. Like Beard, he too had become a conservative defender of the American status quo, but capitalism, in Niebuhr's revised philosophy of history, was part of American tradition. And so the major threat to the American heritage was not capitalism but nazism.

As Niebuhr prepared to support American participation in World War II, he was self-conscious of how different his philosophy of history was from the one he had held on the eve of World War I. He had undergone, he wrote, "a fairly complete conversion of thought which involved rejection of almost all the liberal theological ideals and ideas with which I ventured forth in 1915."[19] The conversion, as he understood it, was from Christian "idealism" to Christian "realism." Part of that conversion had occurred by the time he had written *Moral Man and Immoral Society* in the early 1930s. There he had denounced the commitment to nonviolence among his Protestant friends, who continued to believe, as Niebuhr once had, that the Kingdom was to be achieved within history and that the ethics of Jesus, therefore, were normative in everyday life. Scathingly, Niebuhr had declared in 1932 that "what is lacking among all these moralists, whether religious or rational, is an understanding of the brutal character of the behavior of all human collectivities, and the power of self-interest and collective egoism in all inter-group relations. Failure to recognize the stubborn resistance of group egoism to all moral and inclusive social objectives inevitably involves them in unrealistic and confused political thought."[20] Niebuhr used this Christian realism of 1932, however, to urge the use of violence by the proletariat to break down "the stubborn resistance of group egoism" represented by the bourgeoisie.

Therefore, he continued to assume, as did Beard, that the logic of industrial production instilled a sense of public interest and public virtue which was very different from the capitalist ethic of self-interest exploitation. But 1936 marked a crucial change for both men in their implicit faith in the redemptive power of industrialism. In Beard's American jeremiad, industrialism was to provide the energy to revitalize the promise of the colonial agricultural democracy. But the power of Roosevelt's leadership in directions that Beard had not expected dramatically changed the emphasis of his rhetoric. In 1932, he was engaged in prophecy, pointing the way out of declension, to the fulfillment of the promise. After 1936, he was defending the promise against the false prophet Roosevelt. The pattern of Niebuhr's rhetoric was the same. In 1932, he was prophesying the victory of the proletariat and the fulfillment of the promise. After 1936, his central concern also was the protection of the promise against false prophecies.

When Niebuhr lost faith in history as progress after 1936, he focused his writings on a condemnation of the ominous future offered by the fascists. And he used the Christian realism of 1932 to justify the use of violence against Nazi aggression; once more he exhorted Protestants to reject pacifism. This just war, however, was not between classes, and it was to abort, not fulfill, prophecies. His Christian realism now seemed to point toward a self-conscious conservatism which opposed all prophecies that promised they could overcome the present state of declension in the name of a better future.

After the United States had entered the war in 1941, Niebuhr began a reconstruction of American political theory that would separate the American democratic tradition from all Progressive jeremiads, whether derived from Marxism, as in his own past, or from the tradition of republican virtue, as in Beard's case. This intellectual enterprise brought Niebuhr a much wider audience than he had reached either as a social gospel writer in the 1920s or as a Christian Marxist in the 1930s. Beard had reached his greatest popularity when he renounced his pre-World War I vision of American history as part of a universal history and began, after 1920, to celebrate an organic American national tradition that was democratic. Now Niebuhr, after 1940, was renouncing his loyalty to a Marxist theory of universal history. And he had begun to celebrate an organic American national tradition that was democratic. It is obvious, of course, that Niebuhr was offering the nation a different organic tradition from that which Beard had so poetically evoked in the 1930s. Why Beard's version was false and Niebuhr's true became the theme of Niebuhr's most influential book on political theory, *The Children of Light and the Children of Darkness: A Vindication of Democracy and a Critique of Its Traditional Defense*, published in 1944.[21]

After 1920, when Beard rejected his earlier philosophy of universal history and began to construct a new philosophy of organic, national history, he nevertheless carried over the same definition of political virtue. Continuing Turner's commitment to the republican tradition, he insisted that an American "people" had existed from colonial times to the present. They were essentially classless, with an equal distribution of power. The corrupting influence of class and power existed in the United States only because of the presence of a capitalism that was alien to the national tradition. But when Niebuhr, after 1940, rejected his earlier philosophy of universal history and began to construct a new philosophy of organic, national history, he carried over his theology of Christian realism which denied that there could be the kind of "innocent people" postulated by Beard. Democracy was not to be defined as a perfectly virtuous society.

Niebuhr, of course, in contrast to Turner and Beard, had always seen capitalism as a major element in American history. When he was a Christian Marxist, he had expected that democracy would come to the United States from abroad and replace the destructive heritage of capitalism. It is not surprising, therefore, that after Niebuhr came to believe that Hitler, rather than Marx, was the major voice of revolutionary change, he concentrated on defending the status quo against the dyamism of fascism and began to find democracy in an American past dominated by capitalism. If democracy was not to be a future partnership in equality by producers, perhaps it was to be found in the economic and social pluralism that inevitably flowed from a capitalist economy. His Christian realism, once it was separated from his previous belief in history as inevitable progress, offered the hope that the evil results of the selfishness and ambition for power characteristic of the human condition could be minimized in a system in which power was decentralized. Niebuhr's vision in *The Children of Light and the Children of Darkness* was the absolute opposite of a homogeneous and virtuous citizenry envisioned by both American liberals and Marxists.

These Children of Light failed to recognize their own imperfections. This self-deception led them either into attempts to isolate themselves from evil or into attempts to impose their presumed purity on others. Failing to recognize the inevitable intermixture of good and evil, the Children of Light were vulnerable to attacks by the Children of Darkness, who assumed that there were no moral standards but only the naked use of power. This 1944 book, therefore, gave meaning to American participation in World War II. Americans, as Children of Light, had tried to isolate themselves from a corrupt world. They had failed to recognize their responsibility to defend a pluralistic world order as the necessary basis for their own democracy as well as other democracies against the Children of Darkness, who had ambitions to impose their totalitarianism on all people. Almost by accident, the United States had entered the war. Americans still suffered from the delusion that democracy was a state of perfect virtue. Now they must use the experience of the war to learn to identify democracy with pluralism, with a system of checks and balances that limited the ability of any group at home or abroad to achieve tyrannical power. Unless Americans learned this lesson, they would be as disillusioned at the end of the war as they had been in 1919 and would fall back into the philosophy of innocence and isolation that had dominated the 1920s and 1930s. But the expectations of Americans in 1917 were bound to be frustrated. They had prophesied a millennium of world unity, as well as a virtuous democracy at home. But, for Niebuhr in 1944, the differences between nations did not represent declension from an original promise of perfect unity. Nor did the less than perfect democracy within the United States indicate declension. For him, nothing was more dangerous than the definition of the status quo as a state of declension. Nothing was more delusive than prophecies that the present could be molded into the shape of some abstract ideal that was supposed to give meaning to history.

The true American national tradition of 1944, in contrast to Beard's false tradition, was that of a pluralist democracy based on the development of capitalism within the unique geographic environment of North America. In 1941, Americans found themselves in military alliance with England and Soviet Russia, both of whom had very different national histories. Since this alliance was organic, unplanned, and defended a pluralist status quo, all good characteristics to Niebuhr, this pragmatic situation should become the basis for America's foreign policy when the war ended. The wartime alliance should become a peacetime alliance. Since the Allies, the United States, England, and Soviet Russia, were more powerful than other nations, they had the responsibility to use that power to ensure stability within the community of nations.

As Niebuhr struggled between 1936 and 1944 to rid himself of his lifelong commitment to one or another Progressive jeremiads, he in effect identified the real American democracy with what he had once defined as a state of declension. And he dismissed the promise and the prophecy of the jeremiad as sheer fantasy. Beard's American "people" had never existed. Compared, then, to the organic reality of a pluralist democracy based on capitalist enterprise, Beard's vision of a virtuous democracy must be considered as having no substance, no reality. There should be no question of revitalizing that dream of a virtuous democracy after Americans had learned the importance and value of their existing pluralist democracy. And by 1944, he had persuaded himself that the same conflict between organic, national tradition and abstract visions of a perfect future had been fought in Russia with the same conclusion as in the United States. Stalin and the Russian people had waged World War II to protect the national integrity of their country. The communist dream of a perfect international order was as alien to the spirit of Russian nationalism as it was to the spirit of American nationalism. The Children of Darkness, through the agency of World War II, had taught the American and Russian Children of Light that they must give up their delusions about forcing history to fit an ideal model to be projected on the future. "Russia, as a nation," Niebuhr declared, "is not aggressive."[22]

Niebuhr felt betrayed, therefore, when he came to believe that revolutionary communist theoreticians were taking control away from a conservative nationalist such as Stalin who had cooperated so well with the conservative nationalists Winston Churchill and Franklin Roosevelt. As he became increasingly angry at what he saw as the revitalization of the Progressive, international jeremiad in

Soviet Russia, he also came to believe that the United States must exercise more force throughout the world to sustain the status quo of international pluralism. By 1947, when he declared that "we cannot afford any compromises" with Soviet Russia, he had begun to spend considerable energy educating Americans on the messianic pretensions of a communist faith that would use bloody revolution to achieve heaven on earth. Americans, he declared, "cannot imagine a political religion so consistent in its dogmatism that it is able to discount in advance any approach which varies from its dogmas."[23]

In 1944, Niebuhr had insisted that after the war the United States should respect the variety of national traditions throughout the world and recognize that the countries of Asia, especially, would always have cultures that were drastically different from that of America. Even the countries of western Europe, those most similar to America, had incorporated much more socialism in their national traditions than had the United States, and America must not attempt to force its more capitalist national tradition on them. But Niebuhr, by 1950, was becoming a more strident advocate of capitalism as a model for other countries. Why, Niebuhr asked himself, were some nations more likely than others to become aggressors in the international community? And the answer he developed was that respect for international pluralism was deeper in the nations that were more pluralistic in their domestic arrangements. This explained why in contrast to Germans or Russians or Japanese, Americans "do not have a philosophy of life which makes us constitutionally fanatical and self-righteous." And that sense of national humility could be linked to the pluralism inherent in capitalism. " 'Self-interest'," Niebuhr insisted as he entered the 1950s, "must be allowed a certain free play for the additional reason that there is no one in society good or wise enough finally to determine how the individual's capacities can best be used for the common good."[24] Niebuhr, therefore, as he approached the age of sixty and was about to sum up his new appreciation of the United States as a capitalist democracy in his book *The Irony of American History*, was in a difficult position regarding his country's role in foreign affairs. He believed that the world community would never become uniform; national distinctions would exist until the end of history. But the United States, the nation with the most pluralistic domestic history, must engage in a cold war against the attempt of communist Russia, the most totalitarian government, to impose uniformity on all nations. The cold war, for Niebuhr, justified the use of limited violence to stop Marxist subversion in other nations or even to keep a nation from voluntarily choosing Marxism. Capitalism had to be exported if other nations were to become so pluralistic at home that they could appreciate pluralism abroad. But this was not the major irony Niebuhr had in mind when he published *The Irony of American History* in 1952.

As Niebuhr lost faith after 1936 in the power of industrialism to bring an exodus from the Old World of capitalism to a New World of industrial democracy, he entered into a period of intense theological creativity. *Beyond Tragedy: Essays on the Christian Interpretation of History* was published in 1937. His magnum opus, *The Nature and Destiny of Man*, appeared during the years 1939–42. And *Faith and History*, published in 1949, marked the end of this period when Niebuhr felt the need to rethink the relationship of his theological assumptions with his philosophy of history.[25] It was the same period when he was working out his concept of democracy as pluralism rather than virtue. When Hitler's ability to shape the future had destroyed his faith in the inevitable progression of the stages of history, he seemed to be forced back to the view proposed by the tradition of republican virtue, that history was the dynamism of irrational particulars and meaning could be found only by transcending history to achieve unity with rational universals.

But Niebuhr denied that science could achieve such unity, and he also denied that Protestants, as a Chosen People, could escape the flux of history. Niebuhr insisted, however, that history was mysterious rather than meaningless. God, although transcendent, existing before and after time, also acted in history. It was only because of the presence of God in history that humans were fulfilled through their participation in the sea of time, which was not proceeding in a predictable fashion toward salvation. Divine action in this world did not end our inability to fully understand or control the patterns of historical change. "God, though revealed, remains veiled; His thoughts are not our thoughts nor His ways our ways," he declared, and "every revelation of the divine is relativised by the finite mind which comprehends it." Humans, he continued, given the divine gift of creativity, necessarily expressed themselves in the construction of the variety of social patterns we call history. But they refused to admit that they were creatures as well as creators, and that their finite creations were always bounded by time. This, he maintained, is the meaning of original sin. "Man is a sinner not because he is one limited individual within a whole, but rather because he is betrayed by his very ability to survey the whole, to imagine himself the whole. . . . The truth," he insisted, "as it is contained in the Christian revelation, includes the recognition that it is neither possible for man to know the truth fully nor to avoid pretending that he does."[26]

This was the theological foundation on which Niebuhr constructed the political philosophy of *The Children of Light and the Children of Darkness*. "The thesis of this volume," he wrote, "grew out of my conviction that democracy has a more compelling justification and requires a more realistic vindication than is given it by the liberal culture with which it has been associated."[27] The Children of Light, he continued, naively have believed that democracy was possible because humans were capable of making rational decisions in which they would choose the public interest over the irrational and selfish. Perhaps recalling his own shocked surprise at Hitler's ability to destroy the socialist opposition in Germany, Niebuhr pointed to the wisdom of the Children of Darkness, who understood that humans could always be called into political action by appeals to their irrational fears and hatreds and to their immediate self-interest. Demagogues forgot, however, that people are capable of rising above their baser instincts and that there were times when the world chose the good rather than the evil. Democracy, therefore, is a balance of light and darkness; it "prospers best in a cultural, religious, and moral atmosphere which encourages neither a too pessimistic nor a too optimistic view of human nature." This, then, was the theological basis for his famous aphorism, "man's capacity for justice makes democracy possible; but man's inclination for injustice makes it necessary."[28]

Given the need to balance the human capacity to be both creative and destructive, Niebuhr maintained that "a healthy society must seek to achieve the greatest possible equilibrium of power, the greatest number of centers of power, the greatest possible social checks upon the administration of power and the greatest possible inner check on human ambition." Of all the forms of government, democracy came closest to providing the necessary political structure for such a society because it embodied "the principle of resistence to government within the principle of government itself." Civil liberties gave the individual the right to criticize the government, and acceptance of political conflict between parties meant that "new forces may enter into competition with the old and gradually establish themselves peacefully."[29]

Niebuhr, by 1944, believed that Americans had always experienced democracy as a pluralism of competing interests and not as a state of perfect public interest. Many Americans, however, had dwelled in a realm of false consciousness, assuming that a virtuous democracy, free from self-interest, had existed in the past and would exist again in the future. By 1950, as Niebuhr came to accept the cold war as a permanent part of American life, he feared that Americans would respond to the fanatical resurgence of the Progressive jeremiad in Russia by revitalizing their own intellectual heritage, both secular and Protestant, of the Progressive jeremiad. If Americans were to define themselves as a redeemer nation, the catastrophe of nuclear war was inevitable. Niebuhr hoped, therefore, to convince Americans with his argument in *The Irony of American History* that their experience with the relative particulars of democracy as a timeful pluralism was more meaningful than their dreams of a democracy that embodied timeless universals. Americans must not define the present, at home or abroad, as a declension from an extrahistorical norm. They must accept the present as one of those provisional goods that humans are capable of constructing.

He began *The Irony of American History* by describing three forms of historical experience: pathos, tragedy, and irony. A person or people were pathetic when they were powerless victims of fate. But Niebuhr's theology as he had developed it between 1935 and 1950 insisted that all persons were endowed with creative capacities. Acting, making choices, they gave history its dynamism. Pathos, therefore, was never a significant part of human history. The real possibilities of historical experience were tragedy and irony. "The tragic element in a human situation," he wrote, "is constituted on conscious choices of evil for the sake of good." In contrast, the ironic situation "is differentiated from tragedy by the fact that the responsibility is related to an unconscious weakness rather than to a conscious resolution." Niebuhr's intention was to alert his fellow citizens to their "unconscious weakness." This was necessary, in his estimation, because irony was only a momentary experience. "An ironic situation must dissolve," he declared, "if men or nations are made aware of their complicity in it. Such awareness involves some realization of the hidden vanity or pretension. This realization," he concluded, "either must lead to an abatement of the pretension, which means contrition; or it leads to a desperate accentuation of the vanities to the point where irony turns into pure evil."[30]

To avoid tragedy, Americans had to become self-conscious of the central irony that their mortal enemy, Soviet Russia, was preaching the same doctrine of human perfection that had informed American intellectual history. The great "hidden vanity or pretension" of the American people was that they were pure and virtuous, whereas all their neighbors were corrupt. It was this sense of particular virtue that had provided the justification for American isolation in 1940.

Niebuhr hoped to desanctify this pretense to unique American virtue by demonstrating that it was Europeans who were responsible for American identity. The development of a bourgeois culture in Europe had sent Puritans to America in search of the Promised Land. It was the European Enlightenment, he insisted, that defined the American Revolution as the achievement of harmony with the rational and universal laws of nature. These Reformation and Renaissance traditions of American innocence, Niebuhr continued, were reinforced at the beginning of the nineteenth century when the European middle class constructed the theory that a marketplace existed where the pursuit of self-interest automatically worked for the welfare of the entire community. And they immediately convinced Americans that the United States was the first model of such a marketplace society. Only the chance circumstance of vast natural resources, Niebuhr admonished, had kept this capitalist party in the United States from being severely challenged by Marxism to the same extent that it was in the less richly endowed European nations.

The United States, therefore, had been, up to 1940, blinded by the intellectual heritage of Puritanism, the Enlightenment, and free marketplace capitalism to the realities of power and responsibility. If Americans had only this history of utopian ideas to sustain them in the sudden transition from the illusion of innocence and isolation to the problems of world leadership, Niebuhr would have had little hope that Americans might escape moving from the ironies of that position to the tragedy of attempting to achieve a resolution of the cold war by waging an atomic war. But Niebuhr was optimistic for this reason: "If the prevailing ethos of a bourgeois culture also gave itself to dangerous illusions about the possibilities of managing the whole of man's historical destiny, we were fortunately and ironically saved from the evil consequences of this illusion by various factors in our culture."[31] The most important of those factors, he declared, was the existence of democratic political machinery, which the bourgeoisie had created to overthrow the feudal aristocracy and which was now used by lower-income people against the capitalists. "The American democracy," Niebuhr asserted, "had learned to use the more equal distribution of political power, inherent in universal suffrage, as leverage against the tendency toward concentration of power in economic life. Culminating in the New Deal, national governments, based upon an alliance of farmers, workers and middle class, have used the power of the State to establish minimal standards of 'Welfare' in housing, social security, health services." This meant, for Niebuhr, that despite the predominant bourgeois ideology of innocence and virtue, Americans had exercised power. They had continually engaged in compromises and the balancing of interests. "In our domestic affairs," he concluded, "we have thus builded better than we know because we have not taken the early dreams of our peculiar innocency too seriously."[32]

In Niebuhr's estimation then, the future of the world depended upon a "disavowal of the pretentious elements in our original dream, and a recognition of the values and virtues which enter history in unpredictable ways."[33] In domestic history, Americans had always accepted limited, provisional goods despite a rhetoric of unlimited perfection. Facing the problems of foreign policy for the first time, Americans had also accepted limited, provisional goods. Niebuhr was straining to persuade Americans to bring a drastically lowered set of expectations to foreign policy because he visualized only increasing frustrations in the cold war effort to contain Soviet Russia. The nations of the world that had not become industrialized, Niebuhr wrote, mistakenly believed that their poverty was the result of Western imperialism. They did not understand that the wealth of the United States and the Western nations came from their vast resources of industrial production rather than from the exploitation of Asia, Africa, and Latin America. And because of their backward economies and non-Western cultural heritages, these countries did not appreciate civil liberties and the competition of free elections. For all these reasons, Americans must anticipate that the nations that were once under European imperial control would look more favorably to the Soviet model of dictatorial modernization than to that of American democracy. We must be patient, he admonished, and then even more patient because Americans, along with all other humans, could not force history to fulfill their desires. Refuting the metaphor of two worlds, Niebuhr offered Americans a single world of constant frustration and disappointment. If we accepted such a reality, he affirmed, "we might acquire the necessary patience to wait out the long run of history while we take such measures as are necessary to combat the more immediate perils."[34] Such patience, of course, was incompatible with the Progressive jeremiad, American or international. The denial of two worlds, for Niebuhr, made it impossible to propose an exodus from the present as a state of declension into a future where promises would be fulfilled. Joining capitalism and democracy, Europe and America, Niebuhr offered contrition as the alternative to tragedy. His rhetoric now seemed closer to the conservative medieval jeremiad described by Bercovitch than to that of the Puritans or of Charles Beard.[35]

Richard Hofstadter: American Democracy or American Capitalism, 1940–70

5

Richard Hofstadter was the most influential of the younger historians who became identified with the Consensus, or Counter-Progressive, school of American historical writing during the 1950s. He began his graduate studies at Columbia University in 1938 under the direction of Merle Curti, an admirer of Charles Beard. As was common among his contemporaries, Hofstadter acknowledged Beard's intellectual leadership in the profession. "I took up American history," he later recalled, "under the inspiration that came from Charles and Mary Beard's *The Rise of American Civilization*." [1]

His historical writing, which began in about 1940, illuminates, therefore, the devastating impact of the American entry into World War II on those young historians who had accepted Beard's concept of an American national democracy in conflict with international capitalism. By the end of the war, Hofstadter, like so many of his contemporaries in the historical profession, could no longer use Beard's definition of the metaphor of two worlds as the structure for his narratives. An enthusiastic participant in Beard's American jeremiad when the war broke out, Hofstadter, by the war's conclusion, was joining with Niebuhr to denounce the American jeremiad as a snare and a delusion. Then, by 1950, he began the slow and painful process of groping toward a way to unite capitalism and democracy.

His life was cut short by illness in 1970, but he had plans to write a synthesis of American history from beginning to end which would surpass Beard's *The Rise of American Civilization* in scope. He had become confident that Beard's thesis of the colonial promise of a virtuous democracy, threatened by declension into capitalism, could be replaced by the thesis that the colonial promise, which gave meaning to all subsequent American history, was that of a pluralist democracy in harmony with capitalism. Hofstadter had begun his career as a professional historian with *Social Darwinism in American Thought*, which illustrated the validity of Beard's *The Rise of American Civilization*. When his career ended, his books were illustrating the validity of Reinhold Niebuhr's *The Irony of American History*.

Social Darwinism in American Thought, a revision of his doctoral dissertation, was published in 1944 and received an award from the American Historical Association. Merle Curti, his thesis adviser, was one of the original historians of ideas within the profession, and he encouraged Hofstadter's interest in exploring more extensively that bitter conflict of democratic and undemocratic ideas in America between the Civil War and World War I which the Beards had briefly discussed in *The Rise of American Civilization*. The narrative structure he used for his analysis was that of Beard's post-1920 American jeremiad. And the specific descriptions of the promise, the declension, and the prophecy for the years 1865–1917 were almost identical to those employed by the Beards. In a foreword written for a revised edition, published in 1955 after he had broken from Beard's influence, he admitted that the 1944 book, "although . . . meant to be a reflective study rather than a tract for the times . . . was naturally influenced by the political and moral controversy of the New Deal era."[2] It is interesting, however, that he did not link that political and moral controversy explicitly to Beard's position in 1940.

Although the book directly addresses early twentieth-century ideas from the perspectives developed by Beard, it is apparent that the shadow of Beard's crisis, his fear of President Franklin Roosevelt's charismatic power over foreign policy, darkens Hofstadter's story. Ostensibly, he had written a successful Progressive national jeremiad. He began, like Beard, with the American democratic promise. "The dogmas of the Enlightenment had been traditional ingredients of the American faith," he declared; "American social thought had been optimistic, confident of the special destiny of the country, humanitarian, democratic. Its reformers still relied upon the sanctions of natural rights."[3]

Then there was declension. Following the conventions of the American jeremiad with which Beard had replaced his pre-1919 international jeremiad, Hofstadter stressed that this democratic promise had been the American experience until the Civil War. After that, this century of political virtue based on universal natural laws was attacked by American thinkers, chief among them William Graham Sumner, who used the ideas of English capitalist philosophers to deny the intellectual validity of those principles. "It was Sumner's function to take the leadership in a critical examination of these ideological fixtures," Hofstadter continued, "using as his instrument the early nineteenth-century pessimism of Ricardo and Malthus, now justified with the tremendous prestige of Darwinism." Hofstadter's understanding of this conflict of ideas—American versus English, democratic versus capitalist, universal versus particular, public interest versus private interest, virtue versus corruption—was very similar to that tradition of eighteenth-century republicanism described by Pocock. Sumner, the Yale economist, Hofstadter continued, "tried to show his contemporaries that their 'natural rights' were nowhere to be found in nature, that their humanitarianism, democracy, and equality were not eternal verities, but the passing mores of a stage of social evolution."[4]

Again, like the Beard of the 1920s and 1930s, Hofstadter stressed that the ideology of particular and irrational self-interest that characterized English capitalism could not have become dominant in the United States after the Civil War unless the economic system of English capitalism had defeated that American economic system of agricultural democracy whose passing was mourned by Turner. American academics, like Sumner, successfully preached the doctrines of social Darwinism as they had received them from the English social philosopher Herbert Spencer, only because capitalists controlled the American economy by the 1880s. "With its rapid expansion, its exploitive methods, its desperate competition, post-bellum America was like a vast human caricature of the Darwinian struggle for existence," Hofstadter lamented, as "successful business entrepreneurs seem to have accepted almost by instinct the Darwinian terminology which had emerged from the conditions of their existence."[5]

Hofstadter, in 1940, had succeeded where Turner had failed to create a convincing prophecy that this declension from the original democratic promise would be replaced by a more glorious democratic future, as earlier Beard had so succeeded, by assuming that the undemocratic economic system of capitalism would be replaced by the democratic economic system of industrialism. But Hofstadter's confidence in industrialism was not that of the Beard of 1900 who saw it as a force bringing an international democratic order. Instead, he stood with the later Beard, who was concerned only with the relationship of industrialism to the national tradition of democracy within the borders of the United States. And, in 1940, he explicitly shared Beard's identification and rejection of an international, industrial democracy based on the doctrines of Karl Marx.

The first half of *Social Darwinism in American Thought* is characterized by Hofstadter's description of the clash of ideas between William Graham Sumner and Lester Frank Ward. A pioneer sociologist, Ward, according to Hofstadter, developed his ideas, in contrast to Sumner, outside the academic establishment that was providing the major apologetic for the new capitalist order that had come from England. Ward shared with Spencer and Sumner an acceptance of Darwin's theory of evolution. But he interpreted evolution in a totally different way than they did. For instance, Ward insisted that the major characteristic of evolution was cooperation rather than competition within species. If Darwin represented the new authority for defining natural law, it was crucial, Hofstadter insisted, to establish that public interest rather than private interest was in harmony with Darwin's description of the natural. Ward's "opposition to the biological argument for individualism stemmed from his democratic faith,"[6] Hofstadter declared, and that faith enabled him to see that Darwin did not contradict the colonial definition of the natural as rational.

Related to Ward's emphasis on the role of cooperation in the evolutionary process was his affirmation that humans played a creative role in the evolutionary process rather than the passive one defined by the conservative social Darwinists. Implicit in Hofstadter's analysis was the idea that Spencer and Sumner were justifying the capitalist declension from the democratic promise by arguing that this chaotic and competitive present was the only reality. But Ward's understanding of evolution was consistent with Hofstadter's use of the rhetorical ritual of the American jeremiad to shape his historical narratives. Ward, in contrast to Spencer and Sumner, assumed that a democratic promise gave meaning to natural history. And Ward, unlike the apologists for the status quo, could prophesy that the current declension of competitive capitalism would be overcome as evolution brought a cooperative industrial democracy into existence. For Ward, the ability to use the original promise to forecast the future gave humans the opportunity to participate actively in the evolutionary process. American democrats understood the capitalist declension as evidence of cultural lag. And they also understood that they could help build a new culture in harmony with the new stage of history emerging from the evolutionary process. "Man's task," in Ward's opinion, was "not to imitate the laws of nature, but to observe them, appropriate them, direct them."[7]

Ward, however, in Hofstadter's presentation, "broached his collectivism almost two decades too early to reach a fully receptive audience." His prophecy came before most Americans moved from the experience of capitalist self-interest to the experience of industrial cooperation. But "the transition to solidarism, which was part of a larger reconstruction in American thought, became apparent in the 'nineties."[8] Although he praised the social gospel ministers who helped to replace Sumner's idea of competitive self-interest with that of cooperative democracy, he expended most of his analysis on such secular philosophers as John Dewey. These pragmatists, for Hofstadter, were the true prophets of the coming collectivist democracy, in which a virtuous public interest would replace the corrupt private interest of capitalism.

Hofstadter stressed that the conservative Darwinism of Spencer and Sumner was "the philosophy of inevitability," whereas the reform Darwinism of Ward and Dewey was "the philosophy of possibility." Spencer and Sumner preached a conservative jeremiad that declared there was no alternative but to suffer the consequences of competition. But Hofstadter, like Ward and Dewey, knew that the declension of the capitalist establishment was not in harmony with evolution. In 1940, Hofstadter could prophesy a democratic future and work to bring it into existence because, like the Progressives of 1900, he was certain that the development of industrialism was undermining capitalism and preparing the foundation for a democratic society. Again and again, he stressed that prophets such as Ward and Dewey could not bring democracy into existence. It was factory workers who first felt the cooperative rhythms of an industrial production that expressed the laws of evolutionary nature. It was the laborers who were the true pioneers of collective democracy. "The change in the political outlook of the common man," Hofstadter declared, "was responsible for a change in the fundamental mechanisms of thought among workers in the social sciences."[9] At this point, Hofstadter asked his readers not to confuse American progressivism with Marxism. Only in the United States could productive workers and the productive middle class overthrow parasitical capitalism in a bloodless revolution.

Hofstadter's narrative, after establishing the debate between Ward and Sumner, had become the joyful report that by 1900 the capitalist declension from the early American agrarian democracy was being overcome by a new industrial democracy supported by progressive intellectuals, factory workers, and productive middle class. But Hofstadter's narrative, like that of Beard in *The Rise of American Civilization*, had to abort this successful exodus from declension because of World War I when, for Hofstadter, "the reformers of the era were destined to tragic failure." He had to admit that reform Darwinism, apparently triumphant over conservative Darwinism in the Progressive years between 1900 and 1916, was being undermined by the continued power of conservative Darwinism in the area of foreign policy. Beard, of course, after the failure of his prophecy that World War I was the threshold into industrial democracy, had decided that capitalism gained strength from war. Now Hofstadter, in 1940, was preparing his readers to understand why the Progressive movement had been frustrated by American participation in World War I when conservative Darwinism was "being made to fit the mold of international conflict just when its inapplicability to domestic economics was becoming apparent." The momentum of the movement toward industrial democracy was broken, therefore, when America entered the war in 1917. But Hofstadter concluded his first book with the promise that the prophecy would be fulfilled. "Despite the interruption of the 'twenties,' he maintained, "the trend toward social cohesion kept growing."[10]

On the eve of World War II, Hofstadter fully accepted the thesis of Beard's *The Rise of American Civilization*. Progressivism, the movement to replace the self-interest and corruption of capitalism with the virtuous public interest of democracy, had been revitalized during the Great Depression. In 1936, as in 1912, the threshold was about to be crossed. But *Social Darwinism in American Thought* provided a detailed object lesson of the way in which war could revitalize capitalism. And Beard had been warning, after 1936, that history might repeat itself. Beard, however, had expressed the fear that the defeat of democracy by capitalism would be more disastrous in 1941 than in 1917. Would it be possible, then, for Hofstadter and Beard's disciples to sustain their faith in the Progressive American jeremiad when President Roosevelt was successful in leading the nation away from the continentalism so passionately advocated by Beard?

The answer, revealed in his second book, *The American Political Tradition*, published in 1948, was that Hofstadter had quickly gone beyond the stage of doubt to outright rejection of the narrative structure of *The Rise of American Civilization*. This book was as anti-Beard as *Social Darwinism in American*

Thought had been pro-Beard. The tone of *The American Political Tradition* is one of angry rejection, even of betrayal.

The position he now used to criticize the Progressive American jeremiad, however, was very similar to the Marxist jeremiad that Niebuhr had embraced around 1930 after a decade of disillusionment with the virtue of the American people. Niebuhr had become a Marxist when he was no longer able to believe that the middle class was more committed to democracy than to capitalism. Looking back at his second book, Hofstadter accurately recalled that "my own assertion of consensus history in 1948 had its sources in the Marxism of the 1930s." This, then, was a consensus that was totally different from that expressed in his 1955 book, *The Age of Reform*.[11] By then, Hofstadter would share the outlook of Niebuhr's *Children of Light and Children of Darkness*, rather than that of *Moral Man and Immoral Society*. In 1955, he too found democracy and capitalism complementary. But as of 1948, he was still discovering that the politics of the United States from the founding fathers to the New Deal had been dominated by capitalists who hid behind the mask of democracy.

The American Political Tradition provided an answer to the questions that young historians, such as Hofstadter, must have been asking about the way in which Beard, as their intellectual hero, explained the flow of events from 1933 to 1941. According to Beard, the democratic tradition in America was more powerful than that of an alien capitalism. The collapse of the capitalist-controlled economy between 1929 and 1933 gave democracy, the authentic value system of the American people, a golden opportunity under the leadership of Franklin D. Roosevelt to restore the momentum of the Progressive Era toward industrial democracy. But somehow that had not happened. All Beard could do in 1940 to explain the failure of what seemed an inexorable pattern was to point to the political wizardry of the president—his skill as a demagogue and a conspirator. But wasn't a Marxist explanation simpler and more convincing? Beard was wrong about American exceptionalism. American history was part of capitalist history. Capitalism was not an alien force in the United States; there was a capitalist establishment, and it controlled the patterns of American politics as well as economics. The burning question for Hofstadter, however, was why he, in writing *Social Darwinism in American Thought*, had shared Beard's mistaken belief that democracy represented a more profound American reality than capitalism.

Beard, by 1940, was obsessed with Roosevelt's demagoguery. Beard felt that he and the American people had been fooled by Roosevelt in 1932 and 1936. The president had masqueraded as a democrat, when in reality he was a capitalist. Hofstadter, when he began to write *The American Political Tradition* in the mid-1940s, made a major extension of Beard's analysis of Franklin Roosevelt. The American presidents Thomas Jefferson, Theodore Roosevelt, and Woodrow Wilson, whom Beard had identified as spokesmen for American democracy in its conflict with European capitalism, were covert capitalists. Franklin Roosevelt had not betrayed a tradition of political democracy, as Beard asserted; he had only been carrying on a tradition of political capitalism. Beard's *The Rise of American Civilization*, therefore, had no more substance than the campaign speeches of presidents who used democratic rhetoric but who acted as capitalists. Hofstadter had been able to reach maturity as a professional historian without seeing the substance of capitalism because that reality had been masked by major historians as well as by demagogic politicians.

The opening pages of *The American Political Tradition* dripped with bitter irony as Hofstadter declared his independence from Beard's progressivism. That "quest for the American past," he declared, was "carried on in a spirit of sentimental appreciation rather than critical analysis." But "the following studies in the ideology of American statesmanship," he continued, "have convinced me of the need for a reinterpretation of our political traditions which emphasizes the common climate of American opinion. The existence of such a climate of opinion has been much obscured by the tendency to place political conflict in the foreground of history."[12]

Students of American historical writing currently consider the difference between Beard's kind of historical analysis and that of the generation that rejected him to be the difference between an emphasis on conflict and an emphasis on consensus. They speak about a Conflict school and a Consensus school. Clearly, Hofstadter, in the space of a few years, had moved away from the kind of dramatic conflict between capitalist and democratic politics and ideology he had evoked in *Social Darwinism in American Thought*. "The fierceness of the political struggles has often been misleading," he concluded, "for the range of vision embraced by the primary contestants in the major parties has always been bounded by the horizons of property and enterprise."[13] The conflicts that Beard and the young Hofstadter had characterized as those between capitalists and democrats turned out to be only quarrels within the capitalist establishment. Now, using a Marxist perspective, Hofstadter was engaged in unmasking the face of capitalism, which had been disguised as democracy. "Even when some property right has been challenged—as it was by followers of Jefferson and Jackson, the challenge," he asserted, "when translated into practical policy, has actually been urged on behalf of some other kind of property." The depth of his disillusionment became apparent when he complained that ours has been a "democracy in cupidity rather than a democracy of fraternity."[14]

In chapter after chapter, Hofstadter demythologized the democratic heroes. "Thomas Jefferson: The Aristocrat as Democrat" was followed by "Andrew Jackson and the Rise of Liberal Capitalism." He then proceeded to "Abraham Lincoln and the Self-Made Myth." But the most bitter part of his satire came when he reached the presidents of the Progressive Era, especially "Theodore Roosevelt: The Conservative as Progressive." He depicted Roosevelt as an

especially warlike spokesman for the conservative Darwinism that had dominated American foreign policy in the decade before World War I. How, then,
could one explain the admiration that Roosevelt received from the many Progressives, like Beard, who hated imperialism? Theodore Roosevelt, Hofstadter
wrote, was a masterful demagogue who had an "uncanny instinct for unpalpable
falsehoods" and whose speeches contained "a string of plausible superficialities."
Hofstadter was less harsh in his description of "Woodrow Wilson: The Conservative as Liberal," but he suggested that Wilson, like Roosevelt, brought no
integrity to his role as reformer. "Both men," he wrote, "seem to have been converted to the rising progressive philosophy in part because that philosophy was
more opportune for their political careers."[15]

Writing about American capitalism in the mid-1940s, Hofstadter seemed to
be trying to replace the prophetic aspect of a failed American jeremiad with that
based on an international foundation, as Beard had done in 1900 and Niebuhr
in 1930. *The American Political Tradition* did more than unmask a capitalism
that had masqueraded as democracy. It also presented the argument that capitalism had reached a dead end when the economy crashed in 1929. Hofstadter,
therefore, was the most creative in his last two chapters: "Herbert Hoover and
the Crisis of American Individualism" and "Franklin D. Roosevelt: The Patri-
cian as Opportunist." He painted Hoover as a tragic figure whose imaginative
world reflected the realities of the nineteenth century, realities that no longer
prevailed in 1929. "The entire generation of businessmen of which [Hoover]
was a part was under singular disadvantages in understanding the twentieth century," Hofstadter wrote. They were "driven to reiterate with growing futility the
outworn creed upon which they had been suckled." Now these "men who had
made such a fetish of being up-to-date" displayed "archaic, impractical, and
flighty minds."[16] This, of course, was similar to the argument of cultural lag that
he had made in *Social Darwinism in American Thought*. Only now capitalism was
to be replaced by socialism, not by a unique American democracy.

If the defeat of Hoover in 1932 marked for Hofstadter, as it had for Beard,
the collapse of capitalist leadership, Franklin D. Roosevelt must have symbolized the Moses who would lead Americans into the Promised Land of democracy. And when Hofstadter described Roosevelt, he revealed how much he had
expected from him and how disappointed he was. "Franklin D. Roosevelt," he
declared, "stands out among all the statesmen since Hamilton—for his sense of
the failure of tradition, his recognition of the need for novelty and daring. His
capacity for innovation in practical measures was striking, and the New Deal
marked many deviations in the American course." Roosevelt, in Hofstadter's
analysis, as in Beard's, however, did not go beyond his recognition that the old
order was dead. He was not a Moses leading the American people across the
threshold from capitalist bondage to democracy. "But his capacity for innovation in ideas was far from comparable," Hofstadter concluded; "he was neither

systematic nor consistent, and he provided no clearly articulated break with the inherited faith."[17]

It is important to notice that although in 1948 Hofstadter provided biting criticism of Roosevelt for engaging in "month-to-month improvisation, without trying to achieve a more inclusive and systematic conception of what is happening in the world,"[18] he had not criticized Roosevelt for aborting the democratic movement of the 1930s by taking the country into World War II. The Roosevelt presented by Hofstadter in 1948, in contrast to the one presented by Beard in his book of the same year, *President Roosevelt and the Coming of the War*, was not a masterful conspirator successfully manipulating a revitalization of capitalism. This failure to discuss the issue of foreign policy in the 1930s clarifies the tremendous shift in Hofstadter's outlook between 1944 and 1948. His Beardian nationalism in *Social Darwinism in American Thought* had focused on the tragic consequences of American participation in World War I. But in *The American Political Tradition*, he rejected the old culture that "has been intensely nationalistic and for the most part isolationist" and called for a new culture, "corporate and consolidated, demanding international responsibility."[19] In part, Hofstadter's willingness to suddenly surrender the whole pattern of Beardian meaning that had infused his first book and to search for an alternative pattern to organize American history must have come from his rejection of Beard's continentalism. American history, in 1948, for Hofstadter as for Niebuhr, was part of world history.

But in 1948, Hofstadter did not share Niebuhr's rejection of the exodus metaphor. He had expected Franklin D. Roosevelt to provide leadership from an Old to a New World and was disappointed when Roosevelt proved incapable of developing a vision of a socialist democracy. Such impotence, in Hofstadter's view, was caused by the president's unwillingness to accept socialist theory. When Hofstadter rejected Beard's belief that a democratic promise had been embodied in American historical experience, he assumed that a democratic promise based on socialist principles would be constructed in the 1930s since the capitalism that had been the central experience in the American past no longer offered a viable future.

In 1955, however, when Hofstadter's next book, *The Age of Reform*, appeared, he had nothing but praise for Roosevelt's pragmatism. Sometime around 1950, he had joined Niebuhr in rejecting the exodus metaphor. Now he criticized those who believed that a New and virtuous World could be separated from an Old and corrupt World. Concepts of exceptionalism based on such dualisms and dichotomies had become as dangerous for him as they had earlier become for Niebuhr. One can find as many parallels between themes in *The Age of Reform* and Niebuhr's *The Irony of American History* as there were between those in *Social Darwinism in American Thought* and Beard's *The Rise of American Civilization*.

In 1944, Niebuhr had argued that human activity within the particulars of history was both necessary and worthwhile. But his major concern in *The Children of Light and the Children of Darkness* as well as in *The Irony of American History* was not that modern people would deny the meaning in such temporal activity and take a passive stance toward history comparable to that of the Middle Ages or of Asian civilizations. Rather, Niebuhr warned against the modern Western outlook that tried to elevate the particular good into a universal. He was warning against those groups who claimed that they could achieve harmony with the universal. Each of these groups believed that it represented the climax of history and was immune to the historical change experienced by all previous groups.

During the 1940s, Franklin D. Roosevelt emerged in Niebuhr's writings as the ideal political hero. Roosevelt acted vigorously to arrive at provisional goods, but he was never tempted to claim that his accomplishments represented the achievement of an absolute good. And in 1955, Hofstadter made Roosevelt the hero of *The Age of Reform* because he demonstrated pragmatic qualities – the same pragmatic qualities that Hofstadter had criticized in *The American Political Tradition* and Niebuhr had condemned between 1932 and 1940.

The dramatic movement in the philosophies of American reform as recounted by Hofstadter in this major document of the Consensus school was the change from the arrogant philosophies of populism and progressivism, which did confuse the particular with the universal, to the modest philosophy of the New Deal, which accepted the particular as the necessary building block for all human activity. Hofstadter was now teaching the kind of lesson advocated by Niebuhr in *The Children of Light and the Children of Darkness* as well as in *The Irony of American History*: Americans must learn that they are not a Chosen People living in a Promised Land; they must learn that they are not exempt from the terrors of history that beset the rest of humanity; and they must stop preaching the American jeremiad.

In *The Age of Reform*, 1933 remained the pivotal date that it had been in *The American Political Tradition*. But Roosevelt's New Deal no longer symbolized the end of a bankrupt capitalist system whose existence had been masked by the rhetoric of democracy. Now it symbolized the end of a tradition of false consciousness that had invented a continuing conflict between democracy and capitalism throughout much of American history. Borrowing from Henry Nash Smith's terminology, Hofstadter discussed the rhetorical pattern of the Populists as an expression of the myth of the garden. Populists believed that American farmers, the yeomen, were living in harmony with the timelessness of physical nature. In an analysis that anticipated in several important ways J. G. A. Pocock's *The Machiavellian Moment*, Hofstadter argued that the Populists feared the dynamism of capitalism. They believed that it could drag them away from harmony with nature and undermine their rational and virtuous political system. In the manner of Pocock's eighteenth-century republicans, they identified the dynamism of capitalism with conspiracy. And Hofstadter described this outlook as the "paranoid style" of Populist politics.

In *The Age of Reform*, as a sustained criticism of Turner and Beard's use of the American jeremiad, Hofstadter agreed with the Populists, or with the republican tradition that seems to have been the basis for so much of the American political imagination of the nineteenth century, that capitalism did represent the dynamism of history, the dimension of the particular in contrast to the static perfection of the universal. But Hofstadter in 1955, like Niebuhr in 1944, reversed the conventions of the republican tradition. No people had ever participated in even a temporary exodus from the realm of the particular to that of the universal. The only reality humans ever experienced was the dynamic flow of historical particulars.

The republican tradition of the eighteenth century had identified capitalism with particulars, with the irrational, with fantasy. But Hofstadter declared that Populist belief in two worlds, a natural, democratic, and virtuous America and a historical, capitalistic, and corrupt Europe was the great irrational and fantastic element in nineteenth-century American culture. The Populist mind became divorced from reality when it insisted that Americans had escaped from the flux of history. Hofstadter's position in the 1950s, in contrast to that of the 1940s, was one in which the acceptance of the particulars of the historical process, the acceptance of capitalism, was an act of rationality.

Once Hofstadter defined capitalism as synonymous with reality, he had explicitly rejected Beard's view of 1940 that capitalists represented an alien and conspiratorial force in American life; and he implicitly returned to Turner's understanding in 1890 that industrial capitalism was replacing the agricultural frontier as the dominant economic environment in the United States. For Hofstadter in 1955, however, this revolutionary transition did not mean the end of democracy because he now associated democracy with the social and economic pluralism that he assumed was the inevitable result of capitalism. It was not only capitalism, in his analysis, but also the city that encouraged the pluralism necessary for a democratic society. In this respect, he organized his book around a pattern of cultural lag where farmers specifically refused to accept the growing reality of capitalism and many other nineteenth-century Americans refused to accept the reality of the dramatic shift of population from the countryside to the city. Sounding very much like Turner, Hofstadter declared that "at the beginning of the nineteenth century, the yeoman was by no means a fiction," but "between 1815 and 1860 the independent yeoman almost disappeared."[20]

The irony in this situation, for Hofstadter, was that the farmers, who blamed an un-American conspiracy for introducing the capitalism and urbanization that threatened their way of life, were the very individuals who were choosing to engage in a market rather than a household economy and to search for new opportunities in the city. Farmers, by the time of the Civil War, were motivated, he wrote, by a stronger ideal than that of the self-sufficient yeoman. This was the ideal "of opportunity, of career, of the self-made man."[21]

Hofstadter used the terms hard and soft to describe the contradiction between the economic behavior of American farmers in the late nineteenth century and their political fantasies. The hard side of their "commercial position pointed to the usual strategies of the business world: combination, cooperation, pressure politics." But their soft side "pointed to a different direction: broad political goals, ideological mass politics, third parties."[22] In his chapter "From Pathos to Parity," Hofstadter reported that by 1900 most farmers were abandoning the false consciousness of their soft side. They no longer focused on a golden age in the American past characterized by "natural harmonies." And they were no longer obsessed by a "dualistic version of social struggles" and a "conspiracy theory of history." Entering the twentieth century, they had recognized their true identity as pragmatic capitalists.[23]

The Progressive movement was the next subject for Hofstadter's analysis of the ways in which American reformers, before the New Deal, had tried to escape the historical flow of particulars and had constructed an imaginary America where citizens were supposedly in harmony with universals.

Progressives, Hofstadter wrote, were essentially members of an Anglo-Saxon, Protestant middle class. Most of these respectable citizens lived in cities but were uncomfortable in this environment. Like the Populists before them, they were overwhelmed by a sense of declension. "Reality," for these people, Hofstadter declared, "was a series of unspeakable plots, personal inequities, moral failures, which, in their totality, had come to govern American society only because the citizen had relaxed his moral vigilance."[24] In *Social Darwinism in American Thought*, Hofstadter had presented Progressives as practical visionaries who looked forward to a collectivist democracy based on industrial production, whereas he described capitalists as hopelessly nostalgic for nineteenth-century individualism. This pattern was largely reversed in *The Age of Reform*. Progressives were those who were reactionaries, cherishing an outmoded individualism, unable to adjust to the large-scale structures of the twentieth century. They were trying "to retain the scheme of individualistic values that this organization was destroying."[25]

Progressives and Populists, therefore, were very similar. "They had not been brought up to think of the well-being of society—not merely in structural terms—not as something resting upon the sum of its technique and efficiency," Hofstadter maintained, "but in moral terms, as a reward for the sum total of individual qualities and personal merits. This tradition, rooted in the Protestant ethic itself, was being wantonly defied by the system of corporate organization."[26]

Progressives, like Populists, were primarily concerned with virtue. They assumed that a society could be completely virtuous. For these Protestants, the crisis stretching from 1880 to 1920 was the threat to the virtuous republic that still existed when Lincoln was president. Much of Hofstadter's rhetoric was directed toward minimizing this crisis. His strategy, like that of Sumner and the conservative Darwinists whom he had denounced in *Social Darwinism in American Thought*, was aimed at relativizing the Populist and Progressive concern for a declining democracy. Populists and Progressives, he asserted, could not speak for the pluralist America of the 1950s because they represented only one American culture, that of Anglo-Saxon Protestants. Discussing the Populist-Progressive effort to stop the decline of democracy by encouraging new methods to intensify political participation, Hofstadter wrote that "the movement for direct popular democracy was an attempt to realize Yankee Protestant ideals of personal responsibility: and the Progressive notion of good citizenship was the culmination of this Yankee-Mugwump ethos of political participation without self-interest."[27] He further argued that much of this Yankee-Protestant activism was a response to the flow of Catholic and Jewish immigrants into the expanding urban world which would dominate America in the twentieth century. For Hofstadter, the city as well as capitalism encouraged pluralism because it was here that the monolithic Anglo-Saxon Protestant culture first lost its ability to monopolize American identity. In a way, it was the new immigrants from eastern and southern Europe, forming the majority in many northeastern and midwestern cities by 1914, who provided the momentum to move the American reform tradition away from the Anglo-Saxon Protestant commitment to universal laws and absolute virtue toward the pragmatism of the New Deal and its acceptance of the reality of particulars and the necessity of compromise. "Anglo-Saxon thinking emphasized governance by legal rules," Hofstadter stated, "as opposed to the widespread tendency among immigrants to interpret political reality in the light of personal relations."[28]

In *Social Darwinism in American Thought*, Hofstadter had argued that the American entry into World War I made it possible for capitalists to frustrate the momentum toward that industrial democracy prophesied by progressivism. In *The American Political Tradition*, he had presented no such tragedy because the rhetoric of progressivism masked the underlying control of the capitalist establishment. Now, in *The Age of Reform*, he described Populists and Progressives who increasingly behaved as flexible capitalists but who remained prisoners of their rhetoric which promised that the war, as an Armageddon, would restore the perfection of a lost golden age. In 1955, therefore, in dramatic contrast to his viewpoint in 1944, Hofstadter associated American participation in World War I with progressivism. And he no longer presented Wilson as a conservative president masquerading as a Progressive, as he had in 1948. Wilson was a Progressive who anticipated that World War I would result in an exodus from a flawed Old World to a perfect New World. Progressives, led by the president, prophesied that 1917 would mark a threshold experience and then their prophecy failed. Wilson, Hofstadter wrote, "by pinning America's role in the war so exclusively to high moral considerations and to altruism and self-sacrifice, by linking the foreign crusade as intimately as possible to the Progressive values and Progressive language, was unintentionally insuring that the reaction against Progressivism and moral idealism would be as intense as it could be."[29]

A reader of *The Age of Reform* would never suspect that Hofstadter had published a book in 1944 praising progressivism or that Beard's Progressive approach to American history was the single most influential interpretation within the historical profession in 1940. Hofstadter, in 1955, was asking his readers to believe that progressivism had ceased to be a vital philosophy in the United States during World War I. It is also interesting that although he had systematically analyzed and described what he saw as the major interlocking principles of the Populist imagination, he had not done so in his discussion of progressivism. He gave the impression that Progressives, like Populists, believed in a golden age in the American past characterized by a natural harmony of interests. He also pointed out the Progressive willingness to believe in conspiracy and in a world of absolute dichotomies. But he did not choose to develop his narrative so that 1917 represented as dramatic a repudiation of a coherent Progressive ideology as 1890 had for Populist ideology. He intimated that progressivism disintegrated without the same intense spiritual anguish that marked the end of the agrarian myth of the Garden. Progressivism, in *The Age of Reform*, evaporated rather than died. "In repudiating Wilson and the war itself," he concluded, the American people "repudiated the Progressive rhetoric and the Progressive mood. Progressivism had been founded on a mood, and with the reaction that followed the war, the mood was dissipated."[30] By implication, Beard's writings did not represent as coherent a philosophy as Turner's had.

In *The American Political Tradition*, he had emphasized the agony of Herbert Hoover's capitalist worldview when it was shattered by events between 1929 and 1933; and he had criticized Franklin D. Roosevelt for failing to take advantage of this threshold opportunity to move the nation into a socialist democracy. But the struggle of 1933 he evoked in *The Age of Reform* was between a collapsing progressivism, with its nostalgia for an America where each citizen played an equal role in constructing a virtuous public interest, and the New Deal, which recognized that the public interest was built by a government that acted as a broker for the contending interests of the important pressure groups in society. The public interest at any given time represented a particular set of compromises rather than virtuous harmony with natural law.

Perhaps Hofstadter was repressing his personal ideological revolution in giving up, after 1944, the identification of democracy with public interest and the participation of equal citizens in the commonwealth—the philosophy of democracy he had expressed in *Social Darwinism in American Thought* and *The American Political Tradition*. But certainly he was obscuring for his readers the dramatic rejection of this heritage of the eighteenth-century republican tradition that occurred in the 1940s and that was most powerfully symbolized by Niebuhr's efforts in *The Children of Light and the Children of Darkness* to develop a justification of democracy that did not depend upon the virtue of each citizen. Hofstadter was pushing the destructive impact of World War II on progressivism back into World War I, hiding the agony he must have experienced when he lost faith in the progressivism with which he had so passionately informed *Social Darwinism in American Thought*. *The Age of Reform* gave the impression that pragmatism had become so dominant under the leadership of Roosevelt and the New Deal that it was easy for Americans to enter World War II with the realism of limited expectations, in contrast to the millennial expectations of 1917.

The narrative structure of *The Age of Reform*, instead of embodying the American jeremiad as *Social Darwinism in American Thought* had, was organized to illustrate the death of that rhetorical ritual and the birth of a new America that did not judge the present as a declension from an original promise and a prelude to a future in which that promise would be fulfilled. Hofstadter's descriptive language was restrained, however, when he celebrated the role of Franklin D. Roosevelt in leading Americans away from the illusion that an original promise, a golden age in the past, was to be restored in the future. Teaching Americans to accept the present, not as declension but as the best of all possible worlds, was not an experience that could evoke the kind of ecstatic prose Beard has used in *The Rise of American Civilization* to describe the journey into the democratic West led by Andrew Jackson. At best, President Roosevelt was an ironic kind of Moses figure as he led his people away from their delusion that they were a Chosen People who had found refuge in a Promised Land.

Without fanfare and as economically as possible, Hofstadter reported a momentous change in American history. "Granting that absolute discontinuities do not occur in history, and viewing the history of the New Deal as a whole," he wrote, "what seems outstanding about it is the drastic new departure that it marks in the history of American reformism." The New Deal, he continued, was different "because its central problem was unlike the problems of Progressivism, different in its ideas and its spirit and its techniques."[31]

The novelty of the New Deal, he argued, came from the fact that its reforms were not designed to restore morality but to overcome the Great Depression. "Managing an economy in such a way as to restore prosperity is above all a problem of organization," he insisted, "while democratizing a well-organized economy had been an attempt to find ways of attacking or limiting organization." Contrasting Franklin D. Roosevelt with the great Progressive presidents Theodore Roosevelt and Woodrow Wilson, Hofstadter pointed out that the Progressives led crusades against special interest groups, including political machines. But FDR "was thoroughly at home in the realities of machine techniques of accommodation." He praised the president for stepping outside the Yankee-Protestant tradition of moral absolutes. Roosevelt, he wrote, "made no effort to put an end to bossism and corruption, but simply ignored the entire problem." He commended FDR for making economic reality rather than political ideals his top priority. "As for the restoration of democracy," Hofstadter concluded, "he seemed well satisfied with his feeling that the broadest public needs were at least being served by the state and that there was an excellent rapport between the people and their executive leadership." The FDR of *The Age of Reform* never fought for causes but only for results. The president, in Hofstadter's analysis, tried to change the Supreme Court not because it was antidemocratic "but because the Court's decisions had made it seem impossible to achieve the managerial reorganization of society that was so urgently needed."[32]

He used the books written by Thurman Arnold in the 1930s, *The Symbols of Government* and *The Folklore of Capitalism,* to suggest that New Deal intellectuals, unlike those of populism and progressivism, also were engaged in "a sharp and sustained attack upon ideologies, rational principles, and moralism in politics." Quoting Arnold, who claimed that "actual observation of human society indicates the great constructive achievements in human organization have been accomplished by unscrupulous men who violated most of the principles which we cherish," Hofstadter placed FDR and his administration within this amoral perspective. "At the core of the New Deal was not a philosophy but an attitude, suitable for practical politicians, administrators, and technicians."[33] Hofstadter's worldview in 1955, in contrast to that of 1948, was now very similar to that of the "court" theoreticians, discussed by Pocock in *The Machiavellian Moment.* These eighteenth-century apologists for capitalism dismissed as naive the republican belief that a virtuous republic must be characterized by "a perfect partnership of all citizens and all values, since, if it was less, a part would be ruling in the name of the whole, subjecting particular goods to its own particular goods and moving toward despotism and the corruption of its own values." Hofstadter, like Niebuhr, had shared that definition of a virtuous republic with Turner and Beard into the 1940s. But now he had joined with Niebuhr in reversing the exodus metaphor. For Hofstadter and Niebuhr, it was sheer fantasy to believe that a society had existed in which there was a perfect partnership or that such a society could be achieved in the future.

The conclusion of *The Age of Reform* embodied many echoes of Turner's pronouncement in 1893 that American exceptionalism had ended. For Turner, the development of corporations and cities had undermined the pattern of freehold property that had been the economic basis for a virtuous democracy. Hofstadter, in 1955, agreed with Turner that a twentieth-century America, dominated by corporations, labor unions, and government bureaucracies, would be more like Europe than like the United States of the nineteenth century and its colonial foundation. But Hofstadter, in *The Age of Reform*, unlike Turner, refused to be nostalgic about nineteenth-century democracy. Turner had been stoic when his theory of evolution pointed to the necessary replacement of democracy by capitalism. But Hofstadter had found in the large-scale organizations related to the rise of corporate capitalism a pluralism that provided the foundation for a different definition of democracy. Celebrating a pluralist democracy, Hofstadter now expressed his fear of the nineteenth-century democracy committed to majority rule and to the dichotomies of virtue and corruption. Vestiges of this dangerous form of democracy unfortunately continued to exist in twentieth-century America, Hofstadter wrote, but he was pleased to report that they represented the lag of a rural culture which was inexorably being eroded by the evolution of industrialization and urbanization. That evolution was accelerated by the American entry into World War II because Americans were then thrust "into a situation in which their domestic life . . . [was] largely determined by the demands of foreign policy and national defense. With this change came the final involvement of the nation in all the realities it had sought to avoid, for now, it was not only mechanized and urbanized and bureaucratized but internationalized as well."[34]

Having crossed the threshold from the rhetorical world of the Progressive jeremiad, first American and then briefly international, to that of the conservative jeremiad most fully articulated by Niebuhr in *The Irony of American History*, Hofstadter, after the publication of *The Age of Reform*, found himself in the position of having to warn his fellow citizens against a declension from the sanity of the New Deal back into the folly of progressivism, populism, and Jacksonian democracy.

As a secular parallel to *The Irony of American History*, Hofstadter's next book, *Anti-Intellectualism in American Life*, was a long lament that the 1950s were not dominated by the pragmatism of the New Deal but by the hysterical witch-hunting of Senator Joseph McCarthy from Wisconsin. McCarthy, for Hofstadter, had tapped the strong traditions of anti-intellectualism that had developed in the early nineteenth century and that were dominant in American culture until the New Deal. The man who cherished intellect was, in Hofstadter's opinion, the secular equivalent of Niebuhr's Christian ironist. The heroic intellectual understood that the status quo has not brought history to a climax; nor could history be brought to a climax by some future reform movement. The intellectual, therefore, accepted complexity and conflict as a central and enduring reality and defined human society "as a form of equipoise based upon the continuing process of compromise."[35] Only a minority, it now appeared to Hofstadter, a necessary elite of intellectuals, was capable of finding value in the particular without becoming cynical or without idealizing the particular as the universal.

The founding fathers, Hofstadter declared, were such an intellectual elite, aware of both the good and bad aspects of their society. The intellectual had the ability both to be fully involved in the world and to stand outside it and criticize it. This critical distance of the founding fathers had been lost as evangelical Protestantism and Jacksonian democracy insisted that every individual could achieve a full understanding and complete harmony with ultimate truth. "Just as the evangelicals repudiated a learned religion and a formally constituted clergy in favor of the wisdom of the heart and direct access to God," he declared, "so did advocates of egalitarian politics prepare to dispense with trained leadership in favor of the native practical sense of the ordinary man with its direct access to truth."[36]

This attack on the necessity for critical distance, this declension from the pragmatic realism of the founding fathers, this repudiation of the need for the reconciliation of differences and compromise then became institutionalized in the business community as the cult of the self-made man. It was not surprising, Hofstadter continued, that American educational theory at the beginning of the twentieth century, expressed most powerfully by John Dewey, represented these dominant anti-intellectual traditions of evangelical Protestantism, democratic egalitarianism, and the cult of the self-made man in the business community. Dewey's educational philosophy, so influential throughout the twentieth century, was one of innocence that assumed natural harmonies characterized the environment and society. Sounding like Sumner attacking Ward, Hofstadter commented bitterly that "if the new educators really wanted to reproduce life itself in the classroom, they must have had an extraordinarily benign conception of what life is. To every adult, life brings, in addition to some measure of cooperation, achievement and joy, a full stint of competition, defeat, frustration, and failure. But the new educators did not accept the idea that these things too would be embodied in the little community that was to be organized for children in the school."[37]

But, once again, Hofstadter had reached the New Deal when for the first time since the American Revolution, intellectuals, that sensitive elite who recognized the need to stand apart from the immediate situation in order to creatively mediate its conflicts, regained a position of authority and respect which increased during World War II. When the war ended, however, "the long-delayed revulsion from the New Deal experience and the war itself swept over the country," he reported with regret, and "the rapprochement between the intellectuals and the popular democracy once more came to an end."[38]

It is clear that Hofstadter in this book of the 1960s had begun to construct a narrative structure for American history based on a conservative rather than a Progressive jeremiad. In *The Age of Reform*, he had found a realistic America only in the New Deal. In *Anti-Intellectualism in American Life*, however, he had found a usable past, an original promise in the realism of the founding fathers. Interpreting the Populists and Progressives as a declension from that realism, he could describe the New Deal not as a revolutionary rejection of participatory democracy but as a conservative fulfillment of the promise of a pluralist democracy that predated the insane pursuit of virtue in the nineteenth century. Ironically, however, Hofstadter in the 1960s was having as much difficulty in completing the rhetorical ritual of his conservative jeremiad as he had in the 1940s with his Progressive jeremiad. No sooner had he celebrated the New Deal as the prophetic fulfillment of the pluralist promise of the founding fathers than he had to report that declension toward Populist democracy was occurring again.

Hofstadter was now presenting a tragic view of an American society that, because of its nineteenth-century traditions of anti-intellectualism, refused to accept an ironic approach to historical experience. Striving for direct and total harmony of the individual with reality, Americans would not become contrite. The tone of despair that characterized the conclusion of *Anti-Intellectualism in American Life* was intensified by his disappointment with the generation of intellectuals coming of age around 1960. He described them in terms similar to those used by Niebuhr in 1944 to criticize the Children of Light. For Hofstadter, as for Niebuhr, "the dislike of involvement with 'accredited institutions' exhibited by the prophets of alienation bespeaks a more fundamental dislike of the association of intellect with power."[39] These young intellectuals had not learned that they, like the Children of Darkness, could use power without, however, accepting the latter's cynicism.

Anti-Intellectualism in American Life, marking another major shift in Hofstadter's understanding of American history, provided the context for his next book, *The Progressive Historians: Turner, Beard, Parrington*. In it he continued to emphasize that nineteenth-century traditions had not died in 1890 with populism or in 1917 with progressivism, as he had so optimistically reported in *The Age of Reform*. He was now willing to confess that he, as an urban New Yorker, had been strongly influenced during the New Deal years of the 1930s by Turner and Parrington, whose intellectual roots, he argued, were to be found in the Populist imagination, and especially by Beard, whose outlook was shaped by the Progressive movement. He also confessed that he no longer was satisfied with the Consensus perspective which he had used to replace his earlier Progressive one. "I trust," he wrote, "it will be clear that while I still find use for insights derived from Consensus history, it no longer seems as satisfactory to me as it did ten or twenty years ago."[40] But above all, this book on the Progressive historians provided Hofstadter with another opportunity to argue the need for Americans to escape tragedy by returning to the pragmatic approach to historical experience proposed by the founding fathers.

Turner, Beard, and Parrington, he declared, "gave us the pivotal ideas of the first half of the twentieth century. It was these men above all others who explained the American liberal mind to itself in historical terms. Progressive histo-

riography gave it meaning and myth, and naturalized it within the whole framework of American historical experience." The consequence of this mythology,
he continued, was that American liberals were unable to deal with the events
of the 1930s and 1940s because "time is the basic dimension of history, but the
basic dimension of the American imagination is space." And it was Frederick
Jackson Turner who most fully incorporated "the awareness of space, this yearn-
ing for rebirth under natural conditions, into our historical thought." The Progressive historians were fighting to save a timeless democracy supposedly in
harmony with the static laws of nature from the ravages of time as symbolized
by capitalism. "Beard thought of democracy not as a relative matter or as an
unfolding historical reality that must be understood at each point in its temporal
context," he concluded, "but as an external absolute."[41]

Beard's commitment to a timeless democracy caused him, Hofstadter maintained, to misinterpret the meaning of his correct emphasis on the crucial role
that elites played in writing the Constitution. Beard was wrong in arguing that
the elites operated through conspiracy to overturn the existing agrarian democracy. "American society of the 1780s was in fact run by elites," Hofstadter
declared, "but the situation was not that of an established democracy. Rather
it was one of "apathy and inertia" in which the elites " 'took charge of events'
and framed and established the Constitution."[42] Criticizing the young intellectuals of the 1960s whose demand for participatory democracy fed on Beard's
nostalgia for a nonexistent colonial democracy in which all people supposedly
had directly engaged in making all the significant decisions, Hofstadter scathingly commented, "To me it seems that in great modern centralized democracies, direct participation in government becomes a hopeless criterion of the efficacy of democratic institutions."[43]

For Hofstadter, as for Niebuhr in *The Children of Light and the Children of
Darkness*, this emphasis on participatory democracy evaded the necessary and
responsible use of power. It was an attempt to preserve a nonexistent innocence.
And such a pursuit of innocence, as Niebuhr had warned in *The Irony of American History*, must always end in tragedy. This was the moral of Hofstadter's narrative as he traced Beard's increasing hysteria when confronted with President
Roosevelt's foreign policy. Beard was clinging to a belief in an American exceptionalism that supposedly freed America from the responsibility of exercising
power. "In the closing episodes of his career," Hofstadter wrote, "we still find
him given to an excessive preoccupation with the motives and methods of those
in power." Like the irresponsible young intellectuals of 1960, Beard "evaded the
central dilemma of international politics: that the quest for security involves
hazardous competitive confrontations of power, and is not simply a pursuit of
competing interests of trade and empire."[44]

In these two books of the 1960s, Hofstadter had retreated from his assertion
in the 1950s that the American understanding of history as an exodus that had

delivered the nation from the complexities of European history had been disintegrating since the 1890s and had been replaced by the pragmatism of the New Deal. But in his last two books, *The Idea of a Party System in America* and *America in 1750*, he returned to the optimism of *The Age of Reform*.[45] Reinhold Niebuhr in *The Irony of American History* had insisted that Americans had never practiced what they preached. Americans talked about innocence and absolutes, but the practice of their politics was one of realism and compromise. They talked about a participatory democracy of equality and virtue, but they built a democracy in which the individual was protected from oppression by a pluralistic society. The reality was a balance of large-interest groups out of which a provisional public interest emerged. Niebuhr's rhetorical strategy in *The Irony of American History* was not to confront Americans with the absurdity of their ideas of an exceptional and innocent history but to ask them to see how they and their ancestors had acted in history. In *The Idea of a Party System*, Hofstadter abruptly abandoned the confrontational style he had used in *Anti-Intellectualism in American Life* and *The Progressive Historians* and adopted a strategy similar to that of Niebuhr.

When Beard had so suddenly dismissed his international jeremiad in 1919, he had constructed a vision of an organic national identity that could not experience declension. The present was an integral part of the past and the future. The present embodied both the original democratic promise and the prophecy of the democratic future as well. Conflict could not develop within this organic community. Conflict was always between the nation and its external enemies — international capitalism, international communism, international Catholicism, international Judaism. Hofstadter had developed his conservative jeremiad as the fulfillment of the promise of the political philosophy of the founding fathers, but had found an intellectual history of declension from that philosophy. However, if he placed the promise in the behavioral experience of the colonial period, as Niebuhr had suggested in *The Irony of American History*, the declension into anti-intellectualism was only an ephemeral false consciousness. Americans had always practiced pluralist democracy even though they had occasionally dreamed of virtuous democracy. There was never a real declension from the practice of interest-group democracy. The New Deal did not mark the end of a long, unusable American past and the beginning of a new, viable American history. The New Deal only expressed in self-conscious philosophy what Americans had always practiced. Hofstadter had now gained a vision of an organic national history in which capitalism encouraged the pluralism necessary for the only kind of democracy possible within the flux of time. By incorporating capitalism within an organic national history, Hofstadter had escaped from Beard's fear that American democracy might be corrupted by an alien way of life.[46]

The dramatic result of this shift was two books that celebrated the American past as intensely as the previous two books had condemned it. Although Niebuhr used the founding fathers and the New Dealers, after 1944, as models of the kind of pragmatic political thought that Americans ought to accept, he pointed in *The Irony of American History* to a theoretical weakness in the founding fathers. They had rejected the idea of political parties. Niebuhr, however, used their erroneous outlook to convince his readers that American political behavior was much better than American political theory. Despite the warnings of the founding fathers, Americans at the beginning of the nineteenth century busily engaged in the construction of political parties. Such competing political parties contradicted, of course, the American belief in the possibility of a public interest representing the unanimity of all virtuous citizens. But Niebuhr celebrated the fact that the parties provided a way of escaping from this simplistic vision of democracy as the direct expression of the will of the people to the realistic democracy of pluralism, contending interests, and compromise.

Hofstadter, in *The Idea of a Party System*, took up this theme and explored in detail the development of political parties in the first decade of the nineteenth century. He was no longer writing the history of ideas but rather the history of institutions. And the story he told was that of the victory of institutions over ideas. In *Anti-Intellectualism in American Life*, he had bitterly condemned the Jacksonians for rejecting the realism of the founding fathers and beginning the ideological declension into Populist democracy which was temporarily reversed by the New Deal before its resurgence in the 1950s and 1960s. Earlier, in *The Age of Reform*, he had found that it was the Jacksonian period that produced the myth of the Garden. The nineteenth-century patterns of political paranoia, which he so despised, all had their origins in this belief in a golden age that must be defended against the conspiracies of evil men. Now, writing at the end of the 1960s, Hofstadter had nothing but praise for the creativity of Americans during the Jacksonian period. They were responsible for the development of a political system in which competition was accepted as legitimate.

Aware of the recent scholarship about the republican tradition in England and the English colonies upon which Bernard Bailyn had based his book *The Ideological Origins of the American Revolution*, Hofstadter now placed the founding fathers explicitly within the tradition of republican virtue. It was this tradition, developed by the "country" party in England, that demanded a unified public interest. And because the Revolutionary generation was loyal to it, a major crisis erupted in the new nation during the 1790s when it became apparent that there were competing theories of the public interest. Republican ideology taught the leaders of 1789 that their opposition represented a conspiracy of evil men. But the founding fathers were able to temper their political theory with their experience. They knew that diversity existed and that it must be accepted. Whatever their fears and misgivings, the Federalists accepted their defeat by the Jeffersonian republicans in 1800, and the United States "gave the world its first example of the peaceful transition of a government from the control of one popular party to another."[47] For Hofstadter, the United States in 1800 provided a political model of a pluralist democracy to the world because its leaders had chosen not to live by the European ideology of the republican tradition, which declared the possibility of harmony with the universal, but by the encounter with the dynamic flow of particulars, which was their American experience. "I do believe," Hofstadter affirmed, "that the full development of the liberal democratic state in the West required that political criticism and opposition be incarnated in one or more opposition parties, free not only to express themselves within parliamentary bodies but also to agitate and organize outside them among the electorate, and to form permanent, free, recognized oppositional structures." This, he affirmed, was "something new in the history of the world; it required a bold new act of understanding on the part of its contemporaries."[48]

After reviewing the recent historical literature on the antiparty positions of the Anglo-American republican tradition, Hofstadter explored the development of parties from the 1790s to the 1820s. By that later decade, he suggested, a younger generation of politicians, chief among them Martin Van Buren, had grown up with the experience of political parties. And for them, that experience was more important than the antiparty philosophy that they had inherited from the founding fathers. They were ready, therefore, to replace the links between political virtue and a homogenized public interest which the republican tradition demanded. James Madison, Hofstadter continued, as an exceptional member of the Revolutionary generation, had seen the need for pluralism and parties, but "he failed to see that the parties themselves might become great, bland, enveloping coalitions, eschewing the assertion of firm principles and ideologies, embracing and muffling the struggles of special interests; or that they might forge the coalitions of majorities that are, in fact, necessary to effective government into forces sufficiently vulnerable to be displaced in time by the opposing coalition."[49]

More than any of his contemporaries, it was Martin Van Buren, according to Hofstadter, who proposed such a positive view of political parties. He was "a man without aristocratic antecedents or the habit of command, without impressive stature or personal elegance, with keen intelligence but no notable intellectual brilliance," and "Van Buren therefore adopted a mode of address that relied upon friendly fraternal persuasion, a feeling for the strengths and weaknesses of others, a spirit of mutual accommodation, and a certain relish for the comedy of human encounters of the sort one sees daily in the country courthouses or the country town."[50] But Hofstadter wanted to stress that this humble professional politician had developed a profound apology for the existence of political parties. "In the ethos of the professional politician, the party became a means not merely of institutionalizing strife within manageable limits but also of cementing civic loyalty and creating a decent and liveable atmosphere." He saw, Hofstadter concluded, "the necessity of giving up the ancient ideal of social harmony that had haunted men from Bolingbroke to Washington, and accepted the useful, the constructive contributions of political competition and conflict."[51]

It is not surprising, therefore, that in 1970, when his life was cut short by leukemia, Hofstadter had begun work on a multivolume history of America. He now firmly believed, as he had tried to demonstrate in *The Idea of a Party System*, that the major theme of American history was not that dream of a perfect New World that he had so severely criticized in *The Age of Reform, Anti-Intellectualism in American Life*, and *The Progressive Historians*. That had been the dream imposed on America by Europe, but it existed only as relatively harmless nostalgia after 1800. It represented a cultural inheritance which lagged behind the development of a new American reality. His major concern now was the experience and acceptance of pluralism. At one level, Americans had related democracy to the European dream of a New World and assumed the necessity of a uniform public interest. But at a more profound level, they acted as if democracy was the political mechanism by which they reconciled the perpetual conflict of different interests in a pluralistic society.

In *Anti-Intellectualism in American Life*, Hofstadter had been particularly disturbed by the role that Protestant theology had played in convincing Americans that they were saints who had escaped the imperfections of the Old World. But in *The Idea of a Party System*, he tied his new appreciation for the institutions of Jacksonian politics to an appreciation of Protestant institutions. The colonial "traditions of dissenting Protestantism," he wrote, "had made an essential contribution to political pluralism." That fragment of his large synthesis, which he managed to complete before his death, was published as *America of 1750: A Social Portrait*. In it he had begun to develop his narrative around the thesis he had asserted in *The Idea of a Party System*, that the real American history expressed a unique pluralism and that experience with that pluralism was more important to Americans than the ideas of uniformity the first colonists had brought from Europe. In *America in 1750*, he had begun to write about Protestantism as he had written about politics: "it was one of those pragmatic American innovations, based upon experience and experiment, which one usually finds keyed closely to changing institutional necessities." "Religious tolerance, and after it religious liberty," he concluded, "were the creations of a jumble of faiths too complex to force into any mold. Puritanism, after all, was not America's gift to the world but England's; what America brought was the separation of church and state."[52]

Had Hofstadter lived to complete his multivolume history, it is possible that it, like Beard's *The Rise of American Civilization*, would have been a celebration of an organic democracy stretching from the colonial past to the immediate present. Beard and Hofstadter both insisted that American democracy was founded on experience rather than on ideas. But Beard's democracy was based on the common experience of first agricultural and then industrial production. It was such common experience that made it possible for a majority to share a sense of public interest. And this democracy was always threatened by capitalism, which encouraged people to follow their selfish interests rather than act for the public good.

Hofstadter's American democracy, in contrast, was built on the plurality of interests, religious and economic, that were an integral part of the colonial past. Capitalism, Hofstadter had been arguing since *The Age of Reform*, was the enemy only of a vision of a perfect, participatory democracy that had never been part of the American experience but existed in the imagination of Americans, expecially the Progressive historians, Turner, Beard, and Parrington.

There were no periods of declension in which the productive American people temporarily lost control to parasitical alien capitalists. There was only the false consciousness of the Progressive jeremiad that fantasized that there existed perfect harmony of interests in the past that could be regained in the future. As an alternative to Beard's use of a Progressive jeremiad to structure his narrative, Hofstadter had substituted a conservative jeremiad which defended the status quo against efforts to use either the past or the future as the basis for criticism of the present. But at the end of his life, Hofstadter did not feel the need to warn Americans against the attempt of Progressives to escape history by efforts to predict and control it. Throughout their history, Americans had understood, better than Europeans, the need to be realistic, to make the best of the situation in which they found themselves, to compromise. Americans, except for a handful of intellectuals, had learned as early as 1750 that history did not need to be the tragic record of broken dreams, illusions, and pretensions. The experience with pluralism had persuaded the colonists to cherish the modest hopes characteristic of those who embraced an ironic and contrite approach to history.[53]

William Appleman Williams: Universal Capitalism, Universal Marxism, or American Democracies, 1955–80

6

William Appleman Williams, unlike Turner, Beard, and Hofstadter, was a specialist in American diplomatic history. Although Williams was only a few years younger than Hofstadter, the age difference was enough to give him an entirely different view of history as he entered the profession. Hofstadter's initiation had been into Beard's philosophy of organic nationalism. In 1940, he had shared Beard's belief that an elite, which participated in the culture of international capitalism and was alien to the American democratic heritage, had shaped American foreign policy since the late nineteenth century. But Williams, beginning his graduate studies after 1945, did not share Beard's thesis that diplomatic history was peripheral to domestic history. After serving as a naval officer during World War II, Williams seemed to believe that to understand twentieth-century American domestic history, one must begin with the history of foreign policy. Once a self-conscious isolationist, Hofstadter equated his personal view with the nation at large and assumed that his conversion to internationalism paralleled the conversion of the nation. Williams, however, had not done any historical writing before 1945. Accepting the reality of American activity as a world power, Williams assumed that this overseas activisim had a history. Hofstadter had groped slowly and painfully toward the position that American history was not separate from that of the rest of the world. Such an interrelationship seemed, for Williams, to be a given, the foundation on which to build one's scholarship. The metaphor of two worlds would not shape his narratives. It is ironic, therefore, that Williams, who explicitly rejected Beard's belief that an alien, capitalist elite had engaged in a conspiracy to trick the nation into participation in World War II, should emerge in the 1950s as a bitter critic of Niebuhr's support of the cold war, and also of Consensus historians such as Hofstadter. By the early 1960s, Williams was identified as a major theoretician of a New Left school of historians which was challenging the intellectual credibility of the Consensus school.[1] The key to this irony is that Williams, in contrast to Beard, Niebuhr, and Hofstadter, did not view World War II as a confrontation between the tradition of republican virtue and capitalism. When Niebuhr and Hofstadter had lost their faith in a virtuous democracy based on the shared experience of industrial production, they continued to identify capitalism with the particulars of history. But their new conservative jeremiads had reversed the meaning given that relationship by the tradition of republican virtue. The dynamic flow of historical particulars, the inevitable experience of humans, provided the basis for pluralist democracy. But those who were loyal to the republican virtue tradition wanted to create a democracy that embodied universal principles, and their ambition symbolized the self-destructiveness of human pride. History became tragedy whenever a person or a people claimed that their position was eternally valid and that all other positions were in absolute error.

Throughout the 1950s and 1960s, Hofstadter had poured most of his energy into describing and criticizing the various expressions of the tradition of republican virtue from the founding fathers, through the Populists, to Senator Joseph McCarthy in 1950, and the New Left intellectuals of the 1960s. Finally, however, he had decided that these flirtations with historical tragedy, these attempts to transcend the flow of time, were insignificant episodes and did not detract from the main patterns of American history, which were so pluralistic that it would be impossible for any demagogue or band of saints to lead the American people away from their commitment to modest, limited expectations of provisional goods and inevitable compromise.

Hofstadter, like Niebuhr, in evoking a United States of exceptional humility, stressed that pluralist democracy had come by accident and not design. Americans had not tried to impose their will on history. They were merely the children of good fortune. Capitalism, Protestantism, and representative government had been brought from a Europe that had begun to modernize. Although these cultural products of Europe were essential to American national identity, it was the American landscape that allowed them to mix in a way that was impossible in the Old World. Capitalism, Protestantism, and representative government had broken the claim of the medieval church to represent a timeless and universal power. And they had opened the way for a more humble and less tragic experience with pluralism in Europe. But circumstances on that side of the Atlantic were such that demagogues and bands of saints periodically created the horror of holy war within nations and between nations.

It was not surprising to Niebuhr, in 1948, that the most dangerous group of political saints had their headquarters in Moscow and there plotted to redeem the world through bloody violence. Holy war, for the Soviet leaders, could bring a universal democracy of perfect virtue. Hofstadter, at the end of his life, saw no need to lament declension from the experience of pluralist democracy in the United States because declension from experience, unlike declension from a promise, was only false consciousness. But, for Niebuhr, pluralist democracy was not the experience of the rest of the world. Outside of the United States, it existed as a promise, and the declension of totalitarian democracy was a real experience. Americans must resist and contain the declension of totalitarian democracy to keep it from leading to a worldwide catastrophe. With patience and fortitude, they must defend the provisional good against the pretensions of absolute good.

For those like Niebuhr, who were beginning to argue that the experience of American democracy had always been that of pluralism and an appreciation of the need to use limited power to sustain order among the competing interest groups, the tradition of republican virtue had played only a destructive role in American thinking about foreign affairs. The false consciousness that the United States was a virtuous democracy with a homogeneous people all having a common interest had not kept Americans from the responsible use of power at home, but it had kept them from being responsible abroad. Obsessed with the need to segregate their purity from the corruption of the rest of the world, Americans had not recognized that their nation was an integral part of a world community and that they must resist tyranny in that community as they did at home. But in World War II, they had come to recognize that since power had been used at home to defend liberty, it also could and should be used to defend liberty abroad. They must sustain the many centers of countervailing power that were the true nature of the community of nations.

But Williams could not share Niebuhr and Hofstadter's belief that the United States had been forced reluctantly out of an isolationist foreign policy in 1941 which represented the tradition of republican virtue. In contrast to Turner, Beard, Niebuhr, and Hofstadter, he had never visualized an America in which capitalism had not played the dominant role. When Williams, part of the first generation of American historians who felt no loyalty to the republican tradition, looked at the past, the only center of cultural leadership he saw was capitalism. After 1945, Niebuhr and Hofstadter argued that capitalism had been the key element in domestic history. Williams, however, also considered it to be the key element in diplomatic history. And Williams, for whom the republican tradition was meaningless, viewed all attempts in American diplomatic history to overcome the particulars of history, therefore, as expressions of the pride and ambition of that dominant capitalist culture.

Before their conversion to pluralist democracy, Niebuhr and Hofstadter had accepted Beard's thesis that a capitalist elite had been working since the 1890s to develop an American empire. In 1930, Niebuhr, as a Christian Marxist, had discussed this covert, informal empire constructed by American capitalists.[2] And Hofstadter, in *Social Darwinism in American Thought*, had called the American entry into World War I the defeat of American democracy by capitalists who used the ideology of English imperialism. After their conversions, however, Niebuhr and Hofstadter repressed their previous discussions of an aggressive capitalist foreign policy. They no longer wrote about an American democracy that was resisting the efforts of capitalists to destroy the anti-imperialistic tradition of the United States. Forgetting the tension they had once sensed between

American democrats who did not want to impose their will on the world and capitalists who did, their post-World War II writings evoked a monolithic isolation in 1940, represented by people such as Beard, and based on the self-destructive vanity of an assumed American purity.

Williams, however, in accepting the dominant role of capitalism in American history, stood outside this heritage which Turner had passed to Beard and Beard, in turn, to Hofstadter. Turner, in 1890, had seen a unique agricultural democracy being replaced by an America defined in terms of international capitalism. And Beard and Hofstadter, in 1940, were still trying to find a pattern of historical analysis that could refute Turner's thesis that international capitalism was the national future. In contrast, Williams wanted to understand the role played by a capitalism already integral to American culture in 1890 in shaping the foreign policy of the twentieth century. When Williams reviewed the history of American foreign relations from 1890 to the 1940s, therefore, he expected to find a consistent pattern. And because this was a pattern left by a capitalist culture, integral and not alien to the American past, the evidence of this policy must be easily available. It would be a public record since capitalist leadership had not been forced into conspiratorial activity by an antagonistic democracy, as Beard had claimed. But as he began his research into the diplomatic records, Williams, like Niebuhr, was also prepared to place his findings within the analytical framework of ironic, tragic, and contrite history. His dissertation was completed in 1950 and published in 1952 as *American-Russian Relations, 1781–1947*. In it, he expressed an implicit philosophy of history almost identical to the explicit theology of history in Niebuhr's *Irony of American History*, which had appeared in the same year.[3]

Niebuhr, in this book, had warned Americans that they would experience a tragic future if they applied the perfectionist ethic of the tradition of republican virtue to the cold war. To avoid tragedy, Americans, Niebuhr insisted, must apply the compromising spirit of their pluralist democracy to the world scene. They must hope only for modest and partial achievements and not for a total victory. But when Williams examined the foreign policy of Franklin D. Roosevelt, the great symbolic hero of Niebuhr's pluralist and contrite democracy, he saw that Roosevelt was willing to use war, not to sustain the balance of power, but as a means to force the nations of the world to conform to the American vision of an international order. Americans in 1952, Williams argued in his first book, were engaged in a tragic history as they pridefully attempted to overcome the particulars of history and achieve universal order. American leaders, Williams was certain, planned to win a total victory over the Soviet Union in the cold war that had begun immediately after they had forced Germany and Japan into unconditional surrender.

Williams, therefore, hoped to show Americans like Niebuhr that Wilson, in World War I, did not represent the idealism of republican virtue, anticipating an exodus from an imperfect to a perfect world, whereas Roosevelt, in World War II, represented the realism of a capitalist, pluralist democracy which aspired only to the relative stability of a balance of power. He wanted to demonstrate that Wilson's idealism and inflexibility came from his commitment to capitalist values, and that Roosevelt and Truman were continuing a foreign policy that had remained remarkably consistent from 1917, through the 1920s and 1930s, and now into the cold war of the 1940s. And this iron cage of ideology, which had inspired American leaders from 1917 to 1947 in their aggressive effort to control and predict world history, stemmed from capitalism. Niebuhr, therefore, was not a tough-minded critic of the destructive role that pride played in history. He was an apologist for an American foreign policy that flaunted contrition in the name of boundless power.

The principle of balance of power, the recognition of the inevitability of pluralism in a world of continual change, this first principle of that conservative jeremiad developed by Niebuhr after 1940, was the foundation for Williams's narrative. His story moved American foreign policy from the promise of realism in the nineteenth century to a declension into ideology in the early twentieth century. "From 1781 to the present," he wrote, Russia and the United States "have adjusted policy with regard to the conflict between each country's territorial and economic expansion and the actual or potential value of each nation to the other in terms of a world balance of power. Prior to the Bolshevik Revolution of November, 1917, ideological considerations were clearly secondary."[4]

But balance of power considerations, Williams declared, could not explain the rage with which American leaders reacted to that revolution. The new Marxist Russia was economically and militarily weak throughout the 1920s and 1930s. Certainly, it did not share with Japan and Germany the energy or the will to drastically alter the world order. And yet, Wilson had joined his wartime allies in sending troops into Russia in a vain attempt to suppress the revolution. And this absolute hatred of the Soviet Union kept the United States from cooperating with it in the 1930s to contain Japanese and German aggressiveness. Only this kind of rigid ideology could explain "the failure of the United States to collaborate with the Soviet Union against Japanese expansion from 1920 to 1922, during Tokyo's invasion of Manchuria in 1931, and later, when Japan began to wage hostilities against China in 1937."[5]

Williams related this declension from a policy of balance of power to the decision by American leaders in the 1890s that the United States needed an overseas frontier because "the financial and industrial powers of the United States soon came to dominate their domestic market and looked abroad for new opportunities."[6] Implicit in his argument was the desire of American leaders to define and control this overseas market. Assuming that the world's future would be one of corporate capitalism, they were prepared to repress revolutions that did not conform to that ideal and that threatened to create alternative futures. This was their policy toward the Mexican revolution, which began in 1910, and it was, of course, the policy toward the Russian revolution of 1917. Their continued hostility toward the Russian revolution in the 1920s and 1930s stemmed from the fact that the existence of the Soviet Union compelled American leaders to be aware of their inability to totally define and control the development of an international marketplace. And the success of the Bolshevik revolution offered a model to other nations who did not want to define their futures in American capitalist terms. Williams, therefore, had nothing but contempt for those who believed America returned to an isolationist policy in 1919. "The policy of the United States toward the Soviets," he argued, "exemplified the victory of those domestic forces that, though generally labelled isolationist, in fact desired the further and unrestricted overseas expansion of American economic and political powers." "Far from isolation," he concluded, "the American policy of these interwar years was one characterized by decisions and actions taken with sole reference to unilaterally determined goals—decisions and actions for the consequences of which Washington disclaimed all responsibility."[7]

Williams was describing the recent history of the United States as a tragedy. A rigid ideology had prevented an alliance with the Soviet Union which might have preserved the balance of power and contained the aggressiveness of Germany and Japan without resort to war. The perception of an absolute dichotomy between capitalism and communism, which became an established pattern in the 1920s, also kept Americans from using the collapse of their marketplace capitalism in 1929 as an opportunity to rethink the relationship of capitalism and democracy. Williams bitterly condemned "this failure of American leadership—New Deal, business, or labor—candidly and courageously to explore the fundamental problem of economic policy, with all its political and social ramifications."[8]

Reinhold Niebuhr, in his 1952 book, *The Irony of American History*, had explained the development of the cold war as the reluctant response of a pragmatic United States after 1945 to the aggressiveness of an ideological Soviet Union. Williams, in his 1952 book, found the origins of the cold war in the ideological response of American leaders to the Russian revolution in 1917. Niebuhr had warned his readers not to become as obsessed with ideology as their Russian enemies were. If that happened, Americans, mobilizing to achieve a total victory over Russia, would destroy their own pluralist democracy. But when Williams looked at the writings of George F. Kennan, a leading American theoretician of the cold war in the late 1940s, he saw that an establishment figure was indeed calling for such a total victory. Williams's jeremiad, like Niebuhr's conservative jeremiad, warned against intensifying the cold war. Williams, however, did not argue, as Niebuhr had, that current American political leaders were working within a tradition of pragmatism, flexibility, and compromise. From 1917 to 1947, American policy toward the Soviet Union had been ideological, inflexible, and uncompromising. Williams's prophecy in 1952 was that the continuation of this policy would indeed destroy whatever aspects of democracy still existed within the United States. "Freedom," he declared, "is not nurtured by states preparing for war. Rather does it find more opportunity to flower in the atmosphere of mutual accommodation achieved and sustained through negotiated settlements."[9]

Much of what Williams had to say in *American-Russian Relations* about the beginning of a revolution in American foreign policy at the end of the nineteenth century was implicit rather than explicit. But in an article published in 1955, "The Frontier Thesis and American Foreign Policy," he was aware that he was offering a new perspective on the 1890s as a watershed decade in American history. At about the same time, Hofstadter had written an article on the 1890s which explained the Spanish-American War as the explosive result of the frustrations and sense of cultural defeat by both rural and urban Protestants.[10] For Hofstadter, these groups were prisoners of the tradition of republican virtue and had not yet abandoned their ideological "soft" side and accepted their pragmatic "hard" side. Hofstadter suggested that once that conversion took place after 1900, further foreign adventures were no longer needed to escape from problems that could not be solved at home.

Williams confronted this assumption that American imperialism in the Spanish-American War was an aberration. "One of the central themes of American historiography is that there is no American Empire," but, he asserted, "the United States has been a consciously and steadily expanding nation since 1890. A set of ideas, first promulgated in the 1890s, became the world view of subsequent generations of Americans and is an important clue to understanding America's imperial expansion in the twentieth century." And he turned to the writings of Frederick Jackson Turner to provide a way of understanding why the 1890s marked the beginning of systematic overseas expansion by American economic and political leaders. "Turner's frontier thesis," Williams argued, "made democracy a function of an expanding frontier." The response of American decision-makers in the 1890s to Turner's announcement that there was no longer an internal frontier followed Turner's logic—the political health of the nation depended upon the development of an overseas frontier. At the very moment when Hofstadter was attacking Turner because he was a spokesman for a mythical, anticapitalist agrarian democracy and the father of isolationist ideology in twentieth-century America, Williams was attacking Turner for providing the justification for American capitalism to become expansive and imperialistic in the new century. "Turner," Williams declared, "gave Americans a national world view that eased their doubts, settled their confusions, and justified their aggressiveness."[11] Like the Spanish-American War, World War I and World War II were not aberrations from an established anti-imperialist isolation; they were, for Williams, the inevitable price that the shapers of foreign policy were willing to pay for their commitment to the necessity of an overseas marketplace.

This article appeared in the same year as Hofstadter's *The Age of Reform*, which had celebrated the cautious pragmatism of Franklin D. Roosevelt and the New Deal. But when Williams looked back in 1955 at the foreign policy of the New Deal, he saw none of that anti-ideological flexibility. By the late 1930s, he wrote, those New Dealers who were shaping foreign policy had begun to "openly apply Turner's thesis to the new economic situation. An expanding economy became the dogma of an industrial economy." And that expansion demanded overseas markets and overseas sources of raw materials. Niebuhr had described Roosevelt's realistic attitude toward World War II as an acceptance of a policy of compromise within the framework of a world in which power was to be balanced and kept from being concentrated. And Niebuhr, who in 1945 understood Stalin to be advocating the same realistic goals, had then decided that the Soviet leaders had turned back to the ideology of world revolution, forcing the United States into the cold war. But, for Williams, the president "seemed, from the spring of 1942 to the fall of 1944, to base his plans for the post-war era on the idea of a concert of Power. Then, in October, 1944, he in effect reaffirmed the Open Door policy."[12] Contrary to Niebuhr's view, American ideology had preceded Russian ideology.

At a time when many younger members of the historical profession were destroying Beard's reputation, Williams defied his peers in the Consensus school by praising Beard. "Beard," he declared, "was a brilliant student of history keenly aware of the consequences of imperial expansion." Beard recognized that the New Dealers' commitment to an overseas frontier "would lead to war and tyranny" and that "democracy would be negated."[13] Once more, Williams was preaching a conservative jeremiad, but one that differed dramatically from that of Niebuhr and Hofstadter. They had seen Americans renouncing the spiritual arrogance of an imperialistic capitalism that was boundless in its ambitions to control and shape history. But he warned that such a prideful policy was leading toward tragedy. And, as in his first book, he did not prophesy that American leaders would necessarily become contrite; rather, he expressed the desperate hope that as these leaders contemplated a third world war to achieve their global mastery, they also might understand that their atomic weapons would destroy them as well as their enemies. These leaders, he hoped, must be "dimly aware that the United States had finally caught up with History, Americans were no longer unique. Henceforward they, too, would share the fate of all mankind. For the frontier was now on the rim of hell, and the inferno was radioactive."[14]

The Tragedy of American Diplomacy, published in 1959, provided him with the opportunity to present a more complex context for this self-destructive impasse of the American foreign policy which called for victory in the cold war.[15] He had traced the roots of the current tragedy to the 1890s, but he had been unable to clearly define the promise from which the expansive foreign policy was a declension. He did not share Beard's thesis, as Hofstadter had in *Social Darwinism in American Thought*, that the American democratic identity was anti-imperialist but that there were Americans who had abandoned that tradition to accept capitalist and imperialist ideology brought from England. Williams in 1959 could not preach a Beardian Progressive jeremiad, which saw a capitalist declension from a democratic promise and prophesied the fulfillment of that promise when the alien influence of capitalism was purged from the American body politic, because he viewed capitalism as an integral part of American history.

In this second book, however, Williams managed to talk about democracy in the American past, though he had been unable to do so in his first book and the subsequent articles. He now argued that democracy and capitalism were intertwined in the nineteenth century, as Hofstadter claimed in *The Age of Reform*. The United States was both democratic and capitalistic until 1890 when, Hofstadter argued in 1955, the "soft" side of the agrarian majority, its belief in a virtuous, participatory democracy, gave way to the "hard" capitalistic side of the farmers. After the 1890s, they were on their way to accepting the compromising, pragmatic, pluralist democracy linked to capitalism that had always been a part of American experience. But Williams envisioned a dialectical relationship between democracy and capitalism continuing after the 1890s. The result of that relationship, however, once American democracy became committed to spreading American democratic institutions to the rest of the world, was to destroy the balance of democracy and capitalism within the United States. The hegemony of a centralized and arrogant corporate capitalism was the unintended result of attempting to export Amerian democracy.

Niebuhr, in *The Irony of American History*, had written that "the tragic element in a human situation is constituted of conscious choices of evil for the sake of good." Williams found the United States of the 1950s to be in the tragic situation of consciously choosing an evil, war, for the sake of the good. Niebuhr had seen tragedy growing out of an ironic situation, which "is differentiated from tragedy by the fact that the responsibility is related to an unconscious weakness rather than to a conscious resolution." Williams, in *The Tragedy of American Diplomacy*, was describing the United States of the 1890s in such ironic terms. But Niebuhr also had insisted that "an ironic situation must dissolve if men or nations are made aware of their complicity in it. Such awareness involves some realization of the hidden vanity or pretension. This realization either must lead to an abatement of the pretension, which means contrition, or it leads to a desperate accentuation of the vanities to the point where irony turns into pure evil." Williams would claim that the irony of the pretentious foreign policy that had begun in the 1890s became tragedy in the 1930s when war was chosen as a necessary tool for its fulfillment. But he still hoped that it was not too late to replace the movement from irony to tragedy with a movement from irony to contrition.

Since the irony of the 1890s came from a hidden vanity, Williams could give *The Tragedy of American Diplomacy* a shape similar to that of the American jeremiad. There was a democratic promise in nineteeth-century America and a declension from that promise because Americans believed that a developing world would benefit from imitating the United States. And Williams prophesied that the declension could be overcome if Americans gave up that pretension to world leadership. But Williams, seeing no resurgence of democracy in the 1950s, did not prophesy that the promise was being fulfilled. The structure of the book, therefore, has a clear beginning in promise and irony; it has a clear description of declension and tragedy; but it does not conclude with a clear prophetic affirmation of the restoration of the promise and the achievement of contrition.

In beginning his narrative with an America in 1890 that was both democratic and capitalist, Williams did not try to describe the late nineteenth century in any detail. Assuming that foundation, he moved immediately to establish the ironic vanity leading toward tragedy. "The tragedy of American diplomacy is aptly symbolized, and defined for analysis and reflection," he wrote, "by the relations between the United States and Cuba from April 21, 1898" to the present. Americans had gone to war "to free Cuba from Spanish tyranny, to establish and underwrite the independence of the island, and to initiate and sustain its development toward political democracy and economic welfare." But Americans did not realize that the only economic tools available to express these generous impulses were those of corporate capitalism, which soon "dominated the economic life of the island by controlling, directly or indirectly, the sugar industry, and by overtly and covertly preventing any dynamic modification of the island's one-crop economy." The elites in the United States government who were making foreign policy moved swiftly to sustain this corporate domination; they were willing to intervene "with economic and diplomatic pressure and with force of arms, when Cubans threatened to transgress the economic and political restrictions set by American leaders."[16] And the American public, smug in their national pride that their model of democracy and capitalism could liberate all the peoples of the world, refused to criticize this foreign policy which would not tolerate alternative forms of modernization. The unintended consequence of this rigid and narrow definition of how progress must be made was to drive subsequent Cuban revolutionists such as Fidel Castro, and similar revolutionists throughout the world who wanted more democracy and prosperity for their nations, to look toward the Soviet Union for support. The cold war paranoia of Niebuhr, who saw a huge Soviet conspiracy to overcome the particulars of history with a universal order, was a self-fulfilling prophecy produced by the aggressiveness of the United States, which since the 1890s had pretended that its own particular national history could and should become universal.

Niebuhr intended that *The Irony of American History* provide Americans with a new way of understanding their history. They must become aware of their heritage of a pluralist democracy if they were to avoid the tempation of the cold war to become the mirror image of the Soviet Union and aspire to perfection. Williams also intended that *The Tragedy of American Diplomacy* provide Americans with a new way of understanding their history. Becoming self-conscious of the necessity of pluralism, they must see how their foreign policy for half a century had denied that pluralism. If the Soviet Union was striving after a world order built on its national model, it was the mirror image of a United States foreign policy already firmly established in 1917 when the Bolshevik revolution took place. Appealing to history as "a way of learning" and "getting closer to the truth," Williams affirmed that "it is only by abandoning the cliches that we can even define the tragedy. When we have done that," he concluded, "we will no longer be merely acquiescing in the deadly inertia of the past." Since 1945, he delcared, we have been trapped within the myth that the United States was an isolationist nation until 1941. But look at the 1890s, look, he wrote, and see the "broad support for expansion, and particularly overseas economic expansion." See how that support "rested upon an agreement among conservatives and liberals (even many radicals joined for a few years) and Democrats and Republicans from all sections and groups of the country." See how the planning for an overseas frontier "was the most impressive intellectual achievement in the area of public policy since the generation of the Founding Fathers."[17]

Visualizing their new overseas frontier as identical with their western frontier, the generation of the 1890s found the embodiment of their expansionist philosophy in the Open Door notes in which American foreign policy leaders had urged that China should not be broken up, as Africa and much of Asia had been, into parts of European empires. The westward expansion of the United States always had increased the size of the marketplace as an environment for the free flow of trade. In contrast, European empires blocked that flow of trade. China, free from those imperial boundaries that obstructed the world's commerce, was to offer a huge national marketplace, comparable to that of the United States and open to economic activity of all nations. Stopping the momentum of European imperialism in China, American leaders hoped they had begun a new momentum that would disestablish the existing empires. Associating war with imperial competition, American leaders contended that if their Open Door policy for China were accepted as universal policy, wars would cease. Business leaders from the various American states competed as individuals within the national marketplace and not as representatives of their state governments. Their competition, therefore, did not escalate into war between the states. A similar world marketplace embodying Open Door principles would also limit competition to the level of individuals. "In a truly perceptive and even noble sense," Williams declared, "the makers of the Open Door policy understood that war represented the failure of policy." But the policy also "derived from the proposition that America's overwhelming economic power would cast the economies and the politics of the poorer, weaker, underdeveloped countries in a pro-American Mold."[18] Designed to end the continual warfare caused by the imperial ambitions of the great powers, this policy ironically increased world tensions because American corporations, in their search for markets and raw materials, aborted the prosperous development of the poorer nations and then enlisted the United States government to coerce those nations when they rebelled against this pattern of exploitation.

This contradiction in the Open Door policy, according to Williams, did not become clear until World War I. "Given entry into the war on the grounds that 'the world must be made safe for democracy,'" he stated, "the crucial questions became those about the definition of democracy and the means to insure its security."[19] Wilson, however, represented the consensus of American leaders in believing that democracy must include a synthesis of the nineteenth-century marketplace of natural harmonies with the large corporation. Wilson therefore had opposed the Mexican revolution, as subsequent American leaders opposed all revolutions that did not identify democracy with the nineteenth-century marketplace and with corporations. Since, for Williams, world history was a constant flow of particulars, the longer American leaders clung to their vision of American corporate capitalism as the only acceptable model for developing nations, the more they would be frustrated and the more they would be tempted to use war to enforce an Open Door policy that had promised an end to war. Irony was becoming tragedy as the United States entered the 1920s.

Herbert Hoover was the figure Williams used to dramatize this moment in American history when the irony was revealed and American leaders could make a tragic choice: either they continue to use more and more force to achieve an Open Door empire, or, acknowledging the arrogance of their insistence that the world conform to the American model, they become contrite and surrender their effort to shape history in their own image. Shocked by the failure to reshape the entire world through the use of war, or even to suppress the Bolshevik revolution by sending troops into Russia, Hoover recommitted himself to the original intention of the Open Door policy, which was to achieve American influence abroad only through the power of the economy. It was this form of internationalism that Franklin Roosevelt denounced as isolationist in 1941, when he embraced war as a necessary tool for American overseas expansion. Hoover, however, in Williams's analysis, did not have the strength to surrender the Open Door policy even though he was certain that if the United States repeated the experience of World War I, the nation would become permanently militarized. According to Williams, Hoover also recognized the flaw in assuming that the pluralism of corporate capitalism in twentieth-century America could be the same as the pluralism of the nineteenth-century capitalism of many small property holders. Hoover "understood that the American economy was an interrelated and interdependent system, rather than a random conglomeration of individual operations mysteriously unified by the abstract functioning of the marketplace."[20] Because the marketplace could not provide an environment that disciplined the competing corporations, Hoover saw the national government expanding to play that role. Just as Hoover feared that overseas military competition would create a government of unchecked power, so did he fear that dependence on the government as the broker for the competing self-interests of large corporations, unions, and agricultural organizations would lead to such gigantic government bureaucracies, a system Williams called syndicalism, that all liberty for the individual would be lost. Once more, Hoover perceived a tragic future if current trends were not reversed. But again Hoover failed to sound the alarm or commit himself to creating an alternative American future that might avoid the impending tragedy. For Williams, who obviously was identifying his own fears with those of Hoover, Hoover's intense dislike of his successor was well taken. Franklin Roosevelt gave no evidence that he feared the growth of the broker state. And, to Hoover's dismay, government bureaucracies mushroomed from 1933 to 1941 and became even more enormous during World War II. If this was the pluralism Niebuhr and Hofstadter were celebrating, it had, for Williams, no relationship to the pluralism of the nineteenth century.

Nor could President Roosevelt's foreign policy be interpreted as anything but a perversion of the Open Door policy. "Men who began by defining the United States and the world in economic terms, and explaining its operation by the principles of capitalism and a frontier of historical development," Williams wrote, "came finally to define the United States in military terms as an embattled outpost in a hostile world. When a majority of the leaders of America's corporate society reached that conclusion, the nation went to war." Hoover had become aware of the irony in the Open Door policy. Roosevelt and his advisers had cut the tension in the irony with the sword of war. They had deliberately chosen a future that would be tragic. "Beginning in 1938 and 1939," he declared, "the evolving corporation coalition called in the military to execute a policy that they—the civilians—were formulating and adopting. It was the civilians who defined the world in military terms, not the military who usurped civilian powers."[21]

After Roosevelt's death in 1945, the new president, Harry Truman, and his advisers continued to look on war as a successful tool for the Open Door policy. The United States had eliminated Japan and Germany as rivals for world leadership. This left only the Soviet Union as a possible competitor. And they decided on an immediate showdown with Stalin, which would force him to acknowledge that the international future was to be defined in Open Door terms. "This decision," Williams declared, "represented the final stage in the transformation of the policy of the Open Door from a utopian idea into an ideology, from an intellectual outlook for changing the world into one concerned with preserving it in the traditional mold."[22]

Therefore, what hope could Williams offer that there were cultural resources in the United States that might reverse the tragedy of this entrenched foreign policy? When he looked back at the 1890s, he saw evidence of the definition of democracy which had only become fully articulated in the New Deal: that democracy cannot exist without expansion. If advocates of democracy in the United States accepted the necessity of overseas expansion, and if they assumed it was good to teach the American model of national development to the rest of the world, no democrats in 1960 would be ready to challenge the Open Door empire directed by corporate capitalists. The last significant challenge to that policy, according to Williams, had come during World War I when a number of American socialists and liberals had seen the imperial implications of Wilson's advocacy of the Open Door. These dissenting voices had disappeared, however, in the 1920s and the 1930s. "There is at the present time," Williams lamented, "no radicalism in the United States strong enough to win power, or even a very significant influence, through the processes of representative government."[23] This perception of an impotent radicalism perhaps explains why Williams had focused on Hoover as a prophetic figure in the 1920s who saw the impending tragedy. Williams made it clear that the only short-run hope to escape the tragic arrogance of the American effort to control world history lay within the American establishment itself. A policy of restraint must come from men like Hoover—but with more courage and decisiveness—"calm and confident and enlightened conservatives" who "can see and bring themselves to act upon the validity of a radical analysis."[24]

With his first two books, Williams had clarified the insight he had brought to his graduate studies: the United States between 1945 and 1947 had not merely responded defensively to the aggressiveness of Soviet ideology. He now had a comprehensive overview of the origins of the cold war in the development of the American Open Door policy in the 1890s. But what happened before that crucial decade? Did the ironic flaws that led to twentieth-century tragedy have a longer history? Hofstadter had not begun to write a major synthesis of American history until after he had answered his questions about the relationship of participatory and pluralist democracy. But Williams set out in the late 1950s to write a synthesis in order to answer his questions. Intertwined with his need to know the larger, historical context for American expansiveness in the twentieth century was the question whether he could realistically hope for the emergence of enlightened conservatives who would see the catastrophic consequences toward which the aggressive foreign policy was leading. The answers he found in his major synthesis, *The Contours of American History*, were even more disheartening than those of *The Tragedy of American Diplomacy*.[25]

Starting with the premise of the interrelatedness of American and European culture, Hofstadter nevertheless had reached a conclusion in the 1960s which was remarkably similar to that of Turner and Beard. For them, the Old World of Europe, the realm of Egyptian bondage, symbolized power, and the New World of America, the Promised Land, symbolized liberty. Connecting the United States to Europe, Hofstadter had found power in the Promised Land, but it was so checked and balanced that, for him, liberty had become the major experience in America. A modernizing European civilization bequeathed little of its aggressiveness to the United States. Like Hofstadter, Williams also found the roots of the America he confronted in 1960 in the way European culture had taken an American shape in the colonial period. But Williams was searching for the origins of a United States that was carrying on an imperial foreign policy, and he found a major legacy of European aggressiveness.

In *The Contours of American History*, he asked why England developed colonies in North America. The answer, for him, was what he called mercantilism, "a corporate conception of society which stressed the relationships and responsibilities between man and man." The characteristics of mercantilism, which he found so admirable, included the belief that "good fortune did not happen by itself: it was the result of men making good policies," and the affirmation that "the state had an obligation to serve society by accepting and discharging the responsibilities for the general welfare." But these characteristics were undemined by the mercantilist commitment to imperialism because "the chief way for a nation to promote its own wealth and happiness was to take them away from some other nation."[26] Until the American Revolution, however, this commitment to imperialism had not corrupted the mercantilist belief in community as necessarily pluralistic. Williams linked this concern for pluralism to the origins of mercantilism within the context of feudalism, which was, he wrote, "a political system and philosophy involving an interlocking network of freedoms, duties, and obligations between individuals inhabiting specified areas of land." The complex political relationship between the colonies and England, he concluded, was, therefore, essentially feudal. And the great irony of the American Revolution was that it was responsible for the rejection of the feudal-mercantilist "assumption that a small state was the only feasible unit of direct government."[27] The Revolution marked a departure from the philosophy and institutions of pluralism that had been brought from Europe.

In Williams's narrative, mercantilism survived as official national policy until 1828 because the founding fathers "remained publicly committed to the ideal of corporate responsibility and welfare." Beneath the surface, however, the commitment was being undermined by the ability of those American leaders to visualize a vast and rapid imperial expansion of the nation westward. The temptation of this empire of liberty made it impossible to sustain the tension in mercantilism between "the principle of wealth and welfare through expansion and the political axiom that a state had to be small to be representative (or democratic) and the moral definition of welfare that had come down from Christianity."[28]

Jefferson, for Williams, was a major figure in this movement to choose expansion to the exclusion of both a small government and a moral community. Jefferson, he wrote, "personified the dream that was already beginning to haunt Americans: a society of free and independent men made equal and prosperous by the bounty of nature." He quoted Jefferson that America's political success furnished "a new proof of the falsehood of Montesquieu's doctrine, that a republic can be preserved only in a small territory. The reverse is the truth."[29]

Williams, examining the early nineteenth century, accepted Turner's thesis that the West, the great frontier beyond the Appalachian Mountains, had finally freed the American individual from the social philosophies and institutions brought from Europe. And Williams, as completely as the post-1945 Niebuhr or Hofstadter, had no respect for the democracy of Jefferson and Jackson. But Williams, unlike Hofstadter, equated this vision of the West with a space where the individual could be free from social responsibility and free, therefore, to pursue self-interest with Adam Smith's vision of the marketplace and laissez-faire capitalism. The key to the Jacksonian democracy, which acknowledged no need for social responsibility, was both westward and marketplace expansion. But "motion as a substitute for structure," Williams warned, "is possible only so long as there is unlimited room to move in."[30]

In the 1960s, Hofstadter studied the Jacksonian period and found a pluralist democracy of pragmatic compromise led by practical, nonideological politicians like Martin Van Buren. Hofstadter, however, never tried to explain how the Civil War developed out of a political culture committed to reciprocity and reconciliation. For Williams, however, Van Buren's generation was intent on purging the nation of all vestiges of a corrupt past. And when northern Democrats "defined laissez-faire in terms that excluded the South," civil war had become inevitable. His conclusion was that when the generations of Jackson and Lincoln rejected the mercantilist concepts of social responsibility and planning for the public good, they no longer had a philosophy that understood compromise and had no appreciation of how to use institutions to bring about gradual reform. Committed to expansion as the solution to all problems, they had no choice but to use the marketplace metaphor of head-to-head competition as the way to end slavery in a bloody ritual of national purification. The postwar Niebuhr and Hofstadter had rejoiced that a pluralistic America did not allow bands of saints to use violence in attempted purges of evil. But Williams asked them to look hard at the Civil War. "Only a nation that avoided such a conflict," he admonished, "could make a serious claim to being fundamentally different."[31]

The Civil War, Williams argued, had made a mockery of the promise of Jefferson, Jackson, and Lincoln that western expansion could make marketplace competition a benign experience. And after 1865, the bloody nightmare of the war became the metaphor for the cutthroat economic competition of the 1870s and 1880s. This was the America of great social suffering which Hofstadter had lamented in *Social Darwinism in American Thought* but which was no longer present in *The Age of Reform*. The Democratic party of 1890, in Williams's analysis, clung to its laissez-faire principles even though they had brought about the war between neighbors. Escape from these horrors brought by nineteenth-century capitalist democracy, the democracy celebrated by Turner and the later Beard, had to come, therefore, from the leaders of big business who created progressivism within the Republican party. "The spokesmen and directors of the new order, though they accepted the traditional premise of private property and the vital role and necessity of an expanding marketplace," Williams wrote, "defined economic activity as making up an interrelated system. The political economy had to be extensively planned, controlled, and coordinated through the institution of the large corporation if it was to function in any regular, routine, and profitable fashion."[32]

Under the paternalistic neomercantilism of the corporate Progressives, Americans throughout the twentieth century escaped much of the destructive competition of nineteenth-century democracy. But, for Williams, the fatal flaw of colonial mercantilism, its assumption of the necessity of imperial expansion, remained. One of the first signs that the corporate Progressives were evading the need to develop a moral definition of community was apparent in the way in which they slid into a position of encouraging mindless consumerism. "Ostensibly created to facilitate the rational and efficient production of goods to meet the needs of men," he argued, "the corporation (like the sorcerer's apprentice) ultimately began by creating in men the demand for goods they had never seen, observed in use, or even known they needed." "Having defined everything good in terms of a surplus of property," corporate Progressives, he concluded, had the problem "of developing techniques for securing more good things from a succession of new frontiers."[33]

Williams now repeated the analysis of twentieth-century foreign policy that he had presented in *The Tragedy of American Diplomacy*. The hope of corporate Progressives to limit international competition through their Open Door policy was undermined by their inability to provide a moral dimension to the international community, as they had already failed at the national level. Williams identified Reinhold Niebuhr as a symbol of this weakness. Niebuhr, for Williams, combined "selected portions of Catholicism and Calvinsim" in his theology and was a much more responsible theologian than those nineteenth-century Protestants who had rationalized laissez-faire. Niebuhr had placed the individual within the community, but he had no definition for the community other than as the sum of the competing interest groups in a society at any given time. Niebuhr, like the other neomercantilists, refused to give a positive meaning to community. And Williams chided him for not preaching the Christian gospel that "man's world had to be built as a commonwealth in which men were brothers first and economic men second." Niebuhr, Williams concluded, "denied the very utopia offered by Christianity. Like the other reformers, Niebuhr was a heretic."[34]

Niebuhr and Hofstadter had not only praised the interest-group pluralism of the New Deal but celebrated its economic success. But, Williams declared, the New Deal had ended in 1937 "with candid admissions of failure from its very protagonists." He pointed out that when corporate capitalism had failed after 1929, the New Deal had used the taxing power of the national government to raise the capital that the corporations needed for their survival. In 1960, Williams did not see a sound and healthy capitalism but a system that had been saved by a continual series of financial transfusions from the national government. How long, Williams asked, can this dying patient be kept alive by a pattern of coercive taxation which must end by impoverishing the taxpayers, the supposed beneficiaries of the productive capacities of corporate capitalism?[35]

But although Niebuhr, Hofstadter, and other liberals in 1960 were still able to pretend that the normal expansiveness of a healthy capitalism made the positive definition of community irrelevant, they had no such tolerance for fantasy regarding the overseas frontier. "Having defined the frontier as utopia and lived by that ideal for most of their history," Williams declared, "Americans had finally been faced by the harsh fact that the frontier as utopia produced the very stalemate it had been designed to circumvent. The world was no longer a series of frontiers, it was a community which would survive or perish by its own hand."[36]

Concluding *The Contours of American History* with this warning, Williams, however, had no usable past—no significant American traditions of community, no promise on which to construct a prophecy that the declension, the evasion of the need to create a positive community, could be overcome in the future. Colonial mercantilism came closest to offering such a promise, but its commitment to imperial expansion had undermined its tradition of public morality. Nineteenth-century democracy, with its values of laissez-faire capitalism, had been the least responsible period in American history. And although the neomercantilists of the twentieth century, the corporate Progressives, struggled to restore the eighteenth-century values of public virtue, "as long as the would-be Founding Fathers of such a gentry defined the wealth and welfare of their projected commonwealth as a dependent variable of overseas economic empire, they would of necessity have to pay more attention to foreign policy than to building the commonwealth."[37]

Since Williams no longer had the hope in an enlightened American gentry that he had expressed at the end of *The Tragedy of American Diplomacy*, he had to find a future for American community outside American national history. With the publication of his next book, *The Great Evasion*, he gained his reputation as a radical because he asked Americans to use the writings of Karl Marx as such a promise, a standard of judgment by which they could define the declension of their capitalist history, and as a prophecy for the building of a positive community.

Having given up on corporate Progressives such as Hoover, Williams now hoped to change the minds of contemporary Americans who identified themselves as liberals or progressives but who had dismissed the writings of Marx as European with no relevance for America. Academic Progressives such as John Dewey and Charles Beard, Williams wrote, had criticized big business and had warned that capitalism was incompatible with democracy. But they were "socialists of the heart," who tried "to take for their own purposes Marxian socialism's magnificent reassertion of the ideal of a Christian commonwealth without taking its commitment to social property." Beard, Williams would later argue, because he defined capitalism only in laissez-faire terms, threw his support to the New Deal in 1933. Beard confused the new role of the national government in saving the major corporate structures in the economy with the achievement of a fraternal democracy.[38]

Can American liberals and progressives at the beginning of the 1960s explain, Williams asked, the failure of the prophecies of men like Dewey and Beard, who had insisted that there was enough strength in an American democratic tradition to make Marx irrelevant as a critic of the American present and as a prophet for the American future? Who was relevant to that task in the 1960s? Williams's answer, of course, was Marx. Dewey, Beard, and other liberals and progressives were prisoners of Turner's belief in the two worlds of Europe and America with two distinct histories. But, as Williams had tried to demonstrate in *The Contours of American History*, American history was a national variation of the capitalist history that characterized the development of early modern Europe. As long as American intellectuals insisted on American uniqueness, they would never adequately define the causes of the declension of their national culture or create a successful alternative. American academic and religious progressives, Williams insisted, had refused to confront "Marx's central theses about the assumptions, the costs, and the nature of capitalist society. We have never confronted his central insight that capitalism is predicated upon an overemphasis and exaltation of the individualistic, egoistic half of man functioning in a marketplace system that overrides and crushes the social, humanitarian half of man."[39]

Specifically, Williams continued, Marx had predicted that a capitalist society would have an imperialist foreign policy. And, as Williams had demonstrated in his first three books, the record of American diplomatic history proved Marx right. But Williams now wanted to broaden the discussion of imperialism to include the westward expansion of Anglo-American culture. Turner and Beard had used the metaphor of exodus from an Old World of oppression to a New World of liberty to define European migration to America. But when Williams rejected that metaphor of two worlds and described the migration as the transfer of capitalist culture from Europe to America, he also, in dramatic contrast to Turner and Beard, defined European settlement as a process of conquest. The constant succession of wars between the Euramericans and the nations of the American Indians from 1600 to 1880 had, for him, become part of American diplomatic history; and so had the colonial slave trade and the enslaved Afro-Americans within Anglo-American culture. Williams now asked Americans who shared Turner and Beard's unqualified understanding of their history as exceptional, or even the qualified concept of exceptionalism held by Niebuhr and Hofstadter, and who defined that exceptionalism as freedom from the oppressive and violent use of power in Europe, to look at the brutal treatment of the Native Americans and the Afro-Americans and the cultural implications of the aggressive war against Mexico in 1846 by the dominant Anglo-American society.

Marx also had predicted increasing economic misery under capitalism, but American liberals, in 1960, insisted that current national prosperity proved Marx wrong. Williams already had pointed to the role of deficit spending by the national government in providing the illusion of economic vitality. But he urged the progressive yea-sayers to recognize the extent to which poverty existed within the United States and to also consider the dependence of the qualified national prosperity on the exploitation of an external proletariat; these were the citizens of the underdeveloped world whose resources and labor were siphoned off as profits for the developed world.

Finally, Marx had predicted increasing alienation within the capitalist nations. The two major examples of this trend, which Williams chose to stress, were the confusion, anger, and resentment being expressed by the present generation of adolescents and the decline of voter participation in elections throughout the twentieth century. Marx had argued that capitalism must betray its utopian promise to make every individual a productive participant in the economy. The history of corporate capitalism in the United States had fulfilled that prediction with "the loss of any participatory role in the principal decisions of the capitalist marketplace" by a growing and dependent wage-earning force, which had lost "control over any private property which played a part in the productive activities in the system." It was inevitable, Williams concluded, that the loss of meaningful participation in the productive economic system would lead these wage earners to feel alienated from the political system. The average citizen "is becoming a mere consumer of politics as well as a mere consumer of goods." But these workers could not imagine an alternative system in which they would be vital participants in the economy and politics because they were ensnared in a culture in which "the sharing of profits is mistaken for the sharing of direction and control of the enterprise itself, just as the sharing of the leader's charisma is mistaken for the sharing of power."[40]

It was Williams's hope in 1964 that if American liberals and progressives were willing to confront Marx, they would recognize the need to stop the disintegration of their culture. Surrendering the frontier myth of American exceptionalism, they would come to understand that "a free society is that in which the individual defines himself, and acts, as a citizen of a community rather than as a competing ego. In a very real sense, therefore, the frontier for Marx is the space and resources made available for human development by loving thy neighbor as thyself." In envisioning the end of American history as capitalist expansion, Williams advocated drastic decentralization of the nation as a political unit because a "true community is more easily obtainable, and more extensively developed, in small rather than large units." A new America, beginning a new history, "will be beautiful instead of ugly" and "will facilitate human relationships instead of driving men into separate functional elements."[41]

In *The Great Evasion*, Williams had hoped that the teachings of Karl Marx would provide American liberals and progressives with a usable past, a promise by which they could define the declension of their nation, so that they might cease being apologists for the disintegrating status quo. And by becoming radicals, they could build on Marx's prophecy to achieve a truly democratic society. By the late 1960s, however, Williams had begun to separate his jeremiad from that of Marx. If modern American culture was rooted in early modern Europe, the cultural weaknesses of the United States were also those of modern European civilization. Marx, of course, had criticized European capitalism. And Williams had insisted that Marx's criticism applied to American capitalism. But it began to occur to Williams that Marx was offering a variation of the modern values rather than an alternative. Williams, for example, in *The Great Evasion* had accepted Marx's position that industrial capitalism was a necessary stage in history as progress. It was industrial capitalism that created the engines of productivity that made affluence possible for all the people of the world rather than for a privileged few. But Williams had criticized the growth of an American empire, first in the West and then overseas, which promised increasing wealth. And the bureaucracies necessary for that expansion and that accumulation of wealth destroyed the possibility of true community. Did Marx's advocacy of unlimited wealth also lead to huge bureaucracies in socialist and communist countries? Were Marxists also frontierspeople unable to stop and define spiritual community as they pursued a future of greater material goods? In *The Great Evasion*, Williams had explicitly separated Marx's teachings from the political practice of the Soviet Union. But now he believed that he had been mistaken. The Soviet Union, with its vast bureaucracy, had become the mirror image of the United States because Marx, in the manner of capitalist philosophers, believed that democracy was possible only in an environment of increasing wealth.

In his 1972 book, *Some Presidents from Wilson to Nixon*, Williams, therefore, was developing his own jeremiad, one free from the ironic weakness in that of Marx which had led to the tragic culture of the Soviet Union. Here Williams disassociated his commitment to political decentralization from the magic of industrial productivity which could come only from those centralized economies of scale that overwhelmed and destroyed the human dimension in the United States and the Soviet Union. Instead, he related what seemed to be the permanent crisis of the presidency to the crisis of an overextended political system linked to an overextended economic system. Increasing wealth depended upon forcing the particulars of history to conform to the logic of industrial rationality and efficiency. If industrial production were to continue to grow, political power must be extended to force individuals, as well as physical nature, to imitate the universals implied in the logic of rationality and efficiency. But, for Williams, there were inevitable limits on the ability of political power to dominate the human and natural diversity that was characteristic of the earth. "There are only two ways to govern a continent," he declared. "One is to assert the will of a minority as a well-organized plurality. The other is to divide the continent into natural regional communities and allow each people to decide its own fate – including its relationships with other social communities." Again Williams urged Americans to view the tragic failures of their presidents from Wilson to Nixon as evidence of the failure of a political system that tried through the triumph of the will to force unnatural uniformity on natural diversity. Again he was urging political diversity as a system more in harmony with human and physical experience.[42]

In his 1976 book, *America Confronts a Revolutionary World*, he extended the moral of presidential failure to impose uniformity within a geographic area as diverse as the United States; now he noted the failure of the presidents since Wilson to force all the revolutions that had occurred in the twentieth century to imitate the American Revolution. Refusing to acknowledge that history was composed of particulars and not universals, they pursued foreign policy goals that always ended in frustration and defeat.[43] And in his 1978 textbook, *Americans in a Changing World*, Williams tried to teach Americans that the pursuit of uniformity not only led to the frustration of their domestic politics and foreign policy but also to the frustration of their personal lives when they permitted themselves to be uprooted from their families, neighborhoods, and geographic localities, becoming individual units who fitted the uniform standards of the marketplace. He now called on the history of the Native Americans for a usable past to define the current declension and to provide a prophecy for a less destructive future. "Not only were" the first Americans "good farmers (who cleared enough land to let half lie fallow)," he declared, but "they demonstrated a sophisticated understanding of how to create and sustain a symbiotic relationship with the land." These "first Americans," he wrote, "had painfully evolved a sense (and the rituals) of time, place, and pace that could have helped the majority of twentieth-century Americans sustain their own traditions of community and common humanity during the process of urbanization and industrialization."[44]

But asking Americans in 1980 to define their present situation as a declension from the Native-American world of decentralized communities was an almost impossible task. In his 1980 book, *Empire as a Way of Life*, he lamented that "once people begin to acquire and take for granted and waste surplus resources and space as a routine part of their lives, and to view them as a sign of God's favor," it is difficult for them to give up the philosophy that more is better. But, he affirmed, we must nevertheless try to "create a culture on the basis of agreeing upon limits." Williams had made clear how far he had moved from 1964 when he had joined Marx in promising a cooperative community with great affluence. Now he declared that the promise of a decentralized America meant that everyone must make tremendous economic sacrifices. But what was the choice? The pursuit of rising standards of living had led to an empire and to an arms race with Soviet Russia. "Empire as a way of life," he insisted, "will lead to nuclear death." The promise and the prophecy, which offered an alternative to the declension of internal and external chaos caused by our national and international centralization, was decentralized community. And "community as a way of life will lead for a time to less than is necessary. Some of us will die. But how one dies is terribly important. It speaks to the truth of how we have lived."[45]

Entering the 1980s, the fifth decade of his academic career, Williams did not expect that Americans were about to create a contrite culture which would express its newfound humility by dismantling the nation-state, thereby destroying the major mechanism used by prideful people in their attempts to impose their will on the diversity of human experience. But he seemed prepared to speak and write as long as there was breath in his body. He had to warn of the catastrophe that must result from this arrogant attempt to control history. And he must point to the alternative that could save his fellow Americans and perhaps humanity from self-destruction. In a 1981 essay, "Radicals and Regionalism," published in a recently established journal, *Democracy*, Williams provided political specificity to the ideas he had been developing since the publication of *The Great Evasion*. He began by asking why the New Left of the 1960s, "despite its moral commitment, its marvelous energy, and its promising ideas, failed to evolve beyond the single-issue politics of opposing the imperial war in Vietnam?" His direct answer was the New Left's dependence on the bankrupt ideas of Marx. Human existence, Williams wrote, is "defined by four variables: place, time, space, and scale." And Marx shared the assumptions of modern capitalism about each of them: that place must be defined as the "nation-state," that time was "the present defined as the future," that space was to be "the world," and that scale was to be "various nation-states competing to unify the globe." This is why, he continued, the Soviet Union, Marx's ideological child, imitates that self-defeating logic of the capitalist nations that "leads to increasing democratic imbalance, the supercentralization of power, and the destruction of community."[46]

American radicals, if they wanted to confront the establishment, Williams insisted, could not do so with ideas that were already held by corporate capitalists. Although they called themselves radicals, they were really conservatives. Paradoxically, therefore, to become truly radical, they must embrace ideas they had always identified with conservatism: localism, rootedness, and a self-conscious religious identity. "Twentieth-century American radicals," Williams complained, had become "so blinkered by Marx's acceptance of the productivity of the capitalist political economy that they had ignored or dismissed ostensibly conservative truth." But if corporate capitalism was pushing for both national and international centralization, "surely a vigorous radicalism," Williams affirmed, "is defined by decentralization and the diffusion of power." American radicals, he continued, "must confront centralized nationalism and internationalism and begin to shake it apart, break it down, and imagine a human and socially responsible alternative."[47]

Radicals, therefore, should consider a constitutional convention in which the centralized nation-state with its international ambitions would be broken down "into a confederation of regional governments based upon proportional representation and the parliamentary system within each region and in the confederation itself." The foreign policy of the confederation parliament would be completely defensive, enabling "each culture to proceed with its self-determined development within its legitimate boundaries."[48]

In the 1940s, Williams had accepted the central premise that underlay Niebuhr's rejection of Beard's Progressive jeremiad. America, Niebuhr preached, was not a unique space in harmony with the universal; it was not a space free from the flow of time, which was expressed by the continual appearance of novelty, the unpredictable in the form of dynamic particulars. America was not a space isolated from the history experienced on other continents. But Niebuhr had insisted that although Americans fantasized that they inhabited such a Promised Land, they had behaved as if they shared an Old World where one did not act as a member of the Chosen People but as an ordinary member of the human race, faced with the continual problems of accommodation, compromise, and reconciliation. And Hofstadter had shifted his intellectual loyalty from Beard's understanding of America as a New World to an understanding of America similar to Niebuhr's. His histories described America in Niebuhrian terms—an intellectual history that insisted on pride and perfection, but an institutional history of compromise and humility.

Williams, however, had searched for such an America of gentle pluralism in his first three books of historical narrative and found, instead, an institutional history of pride and aggressiveness. For him, there were not two segregated American histories, one intellectual and one institutional. The idea of a Chosen People had been translated into the conquest of the West; and when that frontier of institutional expansion had ended, Americans expressed their sense of "manifest destiny" by constructing a foreign policy whose goal was to bring the entire world within their vision of the Promised Land. The postwar Niebuhr and Hofstadter wanted to end American intellectual history to avoid a tragic future. By the 1960s, Williams wanted to end both American intellectual and institutional history to avoid a tragic future.

Niebuhr and Hofstadter, in 1950, preached a conservative jeremiad that defended the reality of the contrite institutional status quo from the prideful Progressive jeremiad and its use of abstract and unreal categories of promise and prophecy to denounce the established order as a declension. If the conservative jeremiad was successful in keeping the Progressive jeremiad from seducing Americans into a quest for perfection, history as tragedy could be avoided. But for Williams, who shared Niebuhr and Hofstadter's desire to avoid tragedy, their conservative jeremiad was itself fantasy. Niebuhr and Hofstadter failed to recognize the trends in American history toward internal centralization and external imperialism. Williams could not preach their kind of conservative jeremiad because, for him, it obscured the way in which Americans' belief in themselves as a Chosen People was expressed in the institutional power of the imperial presidency throughout the twentieth century.

After 1970, Williams was certain that a truly conservative jeremiad must denounce modern ideas and modern institutions, capitalist and Marxist alike, because their logic was endless growth. Niebuhr had confused a commitment to systematic growth with a humble acceptance of time and pluralism. But, for the Williams of 1980, when capitalists and communists embraced time, they did so because they believed they could control the future. Time, for them, was not unpredictable; nor was it the realm of the particular. Both American and Soviet leaders expected their national revolutions to become the basis for a universal order. This was why Williams in 1980 identified his conservative jeremiad as radical. The promise by which he judged the declension of the modern world came from early Christianity and Native-American cultures, both of which had existed before the modern. And his prophecy for a future that escaped the tragedy that must inevitably accompany the desire for boundless expansion was one of nonmodern ideas and institutions. At the end of the nineteenth century, Turner had predicted the end of an American space free from European history. At the end of the twentieth century, Williams predicted the end of a modern

American and European space free from history. Williams, like Turner, was certain that the particular would triumph over the universal.

Such a triumph, for Turner, was tragic because meaning could not be found in the particular. For Williams, however, it was the continuation of the modern quest for the universal that was tragic. Like Niebuhr, Williams believed that meaning could be found in the particular. But, unlike Niebuhr, he believed that local commonwealths, truly pluralistic and comparable to the first Christian communities and Native-American cultures, could be constructed within history. Recognizing in 1980 that "there are not today enough Americans, radical or otherwise," ready to discard the dying modern culture with its ideological and institutional pretensions to the universal, Williams, nevertheless, refused to be a historian, like Turner and Beard and Hofstadter, who could not imagine a dramatically different history from that of 1890 or 1940 or 1970. Williams declared that the end of American history was also the beginning. "The purpose of a radical utopia is to create a tension in our souls," he instructed his readers, and "our first responsibility as radicals is to create a knowledge, individual and then social, that what we are doing is not good enough. Then we must imagine something better."[49]

The 1980s and the Irony of Progress: Limits on the Development of Democracy, but No Limits on Economic Development

7

When I became an undergraduate history major in 1946, my interest was focused on the Progressive Era in the United States. I did not realize then, or for many years to come, that my intense desire to understand the idea of progress, as it had been expressed by so many Americans before 1917, was interrelated with a sense of crisis among my teachers and their peers, in the 1940s, about the central narrative of American history as the story of progress. In retrospect, it seems that my experience as an adolescent caused me to be particularly attuned to that crisis. A family history that had become catastrophic was paralleling the collapse of the Progressive paradigm. And so the metaphor of two worlds that informed Charles Beard's writings in 1940, his vision of a virtuous and benign America separated from a corrupt and malevolent Europe, made little sense to me as a junior in college. The farm on which I was born in 1925 was foreclosed in 1940; my father, at fifty-seven, felt that his life had ended in defeat and he died a year later. When I graduated from high school in 1943, I was immediately inducted into the Army. Oral history in my family, in which grandparents or great-grandparents were immigrants from Europe, had emphasized that America, in contrast to the "old country," was a land of peace and economic plenty. A powerful illustration, which gave substance to this "folk" participation in the metaphor of two worlds, was the heroic flight of my grandfather from Germany to escape conscription. Now I was in military service and in training for the invasion of Germany.

My own doubts in 1946 about the validity of the metaphor of two separate worlds coincided, therefore, with the way in which American participation in World War II had challenged the concept of two histories, American and European, that was a fundamental part of the academic orthodoxy into which my teachers were initiated. The focus of my research and writing, from my senior thesis through my doctoral dissertation, was on the way in which a number of major American social theorists in the years 1890–1920 had defined evolution. The conclusion I reached in *The Paradox of Progressive Thought*, which resulted from that study, was that these intellectuals believed that by looking back at the beginning of the evolutionary process, they could predict its conclusion. From their present position in history, they could see the beginning and the end of the story.[1]

Much has been written recently about the breakdown of narrative among writers in the various modern nations. It has been suggested that the self-confidence, which appeared first in early modern Europe and then spread to other parts of the world, that the modern era represents the climax of evolution, has been eroding, leaving novelists, poets, dramatists, and historians, among others, without stories to tell unless they can develop narratives offering a vision that does not bring evolution and history to a climax with modern civilization.[2] I believe, therefore, that Pocock and Bercovitch exaggerate the way in which ideas about two distinct worlds, generated in Europe during the Renaissance and Reformation, have become peculiarly American.

It is probable, in my estimation, that the development of modern sensibilities in Europe necessarily included the rhetoric of a Progressive jeremiad. The modern outlook always involves a sense of separation from the traditional; a frontier threshold has been, or will be, crossed from an Old World to a New. American intellectuals in 1900 could predict the course of evolution, as could intellectuals in England, Germany, or any modern nation, because they had a vision of the whole of evolution, or history—the past, present, and future. They had a concept of what Bercovitch, in writing about Puritan theology, calls the promise. Among modern intellectuals, the second state of the Progressive jeremiad is the state of declension discussed by Bercovitch. For the secular intellectuals of the various modern nations during the nineteenth century, declension from the promise that the threshold into modern times had been crossed was defined as cultural lag.[3] Frederick Jackson Turner and Charles Beard during the 1890s were participants in an international community that assumed the present could be judged against an understanding of the whole course of evolution. And they claimed that their prophecy that the promise of evolutionary progress would be fulfilled, that declension, or cultural lag, would be overcome, was a scientific evaluation of the laws of evolution.

It is ironic, therefore, that Pocock uses the language of cultural lag in discussing the peculiar strength of the tradition of republican virtue in the United States during the nineteenth century. Pocock's typology is that of medieval, early modern, and modern. The medieval, for him, assumes that there is no reality in the experience of the particulars of history, no reality in the experience of time. Reality is found only in the timeless universals of natural law. According to Pocock, the modern outlook insists that the only reality is to be found in the particulars of history, in the experience of time. For true moderns, in Pocock's analysis, the concept of the timeless universals of natural law is sheer fantasy. He writes, then, about the early modern as a transitional stage that tried to combine natural law and history, the universal with time. For him, this transitional stage was dying everywhere but in the United States by the end of the eighteenth century. And the final crisis of republican virtue was taking place in America by the end of the nineteenth century.

As I indicated in chapter 1, I believe that Pocock is correct about the persuasive power of the republican tradition in American culture between 1790 and 1890. But the implication of his scholarship is that Turner and Beard, faced with the closing of the American West in 1890, should have surrendered the cultural lag of the American political imagination and fully embraced the particulars of history. They should have become as modern as Europeans already were. But Turner and Beard, as I pointed out in *Historians against History*, no longer able to separate time and Europe from nature and America, turned to Europe to find ways of fusing time and nature, the particular with the universal. And there they found the formula for a secular Progressive jeremiad in social theories of evolution. Like Reformation and nineteenth-century Europeans, they could still predict history. Like Renaissance and nineteenth-century Europeans, they could still relate the present to universal laws of nature.[4]

Surely Pocock is wrong about the meaning of modern. This becomes clear when one reads the speeches of politicians and economists given in the 1980s in every modern nation. The language is that of moving from underdevelopment to development. This current language about progress assumes that political and economic leaders can relate that upward, economic movement to an understanding of a coherent relationship between past, present, and future. The social sciences, since World War II, have told a story of progressive modernization, which assumes, as Turner and Beard had in 1900, that time expressed as the evolution of natural law is not mysterious. Progressive time is not the realm of the particular or the irrational. Such time is not the realm of chance or the unexpected. Modern time is not the dimension in which unpredictable creativity takes place.[5]

But the intellectual and emotional torment experienced by such American historians as Turner, Beard, Hofstadter, and Williams, as well as by a theologian like Niebuhr, is not irrelevant to the history of the idea of progress from 1880 to 1980. Although progress remains the most persuasive story for dominant groups in every modern nation, the intellectual biographies of the Americans examined in this book illuminate the major problems confronting the faith in progress during this century. In the 1880s, Frederick Jackson Turner had learned to associate the transition from a traditional, unprogressive world to a modern, progressive one with the exodus of millions of immigrants from Europe and their arrival in the United States. The intellectual heritage into which he was initiated identified the geographic space of the United States not only with the boundless economic resources that separate modern experience from the resource limitations of traditional societies but with the possibility of achieving a society of such social and economic equality that virtuous political democracy was possible.

The crisis of the tradition of republican virtue, expressed by Turner in the 1890s, should be understood, in my estimation, as more than a provincial one. Renaissance and Reformation Europeans had seen American space as an environment in which individuals could enjoy economic plenty, free from large-scale hierarchical organizations. Turner was correct when he predicted in 1890 that the American future, like that of the European nations, would be one of growing bureaucracies. Industrialism, replacing the American frontier as the great source of economic plenitude, could not promise such freedom from large-scale organization. And Beard's hope that the undemocratic hierarchies of corporate capitalism could be replaced by large-scale organizations characterized by democratic participation seems to have been representative of major intellectual currents in western Europe as well as in the United States.

When first Niebuhr and then Hofstadter attacked American innocence, they were attacking that hope of blending participatory democracy with bureaucracy that had been present in all modern nations before 1940. For them, it was American rather than modern innocence because Beard, like so many other American intellectuals, had decided in 1919 that the Industrial Revolution could be blended with participatory democracy only in the United States. Elsewhere the process of modernization was not compatible with social and political equality. The end of American history in the 1940s, for Niebuhr and Hofstadter, therefore, meant the end of the hope for an America that would be an exception to the rule that economic progress and participatory democracy were incompatible. Reality, for them, was to be found in large-scale organizations which did not have workplace democracy and in which the hope for social and political equality was irrelevant to everyday experience. Since the 1950s, the triumph of the theory of pluralist democracy within the intellectual community in the United States has coincided with the conceptual separation of economic plenitude, provided by industrial technology, from political plenitude by political theorists in other modern countries. Escape from the Egyptian bondage of the Old World is to be defined only in terms of an increase in the purchasing power of a nation's citizens, not in a richer political life.[6]

This post-1945 disassociation of economic progress from political progress made it possible for theoreticians, such as Niebuhr and Hofstadter in the United States, to become critical of unlimited political expectations without criticizing unlimited economic expectations. These realists became implicit allies of the modernization theorists even though they explicitly rejected the modernizers' concept of necessary stages of social and economic evolution. From the perspective of those Consensus, or Counter-Progressive, intellectuals, who warned that the attempt to achieve political virtue must end in tragedy because it symbolized an effort to control history, the pursuit of economic self-interest, in contrast, represented a humble acceptance of the fallen nature of humanity. Their conservative jeremiad could warn against political pride, but not against ambition in the marketplace.

This, of course, is the point where Williams's conservative jeremiad diverged so sharply from that of the post-1945 Niebuhr and Hofstadter. They could only imagine the aggressive use of political power to provide alternatives to the marketplace. Since they associated the marketplace with the particulars of history, which they now embraced, all noncapitalist politics were to be defined as prideful and/or sinful. But Williams, unlike the Consensus historians of the 1950s, saw a "political" capitalism. Capitalism, for him, was not merely individuals or groups competing with each other in the marketplace. In his analysis which began in the 1940s, the political power of dominant cultural groups was the key to any understanding of the expansiveness of modern economies. From his perspective, a Consensus historian like Hofstadter continued the tradition of Beard's progressivism which assumed that there was a noncultural economic reality; one that was given rather than artful.[7]

But Williams found economic experience to be as much a part of culture as politics, and that politics and economics were always interrelated within any cultural group. Starting with that premise, and with the principle of the conservative jeremiad that tragedy is the inevitable conclusion to all human efforts to overcome limits, Williams began in the 1960s to warn against the unlimited ambition of the political culture of capitalism in the United States and of the Marxist political culture of the Soviet Union. His thinking paralleled the rapid development in the 1960s and 1970s of a similar ecological conservatism among intellectuals from a variety of disciplines in the United States as well as in other modern countries.[8]

One might suggest, therefore, that the crisis of the metaphor of two worlds depicted in the writings of American historians since the 1890s provides perspective on the larger crisis of modern identity. Until 1890, American historians were certain that the seventeenth-century exodus from Europe to America had brought a Chosen People into a Promised Land of limitless geographic plenitude. And this physical environment would make possible a new kind of politics. After 1890, American historians joined with historians from the European nations in proclaiming that industrialism was the basis of the boundless economic plenitude that awaited those willing or able to cross the frontier threshold from an Old, traditional to a New, modern World. But it has been increasingly difficult for American historians to imagine that the New World of industrialism will also be one of boundless political plenitude. The 1940s were the crucial decade when most American historians abandoned the belief that either an agrarian or an industrial America was the foundation for an exceptional political experience on this side of the Atlantic. But whether as converts to modernization theory or as members of the Consensus school, most historians since the

1950s have not questioned that a migration has occurred into a New World where endless economic growth will take place.[9]

But the principles of the conservative political jeremiad, which became so influential in the 1940s as the basis for the criticism of the Progressive political jeremiad and as an apology for the status quo, can also be used, as Williams has shown, to radically criticize the Progressive economic jeremiad, capitalist or Marxist, so paradoxically advocated by the defenders of elitist politics. In 1984, one cannot say with certainty that the end of American history as an exceptional political and social experience necessarily designates the end of modern history as an exceptional economic experience. But the attack on Beard's understanding of an "innocent" America in the 1940s has led William Appleman Williams to apply the same critical principles of the inevitability of limits to current "innocence." At this point, then, one can only repeat Williams's questions: Can the logic of the argument that there are always limits to human experience be applied to politics without also being applied to economics? Can one criticize the republican and Marxist pretensions to universalism without also criticizing capitalist pretensions to a universal marketplace? Can one hope for participation in economic, political, and social life, for the experience of community, unless one accepts boundaries and diversity?

Notes

Notes

CHAPTER 1. REFORMATION AND RENAISSANCE

1. Gene Wise, *American Historical Explanations* (Homewood, 1973; 2d. ed., Minneapolis, 1980). Thomas Kuhn, *The Structure of Scientific Revolutions* (Chicago, 1962; 1970). For the widespread impact of Kuhn's ideas, see Barry Barnes, *T. S. Kuhn and Social Science* (New York, 1982), and Gary Gutting, ed., *Paradigms and Revolutions: Applications and Appraisals of Thomas Kuhn's Philosophy of Science* (Notre Dame, 1980). For the most complete discussion of the Consensus school, including an extensive bibliography of other historical analyses, see Bernard Sternsher, *Consensus, Conflict, and American Historians* (Bloomington, 1975). Hayden White, *Metahistory: The Historical Imagination in the Nineteenth Century* (Baltimore, 1973), provides another approach to the role of cultural conventions in shaping historical narrative.

2. Sacvan Bercovitch, *The American Jeremiad* (Madison, 1978). J. G. A. Pocock, *Politics, Language, and Time* (New York, 1973), and *The Machiavellian Moment: Florentine Political Thought and the Atlantic Republican Tradition* (Princeton, 1975).

3. The 1940s and 1950s were the decades in which a self-conscious analysis of the metaphor of two worlds became a major theme in American cultural studies. In addition to Perry Miller's *The New England Mind: The Seventeenth Century* (New York, 1939), and *The New England Mind: From Colony to Province* (Cambridge, 1960), there is the work of his student Henry Nash Smith, *Virgin Land: The American West as Symbol and Myth* (Cambridge, 1950). Other important studies on the theme are Lionel Trilling, *The Liberal Imagination* (New York, 1955); R. W. B. Lewis, *The American Adam* (Chicago, 1955); Edmund O'Gorman, *The Invention of America* (Bloomington, 1961); Charles Sanford, *The Quest for Paradise* (Urbana, 1961); Loren Baritz, *City on a Hill* (New York, 1964); Frank Kramer, *Voices in the Valley: Mythology and Folk Belief in the Shaping of the Middle West* (Madison, 1964); Leo Marx, *The Machine in the Garden* (New York, 1964); Ernest Tuveson, *Redeemer Nation* (Chicago, 1968); David W. Noble, *Historians against History* (Minneapolis, 1965), and *The Eternal Adam and the New World Garden* (New York, 1968); Cushing Strout, *The American Image of the Old World* (New York, 1963), and *The New Heavens and New Earth* (New York, 1974); Annette Kolodny, *The Lay of the Land* (Chapel Hill, 1975); John Seelye, *Prophetic Waters* (New York, 1977); and Cecelia Tichi, *New World, New Earth* (New Haven, 1979).

4. This is the analysis that Bercovitch develops in the introductory chapter "The Puritan Errand Reassessed," in *The American Jeremiad.*

5. The books cited in footnote three provide a sense of the central position that the metaphor of two worlds has held in Anglo-American culture from the Puritans to the present.

6. The books by Perry Miller, R. W. B. Lewis, and Leo Marx cited in footnote three, as well as Richard Hofstadter, *The Age of Reform* (New York, 1955), and Marvin Meyers, *The Jacksonian Persuasion* (Stanford, 1957), all limited their analyses of the exodus metaphor to particular periods.

Interestingly, they received much more critical acclaim than did Charles Sanford's *The Quest for Paradise* or Ernest Tuveson's *Redeemer Nation*, which were evidently premature in attempting to interpret the sweep of the Anglo-American cultural outlook as an expression of the exodus metaphor from an Old to a New World.

7. See, for example, Robert E. Brown, *Charles Beard and the Constitution: A Critical Analysis of an Economic Interpretation of the Constitution* (Princeton, 1956).

8. Meyers, *The Jacksonian Persuasion*, and Hofstadter, *The Age of Reform*.

9. Pocock, *The Machiavellian Moment*, chapter 15, "The Americanization of Virtue, Corruption, Constitution, and Frontier," 506–52.

10. Lawrence Goodwyn, in *Democratic Promise: The Populist Moment in America* (New York, 1976), has complained that generations of historians largely ignored populism and that most socialists and Progressives in the years 1890–1920 thought that populism was irrelevant to the political concerns of urban-industrial America. What Goodwyn may have missed in his attempt to understand the Populist reputation is the extent to which their contemporaries believed that the tradition of freehold property as the necessary basis for democracy had become a dead issue by 1890. Charles Sanford, in *The Quest for Paradise*; Major Wilson, in *Space, Time, and Freedom* (Westport, 1974); and John F. Kasson, in *Civilizing the Machine: Technology and Republican Values in America, 1776–1900* (New York, 1976), have explored pre-1890 precedents for Beard's successful avoidance of Turner's dilemma. Henry Nash Smith, *Virgin Land*, R. W. B. Lewis, *The American Adam*, Richard Hofstadter, *The Age of Reform*, and Leo Marx, *The Machine in the Garden*, all described an intense sense of cultural crisis in the late nineteenth century, as did Frederic C. Jaher's *Doubters and Dissenters* (Glencoe, 1964), and Walter La Feber's *The New Empire* (Ithaca, 1963). The most recent study of the rise and fall of the nineteenth-century western frontier is Lee Clark Mitchell, *Witnesses to a Vanishing America* (Princeton, 1981). For insight into the explosion of optimism about a new urban-industrial frontier which provided a context for Beard's outlook in 1900, see Daniel Fox, *The Discovery of Abundance (Ithaca, 1967); Kenneth Roemer, The Obsolete Necessity: America in Utopian Writings, 1888–1900* (Kent, 1976); Samuel Haber, *Efficiency and Uplift: Scientific Management in the Progressive Era* (Chicago, 1964); David F. Noble, *America by Design* (New York, 1977); and David W. Noble *The Progressive Mind* (Chicago, 1970; rev. ed., Minneapolis, 1981).

CHAPTER 2. FREDERICK JACKSON TURNER AND CHARLES BEARD

1. Discussions of Bancroft's philosophy of history are to be found in David Levin, *History as Romantic Art* (Stanford, 1959); David W. Noble, *Historians against History* (Minneapolis, 1965); Richard C. Vitzhum, *The American Compromise* (Norman, 1974); and Merrill Lewis, "Organic Metaphor and Edenic Myth in George Bancroft's History of the United States," *Journal of the History of Ideas* 26 (1965), 587–92. Turner's life and ideas are presented in Wilbur R. Jacobs, *The Historical World of Frederick Jackson Turner* (New Haven, 1968); Ray Allen Billington, *The Genesis of the Frontier Thesis* (San Marino, 1971); and *Frederick Jackson Turner* (New York, 1973). *Pastmasters* (New York, 1969), ed. Marcus Cunliffe and Robin Winks, contains an essay on Turner as well as on Beard and Hofstadter. In addition to Henry Nash Smith's exploration of Turner's underlying assumptions in *Virgin Land*, see the essays by Rudolph Freund "Turner's theory of Social Evolution," *Agricultural History* 19(April 1945), 78–87; Gilman Ostrander, "Turner and the Germ Theory," *Agricultural History* 32(October 1958), 258–61; Robert F. Berkhofer, Jr., "Space, Time, Culture, and the New Frontier," *Agricultural History*, 38 (January 1964), 21–30; and William Coleman, "Science and Symbol in the Turner Frontier Hypothesis," *American Historical Review* 72 (October 1960), 22–49. Other studies are Lee Benson, *Turner and Beard* (Glencoe, 1961); Richard

Hofstadter, *The Progressive Historians: Turner, Beard, and Parrington* (New York, 1968); and Gene Wise, *American Historical Explanations.*

2. Studies of this revolutionary change in Anglo-American culture are Mary O. Furner, *Advocacy and Objectivity* (Lexington, 1975); Burton J. Bledstein, *The Culture of Professionalism* (New York, 1976); Thomas L. Haskell, *The Emergence of Professional Social Science* (Urbana, 1977); and Charles Rosenberg, *No Other Gods* (Baltimore, 1976). See also Paul Carter, *The Spiritual Crisis of the Gilded Age* (De Kalb, 1971).

3. Frederick Jackson Turner, *The Frontier in American History* (New York, 1920; 1962), 1, 299.

4. Ibid., 299.

5. Ibid., 267.

6. *The Early Writings of Frederick Jackson Turner* (Madison, 1938), 107.

7. Turner, *The Frontier in American History*, 18; *The United States, 1830–1850* (New York, 1935), 30.

8. Turner, *The Frontier in American History*, 261.

9. Wise, *American Historical Explanations*, 203.

10. Recent discussions of the acceptance of the idea of evolution are Paul F. Boller, Jr., *American Thought in Transition: The Impact of Evolutionary Naturalism, 1865–*1900 (Chicago, 1969); Cynthia Russett, *Darwin in America* (San Francisco, 1976); Robert C. Bannister, *Social Darwinism: Science and Myth in Anglo-American Social Thought* (Philadelphia, 1979); and James R. Moore, *The Post-Darwinian Controversies: A Study of the Protestant Struggle to Come to Terms with Darwin in Great Britain and America, 1870–1900* (New York, 1979). For the use of the idea of evolution in a related social science, see William F. Fine, *Progressive Evolutionism and American Sociology, 1890–1920* (Ann Arbor, 1979).

11. See Smith's chapter "The Myth of the Garden and Turner's Frontier Hypothesis" in *Virgin Land.*

12. Turner, *The Early Writings*, 250, 251; *The Rise of the New West* (New York, 1906), 331–32.

13. *The Frontier in American History*, 11. Lee Bensen discusses the influence of Loria on Turner in his *Turner and Beard.*

14. Turner, *The Early Writings*, 222. Michael Steiner, in his essay "The Significance of Turner's Sectional Thesis," *Western Historical Quarterly* 10 (October 1979), 437–66, has asked why commentators on Turner have ignored his increasing emphasis on sectionalism toward the end of his career. A possible answer is that Turner's concern with a pluralistic America or, perhaps, with a number of Americas, did not fit the interests of either the Progressive or the Marxist historians, who believed in an industrial frontier, or of the Consensus historians, who argued for a universal capitalist experience. It is important to notice that Turner lost his academic audience when he could no longer write a narrative about a migration into a single American Promised Land. When Williams turned away from the industrial frontier in the 1960s and began to advocate political autonomy for the several American regions, he also lost much of his academic audience. He was unaware of his parallels with Turner, however, because the intellectual world of historical scholarship had been interested only in Turner's closed western frontier and in an alternative open and expanding urban-industrial frontier. It is also possible that Steiner's concern for regionalism corresponds to Williams's disenchantment with a universal urban-industrial frontier and his rejection of the exodus metaphor. Steiner, for example, has written an article, "Regionalism in the Great Depression," *Geographical Review* 73 (October 1983), 430–46, which explores the widespread commitment to regional roots at the popular level, as well as among intellectuals, that characterized this decade when the urban-industrial frontier no longer offered the promise of an attractive New World.

It is interesting that Walter Prescott Webb, whose writings in the 1920s and 1930s seem to have been inspired by Turner's growing concern for sectionalism, published *The Great Frontier* in 1952. In it, Webb linked the closing of the American geographic frontier in the 1890s with a larger crisis in the modern world. It was Webb's thesis that the worldview generated in Europe during the Renaissance and Reformation could not be sustained in the twentieth century once the experience of massive migrations to new frontiers had ended. Recently, Thomas Bender has asked why Charles Beard was the last public historian seeking and finding an audience of general readers as well as of academic historians. But Webb, and later, William Appleman Williams sought to be such public historians. Bender defines a public historian as one who uses a mythic pattern to give meaning to a larger historical synthesis. Webb, like Williams, was rejecting Beard's mythic pattern of New World exceptionalism whether in its American form or in its European origins. Perhaps Webb, who died in 1958, and Williams tried to create a new mythic pattern, but Bender does not recognize them as public historians because their myth of decentralization has not yet found widespread acceptance with general readers of history or with academic historians. See Thomas Bender, "The New History—Then and Now," *Reviews in American History* 12 (December, 1984), 612–22.

15. Major studies of Beard include Howard K. Beale, ed., *Charles A. Beard: An Appraisal* (Lexington, 1954); Bernard C. Borning, *The Political and Social Thought of Charles A. Beard* (Seattle, 1962); Richard Hofstadter, *The Progressive Historians* (New York, 1968); David W. Marcell, *Progress and Pragmatism: James, Dewey, Beard and the American Idea of Progress* (Westport, 1974); Robert Allen Skotheim, *American Intellectual Histories and Historians* (Princeton, 1966); Cushing Strout, *The Pragmatic Revolt in American History: Carl Becker and Charles Beard* (Ithaca, 1958). Ellen Nore, *Charles A. Beard: An Intellectual Biography* (Carbondale, 1983), is the most recent and fullest description of his public life.

16. Charles A. Beard, *The Industrial Revolution* (London, 1901). For Beard's English experience, see Nore's chapter "Sojourn in England," *Charles A. Beard*, 14–27.

17. Ibid., 21.

18. Ibid., 53, 79.

19. James Harvey Robinson and Charles A. Beard, *The Development of Modern Europe*, 2 vols. (Boston, 1907), 1: 167.

20. Ibid., 2: 405.

21. Beard, "Politics," *Lectures on Science, Philosophy, and Art* (New York, 1908), 9–10.

22. Ibid., 21.

23. Ibid., 30.

24. Beard, *American Government and Politics* (New York, 1910), 1–2.

25. Ibid., 46–47.

26. Quoted in David W. Marcell, *Progress and Pragmatism*, 269. See also Eugene Genovese, "Beard's Economic Interpretation of History," in *Charles A. Beard* (Greencastle, 1976).

27. Beard, *The Supreme Court and the Constitution* (New York, 1912), 88. Beard, book review, *American Historical Review* 18 (January 1913), 379.

28. Beard, *An Economic Interpretation of the Constitution of the United States* (New York, 1913).

29. Ibid., 63.

30. Ibid., 63.

31. Ibid., 154.

32. Beard, *The Economic Origins of Jeffersonian Democracy* (New York, 1915).

33. Beard, *Contemporary American History* (New York, 1914), 305.

34. Ibid., 315.

35. Frederic A. Ogg and Charles Beard, *National Governments and the World War* (New York, 1919), 1, 2, 562, 570. George T. Blakey, *Historians on the Home Front* (Lexington, 1970), and Carol Gruber, *Mars and Minerva: World War I and the Uses of Higher Learning in America* (Baton Rouge, 1975), describe how most of the academic community shared Beard's enthusiasm for American participation in World War I.

CHAPTER 3. CHARLES BEARD

1. Quoted in David W. Marcell, *Progress and Pragmatism*, 309.
2. Ibid., 268–71.
3. This change is discussed in Ibid., 271–81. Quoted in Ibid., 280.
4. Ibid., 284.
5. See the discussion in Hugh Rogers, "Charles A. Beard, the 'New Physics' and Historical Relativity," *Historian* 30 (August 1968), 545–60. See also J. W. Meiland, "The Historical Relativism of Charles A. Beard," *History and Theory* 12, no. 4 (1973), 405–13.
6. Beard, "Written History as an Act of Faith," *American Historial Review* 39 (January, 1934), 219–31.
7. There are major parallels between the organic nationalism of Beard's philosophy of history, 1920–48, and that of Daniel Boorstin as described by John P. Diggins, "Consciousness and Ideology in American History: The Burden of Daniel J. Boorstin," *American Historical Review* 76 (February 1971), 99–118, with the great exception that Boorstin's national consensus, unlike Beard's, includes capitalism.
8. Charles and Mary Beard, *The Rise of American Civilization*, 2 vols. (New York, 1927), 1: 88.
9. Ibid., 256, 264, 299–300.
10. Ibid., 328.
11. Ibid., 514, 516–17, 534, 535.
12. Ibid., 2, chapters 17 and 18, 3–121.
13. Ibid., 198.
14. Ibid., 247, 397.
15. Ibid., 399.
16. ibid., 568, 569, 589.
17. Ibid., chapters 28 and 29, 609–712.
18. Ibid., 758, 794.
19. Ibid., 800.
20. Ibid.
21. Charles and William Beard, *The American Leviathan* (New York, 1930), vii, 3.
22. Beard, ed., *America Faces the Future* (Boston, 1932), 117–39.
23. Beard with George H. E. Smith, *The Future Comes* (New York, 1933), 161–64.
24. Charles Beard with Mary Beard, *America in Midpassage* (New York, 1939), 767, 947–48.
25. Beard with George H. E. Smith, *The Idea of National Interest* (New York, 1934), 85.
26. Ibid., 87.
27. Beard with George H. E. Smith, *The Open Door at Home* (New York, 1934). Beard's participation during the 1920s and 1930s in a larger intellectual community which now regretted its commitment, in 1917, to war as a means of achieving more democracy at home as well as abroad is discussed in Warren Cohen's *The American Revisionists: The Lessons of Intervention in World War I* (Chicago, 1967). Thomas C. Kennedy, *Charles A. Beard and American Foreign Policy* (Gainsville, 1975), provides a detailed description of Beard's attitudes on foreign affairs.
28. Beard, *Giddy Minds and Foreign Quarrels* (New York, 1939), and *A Foreign Policy for America* (New York, 1940).
29. Beard with George H. E. Smith, *The Old Deal and the New* (New York, 1940), 174.
30. Ibid., 279.
31. Beard integrated the founding fathers and the principle of checks and balances into his organic nationalism in his very popular book *The Republic* (New York, 1943).
32. Ibid., 342.
33. Charles and Mary Beard, *The American Spirit* (New York, 1942), 164.

34. Ibid., 354–64.

35. Ibid., see chapter 9, "Nature and Incidence of Foreign Criticisms," 482–549.

36. Ibid., 538.

37. Ibid., 594.

38. Ibid., 652–53.

39. Ibid., 674.

40. Beard, *President Roosevelt and the Coming of the War, 1941* (New Haven, 1948). Beard shared the experience of a second failed prophecy with a wide variety of American anticapitalists when the collapse of capitalism in 1929 had not resulted in the triumph of democracy by 1935. Three important books that explore the difficulty of sustaining a Progressive jeremiad between 1935 and 1941 are R. Alan Lawson, *The Failure of Independent Liberalism* (New York, 1971); Richard Pells, *Radical Visions and American Dreams* (New York, 1973); and Peter Clecak, *Radical Paradoxes* (New York, 1973).

CHAPTER 4. REINHOLD NIEBUHR

1. Studies of isolationism in the 1930s include Selig Adler, *The Isolationist Impulse* (New York, 1957); Manfred Jonas, *Isolationism in America* (Ithaca, 1966); and three books by Wayne S. Cole: *Senator Gerald P. Nye and American Foreign Relations* (Minneapolis, 1963); *America First: The Battle against Intervention* (Madison, 1953); and *Roosevelt and the Isolationists* (Lincoln, 1983).

2. Such a revival did occur in the 1950s, led, however, by economists such as Walt Whitman Rostow. See his influential book *The Stages of Economic Growth* (New York, 1960). By the 1960s, this "modernization" theory had begun to influence a number of historians.

3. Studies of the social gospel include Charles H. Hopkins, *The Rise of the Social Gospel in American Protestantism* (New Haven, 1940); Robert M. Miller, *American Protestantism and Social Issues* (Chapel Hill, 1958); Paul Carter, *The Decline and Revival of the Social Gospel* (Ithaca, 1954); Henry F. May, *Protestant Churches and Industrial America* (New York, 1949). For the destructive impact of World War I on Protestant optimism, see Donald B. Meyer, *The Protestant Search for Political Realism* (Berkeley, 1960), and Martin E. Marty, *Righteous Empire* (New York, 1970). Major books on Niebuhr are June Bingham, *Courage to Change: An Introduction to the Life and Thought of Reinhold Niebuhr* (New York, 1961); Charles W. Kegley and Robert W. Bretall, eds., *Reinhold Niebuhr: His Religion, Social and Political Thought* (New York, 1956); H. R. Landon, ed., *Reinhold Niebuhr: A Prophetic Voice in Our Time* (Greenwich, 1962); Nathan A. Scott, Jr., ed., *The Legacy of Reinhold Niebuhr* (Chicago, 1975); Ronald Stone, *Reinhold Niebuhr: Prophet to Politicans* (Nashville, 1972); Paul Merkley, *Reinhold Niebuhr: A Political Account* (Montreal, 1975); Ernest Dibble, *Young Prophet Niebuhr: Reinhold Niebuhr's Early Search for Social Justice* (Washington, 1979); and Dennis P. McCann, *Christian Realism and Liberation Theology* (Maryknoll, 1981).

4. Quoted in Dibble, *Young Prophet Niebuhr*, 55.

5. Reinhold Niebuhr, "What the War Did to My Mind," *Christian Century* (27 September 1928), 1161.

6. Niebuhr, "European Reform and American Reform," *Christian Century* (28 August 1924), 1109.

7. See Merkley, *Reinhold Niebuhr*, and Dibble, *Young Prophet Niebuhr*, for accounts of Niebuhr's outlook during the 1920s.

8. Ibid.

9. Merkley, *Reinhold Niebuhr*, and Dibble, *Young Prophet Niebuhr*, trace these changes in the late 1920s and early 1930s.

10. Niebuhr, "Christianity and Contemporary Politics," *Christian Century* (17 April 1924), 500.

11. See Merkley's chapter "The Making of a Socialist" in Reinhold Niebuhr, and Dibble's chapter "The Early 1930s: Marxian Analysis for Social Justice" in *Young Prophet Niebuhr*.

12. Quoted in Merkley, *Reinhold Niebuhr*, 79–80.

13. Niebuhr, *Moral Man and Immoral Society* (New York, 1932), 179.

14. Ibid., 222. Niebuhr, *Reflections on the End of an Era* (New York, 1934).

15. See Merkley's chapters "Agonies of a Dying Civilization" and "History Takes Another Path" in *Reinhold Niebuhr*.

16. Ibid., "History Takes Another Path" and "What Should America Do?"

17. Quoted in Merkley, *Reinhold Niebuhr*, 132.

18. Ibid., 145.

19. Niebuhr, "Ten Years that Shook My World," *Christian Century* (26 April 1939), 526.

20. Niebuhr, *Moral Man and Immoral Society*, xx.

21. Niebuhr, *The Children of Light and the Children of Darkness* (New York, 1944).

22. Quoted in John W. Coffey, *Political Realism in American Thought* (Cranbury, 1977), 91.

23. Niebuhr, "A Protest against a Dilemma's Two Horns," *World Politics* 2 (April 1950), 341.

24. Niebuhr, "Hazards and Resources," *Virginia Quarterly Review* 25 (Spring 1949), 203. Niebuhr, "The Christian Faith and the Economic Life of Liberal Society," in *Goals of Economic Life*, ed. A. Dudley Ward (New York, 1953), 446.

25. Niebuhr, *Beyond Tragedy* (New York, 1937); *The Nature and Destiny of Man*, 2 vols. (New York, 1942); *Faith and History* (New York, 1949).

26. Niebuhr, *Beyond Tragedy*, 44–48; *The Nature and Destiny of Man*, vol. 1, 17; vol. 2, 217.

27. Niebuhr, *The Children of Light and the Children of Darkness*, xii.

28. Ibid., xiii.

29. Reinhold Niebuhr, *Faith and Politics*, ed. Ronald Stone (New York, 1969), 147. Niebuhr, *Reinhold Niebuhr on Politics*, ed. Harry Davis and Robert Good (New York, 1960), 182. Niebuhr, *The Nature and Destiny of Man*, vol. 2, 268.

30. Niebuhr, *The Irony of American History*, vii–viii.

31. Ibid., 11.

32. Ibid., 32, 35.

33. Ibid., 79.

34. Ibid., 1–29.

35. Important studies that place Niebuhr's changing political thought within the larger context of intellectual history are Edward A. Purcell, Jr., *The Crisis of Democratic Theory* (Lexington, 1973); Robert Booth Fowler, *Believing Skeptics, American Political Intellectuals, 1945–1965* (Westport, 1978); John W. Coffey, *Political Realism in American Thought* (Cranbury, 1977); and Richard Reinitz, *Irony and Consciousness: American Historiography and Reinhold Niebuhr's Vision* (Cranbury, 1980).

CHAPTER 5. RICHARD HOFSTADTER

1. Richard Hofstadter, *The Progressive Historians* (New York, 1968), xiv. Hofstadter's background and ideas are discussed in Alfred Kazin, "Richard Hofstadter," *American Scholar* 40 (Summer 1971), 397–401; Lawrence A. Cremin, *Richard Hofstadter: A Biographical Memoir* (Syracuse, 1972), 2–9; Richard Gilliam, "Richard Hofstadter, C. Wright Mills, and the Critical Ideal," *American Scholar* 47 (Winter 1977–78), 69–86; and Stanley Elkins and Eric McKitrick, eds., *The Hofstadter Aegis* (New York, 1974).

2. Richard Hofstadter, *Social Darwinism in American Thought* (Philadelphia, 1944), and his author's note to the 2d ed. (Boston, 1955).

3. Ibid., 50.

4. Ibid., 50, 51.

5. Ibid., 30.

6. Ibid., 65.

7. Ibid., 58.

8. Ibid., 55, 84.

9. Ibid., 144.

10. Ibid., 101, 145, 175.

11. Hofstadter, *The Progressive Historians*, 452 n9. Hofstadter, *The American Political Tradition and the Men Who Made It* (New York, 1948). Hofstadter, *The Age of Reform* (New York, 1955).

12. Hofstadter, *The American Political Tradition*, v., vii.

13. Ibid., vii, viii.

14. ibid., viii.

15. Ibid., 227, 241.

16. Ibid., 294, 295.

17. Ibid., viii.

18. ibid., 3.

19. Ibid., x. Marian J. Morton, *The Terrors of Ideological Politics: Liberal Historians in a Conservative Mood* (Cleveland, 1972), discusses Hofstadter and several of his contemporaries. A major difficulty faced by a young historian, like Hofstadter, with a socialist commitment in 1948 was that Marxist theory had become associated with the Soviet Union and that nation was, after 1946, increasingly identified as a demonic threat directly comparable to that posed by Nazi Germany in 1939. For Beard in 1940, the great external threat to American democracy was capitalism. But for most young intellectuals in 1950, the great external threat of nazism had been replaced by that of communism. Robert Skotheim has written about the explosive impact of the totalitarianism of the 1930s on the understanding of reality held by American intellectuals in *Totalitarianism and American Social Thought* (New York, 1971); and Les K. Adler and Thomas G. Paterson, "Red Fascism: The Merger of Nazi Germany and Soviet Russia in the American Image of Totalitarianism, 1930s–1950s," *American Historial Review* 75 (April 1970), 1046–64, describe the intellectual foundation for the cold war outlook in the United States.

20. Hofstadter, *The Age of Reform*, 38.

21. Ibid., 39.

22. Ibid., 46.

23. Ibid., 49–130.

24. Ibid., 202.

25. Ibid., 217.

26. Ibid., 223.

27. Ibid., 261.

28. Ibid., 203.

29. Ibid., 278.

30. Ibid., 281.

31. Ibid., 203.

32. Ibid., 306, 307, 310.

33. Ibid., 319, 323, 325.

34. Ibid., 326.

35. Hofstadter, *Anti-Intellectualism in American Life* (New York, 1963), 134–35.

36. Ibid., 154–55.

37. Ibid., 385.

38. Ibid., 221.

39. Ibid., 426–27.

40. Hofstadter, *The Progressive Historians*, 444.

41. Ibid., xii, 5, 6, 248.

42. Ibid., 226.

43. Ibid., 139–40.

44. Ibid., 318, 325.

45. Hofstadter, *The Idea of a Party System in America* (Berkeley, 1970). Hofstadter, *America in 1750* (New York, 1971).

46. Hofstadter in the 1960s was moving toward the position held by Daniel Boorstin as early as 1948. See the chapter on Boorstin in David W. Noble, *Historians against History* (Minneapolis, 1965), and John P. Diggins, "Consciousness and Ideology in American History: The Burden of Daniel J. Boorstin," *American Historical Review* 76 (February 1971), 99–118.

47. Hofstadter, *The Idea of a Party System*, ix.

48. Ibid., xii.

49. Ibid., 72.

50. Ibid., 215.

51. Ibid., 226, 248.

52. Ibid., 55; Hofstadter, *America in 1750*, xvi.

53. Daniel Joseph Singal provides a useful intellectual biography of Hofstadter in his article "Beyond Consensus: Richard Hofstadter and American Historiography," *American Historical Review* 89 (October 1984), 976–1004). He is more interested in Marxist than in Beardian influence on Hofstadter's historical imagination and does not make Gene Wise's thesis of paradigm revolution central to his discussion of the chronological sequence of Hofstadter's writing. His main focus is on Hofstadter's acceptance of Karl Mannheim's concept of ideology and on how that concept differs from that of the anthropologist Clifford Geertz whose ideas have been used by many historians who are half a generation younger than Hofstadter.

CHAPTER 6. WILLIAM APPLEMAN WILLIAMS

1. See Robert W. Tucker, *The Radical Left and American Foreign Policy* (Baltimore, 1971); Robert James Maddox, *The New Left and the Origins of the Cold War* (Princeton, 1973); and James M. Siracusa, *New Left Diplomatic Histories and Historians* (Port Washington, 1973). Bradford Perkins's informative essay "The Tragedy of American Diplomacy: Twenty-five Years Later," *Reviews in American History* 12 (March 1984), 1–18, provides an overview of Williams's influence, through his writings, students, and supporters, on the historiography of American diplomacy, and a bibliography of writings about this Williams school.

2. See the discussion of Niebuhr's views in Paul Merkley, *Reinhold Niebuhr: A Political Account* (Montreal, 1975), 116–20.

3. William Appleman Williams, *American-Russian Relations* (New York, 1952).

4. Ibid., 3–4.

5. Ibid., 106.

6. Ibid., 23.

7. Ibid., 157, 192.

8. Ibid., 233.

9. Ibid., 283.

10. Williams, "The Frontier Thesis and American Foreign Policy," *Pacific Historical Review* 24 (November 1955), 379–95. Richard Hofstadter, "Cuba, the Philippines, and Manifest Destiny," in *America in Crisis*, ed. Daniel Aaron (New York, 1952).

11. Williams, "The Frontier Thesis and American Foreign Policy," *Pacific Historical Review* 24, (November 1955), 379, 380, 383.

12. Ibid., 389, 390, 391.

13. Ibid., 390.

14. Ibid., 395.

15. Williams, *The Tragedy of American Diplomacy* (New York, 1959; 1961).

16. Ibid., 1, 2.

17. Ibid., 9, 21, 22, 50.

18. Ibid., 49.

19. Ibid., 83.

20. Ibid., 115.

21. Ibid., 158–59, 185.

22. Ibid., 205–6.

23. Ibid., 308.

24. ibid., 309.

25. Williams, *The Contours of American History* (Cleveland, 1961).

26. Ibid., 33, 40, 41.

27. Ibid., 56–57.

28. Ibid., 125.

29. Ibid., 177, 179.

30. Ibid., 182.

31. Ibid., 285.

32. Ibid., 350–51.

33. Ibid., 346, 374.

34. Ibid., 385, 472.

35. Ibid., 439.

36. Ibid., 477–78.

37. Ibid., 464.

38. Williams, *The Great Evasion* (Chicago, 1964). For his comments on Beard and the New Deal, see Williams, *Americans in a Changing World* (New York, 1978), 236. Williams's admiration for Beard's opposition to President Roosevelt's leadership in foreign affairs gave way in the 1950s to a more critical position because Beard had not questioned the relationship of democracy and private property. This criticism is contained in his essay "Charles Austin Beard: The Intellectual as Tory-Radical," in *American Radicals*, ed. Harvey Goldberg (New York, 1957).

39. Williams, *The Great Evasion*, 19–20.

40. Ibid., 114, 164.

41. Ibid., 173, 175, 176.

42. Williams, *Some Presidents from Wilson to Nixon* (New York, 1972), 12.

43. Williams, *America Confronts a Revolutionary World* (New York, 1976).

44. Williams, *Americans in a Changing World* (New York, 1978), 81.

45. Williams, *Empire as a Way of Life* (New York, 1980), 58, 213.

46. Williams, "Radicals and Regionalism," *Democracy* 1 (October 1981), 87, 88, 89, 90.

47. Ibid., 91, 95.

48. Ibid., 96.

49. Ibid., 98. Williams discusses the development of his understanding of history in *Visions of History*, ed. Henry Abelove, Betsy Blackmar, Peter Dimock, and Jonathan Schneer (New York, 1984). Williams's "discovery" of an Anglo-American culture, which had originated in England and which had used power to defeat and dominate other American cultures, became widespread within the historical profession during the 1960s. Winthrop Jordan's *White over Black* (Chapel Hill, 1968) was the first influential identification of Anglo-American caste attitudes. Jordan traced the exclusionary and dominating aspects of these caste outlooks from Elizabethan England to the America of Thomas Jefferson's generation. His book was the beginning of an extensive literature that implicitly or explicitly denied the metaphor of two worlds. America was not a Promised Land where the exodus from the Egyptian bondage of Europe resulted in an unprecedented liberty because Anglo-Americans enslaved Africans and rigidly segregated free blacks. Seeing the flow of English culture across the Atlantic necessarily shifted, therefore, the terminology of colonial historiography from the dis-

covery to the invasion of America. Francis Jennings's book on the colonial period, *The Invasion of America* (Chapel Hill, 1975), joined such books as Richard Slotkin's *Regeneration through Violence* (Middletown, 1973); Bernard Sheehan's *Seeds of Extinction* (Chapel Hill, 1973); and led to Richard Drinnon's *Facing West: The Metaphysics of Indian Hating* (Minneapolis, 1980). Once the metaphor of two worlds had weakened to the point that historians perceived a transplanted Anglo-American culture, immigration historians could not continue to use the concepts of Oscar Handlin's *The Uprooted* (Boston, 1951), which assumed that autonomous individuals populated the urban-industrial frontier, as Turner had assumed that such individuals populated the western frontier. In the 1960s, the historiography of immigration shifted, therefore, to the general assumption of a variety of transplanted European cultures. Historians no longer insisted that blacks were autonomous individuals, and, as in Lawrence Levine's book *Black Culture, Black Consciousness* (New York, 1977), they assumed that African cultures had been transplanted in America and formed the foundation for Afro-American culture.

Perhaps the way in which the erosion of the metaphor of two worlds has undermined the thesis of an exodus from European power to American liberty is most dramatically expressed in the area of family history. Throughout the 1950s, it was argued that the American frontier made it possible to move from a European extended family, which demanded the subordination of the individual to the group, to an American nuclear family, which allowed the development of individualism. Since then, the scholarly consensus has shifted, and it is generally accepted that the nuclear family was brought from England and existed in contrast to the extended families of the American Indians and the Afro-Americans. It is also now assumed that the nuclear family was patriarchal, with adult males dominating women and children. If American historiography has become interested since the 1960s in those American cultures that had been dominated by Anglo-American culture and that had remained invisible as long as Anglo-American culture could sustain the metaphor of two worlds and maintain that American history was an exodus from Old World power to New World liberty, it also has become interested in Anglo-American women, whose experience had no meaning within American history as the history of liberty. Throughout the 1970s, more and more scholarship, therefore, has explored the cultures of women and the relationships of dependent women to powerful men. Thinking of the Anglo-American family as a system of power had led to the argument that education is also a system of power. At the beginning of the twentieth century, it was widely argued that compulsory education would facilitate the liberation of the individual from a variety of provincial cultures, including the closing agricultural frontier, to participate in the universal characteristics of the urban-industrial frontier. But because the supposed liberty of that universal order was viewed as the dominating power of a particular Anglo-American, middle-class culture, it has become increasingly difficult to describe schools as offering an exodus experience, an escape from power to liberty. Just as Williams had begun to rewrite the history of American foreign relations at the end of the 1950s, finding power where previous scholars had found liberty, so too did scholars in a variety of other fields of historical research discover power behind the facade of liberty. Few have taken the explicit role of an adversary of the dominant political culture, as Williams has, but implicit in much of their writing is a challenge to the continued use of the metaphor of two worlds by the leading politicians of the two major political parties.

CHAPTER 7. THE 1980s AND THE IRONY OF PROGRESS

1. David W. Noble, *The Paradox of Progressive Thought* (Minneapolis, 1958).

2. Jean-Francois Lyotard, *The Postmodern Condition: A Report on Knowledge* (Minneapolis, 1984), discusses the breakdown of the modern narrative; Judith N. Shklar, *After Utopia: The Decline of Political Faith* (Princeton, 1957), pointed to the crisis throughout the modern West of what I have called the Progressive political jeremiad. *Guilt and Gratitude: A Study of the Origins of Contemporary*

Conscience (Westport, 1982), by Joseph A. Amato II, examines the prevalence of the Progressive political jeremiad in Europe after the Renaissance and Reformation, and its loss of credibility in the twentieth century.

3. The classic statement of cultural lag in modernization theory remains Walt Whitman Rostow's *The Stages of Economic Growth* (Cambridge, 1960).

4. David W. Noble, *Historians against History* (Minneapolis, 1965).

5. Stanford Lyman, *The Black American in Sociological Thought* (New York, 1972), explicitly points to the ahistorical outlook of those American sociologists who assumed the inevitablity of a predictable pattern of modernization, and implicitly illustrates the commitment of those sociologists to the rhetoric of a Progressive jeremiad. The English economist and historian Michael Fores has written extensively on the way in which modernization theory asumes a universal space characterized by industrialism, science, and technology, which is free from the particulars of time. Representative of his many essays on this theme are "The Myth of a British Industrial Revolution," *History* 66 (1981), 181–98; "Technical Change and the 'Technology Myth'," *Scandinavian Economic History Review* 30 (1982) 167–88; and "Science and the 'Neolithic Paradox'," *History of Science* 21 (1983), 141–63.

6. On the central ideological role that economic progress has played in American politics since 1945, see Alan Wolfe, *America's Impasse: The Rise and Fall of the Politics of Growth* (New York, 1981). For the wider role of this concept in the western European nations, see Charles S. Maier, *Recasting Bourgeois Europe* (Princeton, 1975), and "The Politics of Productivity," *International Organization* 31, no. 4 (1977), 607–32.

7. Gabriel Kolko, *The Triumph of Conservatism* (New York, 1963), was one of the first books that applied the concept of political capitalism to the Progressive Era. Since then the concept has become widespread in the historical profession and used by historians of such divergent political persuasions as David F. Noble in *America by Design* (New York, 1977), and Alfred D. Chandler, Jr., in *The Visible Hand* (Cambridge, 1977).

8. See, for example, the books of the economists Nicholas Georescu-Roegen, *The Entropy Law and the Economic Process* (Cambridge, 1971); E. F. Schumacher, *Small Is Beautiful* (New York, 1973); Herman Daly, *Steady-State Economics* (San Francisco, 1977); the historian L. S. Stavrianos, *The Promise of the Coming Dark Age* (San Francisco, 1976); the geographer Warren Johnson, *Muddling toward Frugality* (San Francisco, 1978); the political scientist William Ophuls, *Ecology and the Politics of Scarcity* (San Francisco, 1977); the literary critic Joseph Meeker, *The Comedy of Survival* (New York, 1974); and the legal scholar and political philosopher Roberto Unger, *Knowledge and Politics* (New York, 1975). See also Wendell Berry, *The Unsettling of America* (San Francisco, 1977).

9. Job L. Dittberner, *The End of Ideology and American Social Thought* (Ann Arbor, 1979), provides a discussion of two American social scientists, Daniel Bell and Seymour Martin Lipset, who, after ending their commitment to a Progressive political jeremiad in the 1940s, developed explicit Progressive economic jeremiads.

Index

Index

Educated at Princeton University and the University of Wisconsin, where he earned a doctorate in history and American studies in 1952, David W. Noble has taught for over three decades at the University of Minnesota. His books on intellectual and cultural history include *The Paradox of Progressive Thought* (1958) and *Historians against History* (1965), both published by Minnesota, and *The Eternal Adam and the New World Garden* (1968). He is also co-author, with Peter Carroll, of an interpretive overview of American history, *The Free and the Unfree: A New History of the United States* (1977).